The Unsinkable

HERMIONE BADDELEY

Hermione Baddeley

COLLINS
8 Grafton Street, London, W1
1984

William Collins Sons and Co. Ltd
London · Glasgow · Sydney · Auckland
Toronto · Johannesburg

Every effort has been made to trace copyright
ownership of the illustrations used in this book
where these were not supplied from the author's
private collection.

British Library Cataloguing in Publication Data

Baddeley, Hermione
The unsinkable Hermione Baddeley.
1. Baddeley, Hermione   2. Entertainers –
Great Britain – Biography
I. Title
792'.028'0924   PN2598.B/

ISBN 0 00 216493 0

First published in Great Britain 1984
© Hermione Baddeley 1984

Photoset in Linotron Sabon by
Rowland Phototypesetting Ltd, Bury St Edmunds, Suffolk
Made and printed in Great Britain
by Robert Hartnoll Ltd, Bodmin, Cornwall

For George,
my wonderful
French bulldog

Illustrations

FAMILY AND FRIENDS   *between pages 40 and 41*

With my daughter Pauline, my sister Angela and niece Jane
My mother
Angela
With Angela in California
With David Tennant shortly before our wedding
With Angela, Muriel and Ciggie
David with Eric Dugdale and his wife
My second marriage
Pauline
My son David
With Tennessee Williams
Learning to shoot with Francis De Moleyns
Johnny Rebel
With Robin Maugham
Lottie and George, the two dogs in my life

THE THEATRE   *between pages 72 and 73*

As Clare in *Lord Babs*
In *The Forest*
As Madame Fallover in one of the *Nine Sharp* revues
With the stage hands of *Nine Sharp* . . .
. . . and with the cast
Arriving in Sicily with Leslie Henson's Gaieties E.N.S.A. party
My send-up of Phyllis Dixey
With Hermione Gingold
With Moira O'Neil in *Pagan in the Parlour*
As a drunk in *Grand National Night*
My take-off of Jayne Mansfield

As Mrs Gwynn in *Nell*
With Vanessa Redgrave in *Threepenny Opera*
In *The Killing of Sister George*

FILMS AND TELEVISION   *between pages 120 and 121*

With Richard Attenborough in *Brighton Rock*
With Cyril Ritchard in *Open Ends*
As Mrs Prohack, with Cecil Park as my husband
In *Grand National Night*
My send-up of Doris Day
Laurence Harvey with Heather Sears in *Room at the Top*
In *Do Not Disturb*
In *Mary Poppins*
With James Cromwell in *Maude*
With Donald Pleasance in *The Good and Faithful Servant*
As Kiesier in *The Little House on the Prairie*

JUST ME   *between pages 168 and 169*

Photographed at the time of The Sunday Society Performances
Aged seventeen
Kanelba's portrait of me
In the first *Nine Sharp* revue
Photographed for *London Life*
Aged eighteen
Photographed during the run of *Pagan in the Parlour*
With Elizabeth Ashley
On the Isle of Arran
With my cat Lady Winifred in California

Foreword

When Hermione Baddeley was asked yet again to write her auto-biography I said I'd start it off for her. She is best known as a comedy actress but I knew that in addition to being a comedienne Hermione is a great dramatic actress. Her performance in Tennessee William's *The Milk Train Doesn't Stop Here Anymore* was magnificent and deeply moving. The whole audience rose and shouted for her. I have never seen such an ovation.

From that night onwards I expected Hermione to become a second Eleanor Duse. But she has not because managements insist on offering her comedy roles and because Hermione believes that life is there to be enjoyed – enjoyed by herself and her friends. Her heart is engaged – thoroughly engaged – to the joyous comedy of life.

Robin Maugham
1916–1981

Chapter One

We seemed to have everything. A manor house in Wiltshire called Teffont with sweeping lawns down to the lake, a horse-drawn caravan when we wanted romantic interludes, several splendid motor cars and a Gipsy Moth plane when we were in a hurry. Then there was the mews house in Canning Place with a splendid Matisse in the drawing room, an Augustus John in the hall and, on a side table, a picture of me and the children by Lenare. It had been in all the glossy magazines at the time . . . The Hon. Mrs David Tennant and her babies . . . Mr Tennant is the son of Lord Glenconner of Imperial Chemical Industries . . .

Other pictures of me as Miss Hermione Baddeley, the young actress, appeared in papers like *Picturegoer's Weekly*. That was the part of my life that David called, 'your career'. He liked being married to an actress – it was more fun than being married to the daughter of a duke or a marquess, and David liked fun. We were young, we were rich and we were happy. I knew that I was happy. I loved being a society belle in the wittiest of societies and being an actress on the London stage, but most of all I loved being married to David.

One fine evening at Teffont we were sitting out in the lovely garden waiting for the guests to arrive for a small party we had arranged. It turned out to be a far larger occasion than I had expected. Amongst the many guests were a tall, ginger-haired gentleman and the girl he had brought with him, neither of whom I recognized. Even if I had known who she was, I don't think I could have recognized her for her long, luxuriant hair completely covered her face. Before long, some wag was referring to her as the 'Invisible Lady'. During the course of the evening, I noticed that she was very attentive towards David. When we went into dinner, an enormous rack of lamb was laid out on the table. 'Oooh!' giggled the

Invisible Lady, 'I've never seen such a big lamb chop.' David seemed to find this very funny and laughed uproariously.

I began to wonder whether this person was after my husband. She wasn't alone – it was always happening. I even thought it amusing when someone said: 'I'd like David Tennant next.' And someone or other was always saying: 'Who is that awful girl running after David?' Predatory ladies envied me my good fortune and I couldn't blame them for wanting my husband. He was handsome, he was charming, intellectual and often wonderful to be with. Of course he was spoiled, as sons of rich men often are, but I'd had ten years to get used to that. I soon dismissed these thoughts from my mind. Later on, when the guests had gone, I lightheartedly reminded David that he was married to me. 'Let's not have Russell & Russell again,' I told him, laughing. Some years before, David and I had had a tiff about something unimportant that had blown up into a tempestuous quarrel. David had moved out of our home and gone to stay at the Savoy. Two days later, a letter came from Messrs Russell & Russell informing me that my husband was to sue for divorce. He had named ten most aristocratic co-respondents – it would have been a thoroughly scandalous separation. When the whole silly squabble was over, we used to laugh about my ten phantom lovers.

I met David on the night I went to my first big London party. Quite unexpectedly, at sixteen, I had become a celebrity. I was the star of a runaway success of a play called *The Likes of 'Er*. I was catapulted into instant fame as the little girl with a great future and I was invited everywhere.

My French mother had brought up her four daughters with rules and regulations. The two youngest, Angela and myself, were in the theatre; we'd started performing in public when we were very young, but unlike most theatrical children we had grown up thinking that our lives were perfectly normal and we were expected to conform just as our two older sisters were. Even now, at sixteen, with sudden stardom thrust upon me, my mother considered I was too young to be given my head and she turned down most of the exciting entertainments. I think the main reason I was allowed to accept this invitation to a grown-up party was that the Prince of Wales would be guest of honour. Even my mother couldn't resist the idea of having her daughter present at a party with the heir to the throne.

The party was held at the Chelsea home of Syrie Maugham who had once been married to the writer Somerset Maugham. Syrie was now a fashionable interior designer. One of her gimmicks was to bleach oak furniture to the palest blond. All Syrie's interiors were pale – she loved white and her house was the perfect background for the vividly-dressed Bright Young Things of the twenties. There was exciting music – the brassy trombones, the wailing saxophones of an American jazz band – champagne flowed and the house resounded with laughter. There was a great feeling of joy and gaiety in the air and as soon as I walked into Syrie Maugham's house I knew instinctively that this was for me. I was going to find good parties one of the delights of my life.

Twelve o'clock came all too soon. That was the hour when, like Cinderella, I must leave the party and climb into the hired car waiting for me. I said my goodbyes then dashed to the staircase leading down to the hall. I was half-way down when there was a loud ringing of the front door bell. The butler opened it and a very tall imperious looking young man walked in. He looked up to me, our eyes met, and my hand came to an abrupt halt on the balustrade. There stood the most handsome man I had ever seen. Even today, when I have seen the best that Hollywood, Broadway and London can offer, I have yet to find a man as good-looking as David Tennant. To me he looked like a Greek god. His dark hair was waved back from his forehead, his jaw was strong and resolute. There was an air of such masculinity about him. He was coming up the stairs towards me. He actually barred my way down.

'You can't go yet,' he said with superb confidence. 'We haven't had a dance.'

He removed the flamboyant Spanish shawl I wore around my shoulders – I had snatched it from the top of my mother's piano in a desperate search for an evening wrap – tucked it under his arm and led me back to the ballroom. I found him irresistible. I always did.

David Tennant knew who I was. He'd recognized me standing on the stairs. Some time before he had taken his aunt, Margot Asquith, the wife of the Liberal prime minister, to see my play, *The Likes Of 'Er*. 'What an odious child,' she'd exclaimed after the performance. My best scene, where I hurled china cups and plates across the stage with resounding effect, had shocked her and the rest of the audience. David had not agreed. 'I find her rather endearing,' he'd said.

David's aunt was perhaps even more famous than her prime minister husband, mainly for her dominant personality and her wit. Her luncheons in Bloomsbury were noted social occasions and when David and I were eventually invited to one I naturally hoped that I would make a good impression. Unfortunately David and I were delayed by traffic – even in the twenties – and were quite late.

There was Margot Asquith, the woman who had the ear of half the British Cabinet, kept waiting by us. She sat on a sofa in a drawing room that looked to me, at that moment, the size of a small polo ground. Endless miles of carpet seemed to stretch between me and that famous aquiline profile. Feeling very awkward, I breathed my apologies.

She turned her head an inch or two and gave me the kind of look that had instantly quelled the passions of Winston Churchill and Lloyd George. The other guests leaned forward so as not to miss a word.

'I,' she announced in her regal tones, 'am never late.'

I took a seat well away from my formidable hostess. I whispered to a benign looking gentleman sitting next to me: 'The traffic was terrible, our motor car . . .'

'My dear,' he interrupted, 'you should always take a train. They are much more reliable.'

He was Lord Stamp, the head of the railways. Nothing went right for me that day.

When I was first taken to meet David's parents at their country house, I was naturally very much on my best behaviour. David's mother was a famous beauty, one of the ravishing Wyndham sisters. After the death of her husband, Lord Glenconner, David's mother had married Lord Grey of Fallodon, the Liberal statesman who had been foreign minister at the outbreak of the First World War. Both David's mother and his step-father were so charming and kind that very soon I forgot about my best behaviour and being on approval, and let myself go. Afterwards, Lord Grey told David that he thought I had brains – which pleased me very much – and added: 'She made me feel quite at home in my own house.' All the family were witty, amusing and like David, very good-looking. I remember his younger brother, Stephen, leaning towards me once and saying: 'Of course we have the fatal gift of beauty, darling.'

David was not an ordinary man, nor was ours an ordinary relationship. For a long time we resisted getting married, until David's mother took David away on holiday and tried to pair him off with someone else. When he returned, he told me that he had hated every moment; then he asked me to marry him immediately, before anything else could interfere. I know that my mother was relieved when I told her the news of our engagement. She thought that we had overstepped the bounds of courtship some months before. Bohemian behaviour was all very well, but not for her daughter.

David was much more than a lover or a husband – he was my teacher. He tutored my young mind that had known little formal education, he opened my eyes to the wonders around me and taught me about literature and art. We travelled a great deal and he made every capital of Europe come alive and glowing with the history of our civilization.

Just before we were married, the movie mogul Louis B. Mayer sent a talent scout to Europe to seek out a young actress; I was his choice. The idea was to take me back to Hollywood and turn me into a star comedienne. 'Mr Mayer will make your name famous through the world,' he informed me. David didn't like the idea of a seven year contract. He said it was much too long and they weren't offering enough money.

The reason why my starting salary would be comparatively modest for the first year had been explained in great detail by Mr Mayer's talent scout. Mr Mayer, he said, was going to spend millions of dollars turning me into an international star, so he had to make economies somewhere.

'They'll dye your hair pink and pull out your teeth. Don't go,' said David. But I was tempted, there was no doubt about it. If they had made the contract shorter I might have said yes, for David would then have come to California for some of the time; but seven years was too big a slice out of my life. Anyway, the agent who took over the negotiations on my behalf muddled things up and argued with Louis B. Mayer and, in the end, rather against my will, I had to refuse.

All through the following years, in spite of being happy and successful in England, I was often tantalized by the thought of what might have been had I gone to Hollywood. I did get there, of course, and did make films on their enormous movie lots, but that was much later. There were many journey's and many years between – beginning with the years of my childhood.

One of my earliest memories is of a train journey. My mother with her four little daughters hurried along the platform. Steam hissed from the engine, whistles echoed in the air. I was the youngest, so Angela held me firmly by one hand while Ciggie tugged at the other. Muriel, our eldest sister, bundled us into a compartment, then she and my mother sat down with their backs to the engine.

I remember wondering what all the fuss was about. Why had we been called indoors and suddenly dressed in our best hats and coats? Where were we going? Why were we going? And then I caught Mummy's eye and we smiled at each other. It didn't matter – whatever Mummy did was fun, and as long as she was with us there'd be love and laughter. I felt that there was an air of excitement about this expedition, as if we were running away from someone.

After our home in a quiet Shropshire village with only cows and fields around us, arriving in London was overwhelming. Paddington Station, noise, crowds, pandemonium. It was wonderful – nothing so entrancing had ever happened to us four girls before. Then came the thrill of driving in a taxi-cab through gas-lit streets to a hotel in Russell Square.

The hotel porter, with gold braid on his cap and his jacket, escorted us up the wide staircase to our rooms. He accepted his tip graciously, saluted and wished us all goodnight. My mother closed the door behind him and faced us all. Something in her expression made me turn to Muriel and ask her in a whisper what was happening.

'We've run away from Daddy,' Muriel whispered back.

Next morning Ciggie came out in spots. Ciggie was really called Cynthia, but she was always Ciggie to us. Angela came out in spots by the afternoon and Mummy went downstairs to find a doctor. By the time she came back with him the air was filled with flying feathers. We four girls were having a pillow fight. Order was restored and the spots examined. 'A childish ailment,' pronounced the doctor. 'Measles! The other two will certainly contract the disease. Keep them all isolated.'

Keeping four children isolated in a hotel bedroom was not easy. No one was pleased and the hotel least of all. We children were utterly dismayed – all we could see of thrilling London was through a grimy hotel window. When we got better Mummy decided that we all needed cheering up so she took us off to Selfridges to buy new clothes. It was like being in Paradise. We'd never seen anything like Selfridges before and we spent an entrancing day, each of us choosing a new outfit – a frock, a coat and new ankle boots. Afterwards we had tea in a tea-shop in Piccadilly. It was a wonderful day out. Next morning we all sat with our noses pressed against the hotel windows waiting for the Selfridges horse-drawn van to arrive loaded with packages. It didn't come that day. It didn't come the next day or the next. We were awfully disappointed and asked my mother why the packages didn't come. She sighed and told us that her credit wasn't very good.

Fortunately my mother had connections, well born and wealthy friends and relations. There was an air about my mother: she could really be very grand and no matter how poor we might become she never let us forget that her forebears were distinguished people and we must not let them down. Appearances must be kept up. This maxim has stayed with me all my life. Hold your head high, even if you haven't a penny in your purse, never let on. Discipline had a lot to do with it and running away to London with very little money and four children to support needed an iron determination.

One day my mother piled us all into a taxi-cab and off we drove to a large imposing house in Lancaster Gate. That we should have a home by Hyde Park, that all the rooms were well furnished and that there were servants to clean these rooms seemed quite natural to us. Mother never allowed her worries to cast a shadow over our lives, but what did rather surprise us was the number of friends Mummy had to stay. The spare bedrooms – and there were plenty of them – were filled with guests, and we had friends to lunch and dinner and even to breakfast. It was a delightful state of affairs. We loved company and Mummy's friends seemed such nice friendly people.

What my mother was actually doing, I later understood, was running a smart guest house for congenial gentlefolk. She'd borrowed the money from some of her friends to set up in business, thinking that any fool could run a boarding house and that it would be a home for her children at the same time. It seemed to work and if she had her problems she never let us know. Running a boarding house, no matter how refined, to support herself and her daughters was certainly not the life she would have chosen. But, as she told us, if she'd wanted a boring uneventful life she would have stayed in Scotland and married a Laird.

My mother was a great one for running away. She'd even run away with my father, which in 1900 was an unforgivable thing to do. But behind all this running had been her determination to get on the stage. Mummy, you see, had always been stage-struck.

My mother was French. Her name was Louise Bourdin and her father was a captain in the French army; both her father and mother had connections in England and Scotland. Being in the army there were tours of duty in the French colonies and my mother had an exciting and colourful life while she was growing up. She had a lovely singing voice and, when she was old enough, began to take lessons – I think that was when she began dreaming of the stage. Then, by a cruel twist of fate, her happy, carefree life ended abruptly: her father was killed in battle and her mother died soon afterwards.

The orphan girl was left in the care of an aunt, who decided to accept the offer of family friends in Scotland. These people, the Maxwell-Stuarts, were anxious to make Louise their ward so Louise went to live with them. They were kind, worthy people but their way of life was completely alien to her. On Sunday evenings the maids would assemble in the dining room and the master of the house would read evening prayers. She used to look through the windows and outside would be nothing but mist, swirling Scottish mist, a world away from the hot sun and the palm trees of Algiers.

She was sent off to boarding school. It was a very strict establishment and the little French girl's heart quailed at the harsh restrictions, but she soon made warm friendships with the other pupils. These friendships made school endurable. The other girls, mostly from influential and rich families remained her friends throughout her life. One of them became the Duchess of Norfolk. They used to send us parcels of the most beautiful clothes, which Angela used to describe as 'sent ones'. When her friends, full of envy, asked her where she had got one of her lovely dresses, as often as not she would reply: 'It's a sent one.' I don't suppose her friends were any the wiser.

When Louise came home from school for good the Maxwell-Stuarts saw that she had become a beauty. She had glossy black hair and wonderful blue eyes, eyes so blue that in some lights they appeared violet. Young men came calling. There were plenty of eligible suitors, but Louise turned them all down and told the Maxwell-Stuarts that she wanted to take singing lessons.

Her guardians looked at each other in consternation. 'But that would mean going to Edinburgh.'

'Oh, no!' said Louise. 'London! I want to study at the Royal College of Music.'

'Impossible!' thundered the master of the house.

Money was no problem for her parents had left Louise comparatively well-off, but she did not want to hurt the Maxwell-Stuarts, so she arranged for an invitation to come from a school-friend to stay with her in London. She had decided that while she was there she would enquire about singing lessons.

She left Scotland knowing that if she had her way she would never return and almost as soon as she arrived she went along to the Royal College of Music and demanded to see Signor Vazetti. He was, she had decided, the best singing master in London.

The girl's audacity amused Vazetti and when she sang for him he discovered that she had perfect pitch and that her voice had the makings of a lovely soprano. So Louise began her singing lessons. She was well chaperoned and led a circumspect life, but there was a social life too and she had plenty of admirers. One of them was Edward Marshall Hall, who was to become England's leading criminal lawyer, and another was Edmund Gosse, the writer. In a letter he described my mother as 'a great beauty with jet-black hair and violet eyes'. Invitations to sing at concerts came her way and twice she sang before royalty. Then she was asked to go on tour with Gilbert and Sullivan: her first part would be Yum Yum in *The Mikado*. She told her latest admirer of the offer. Not only did he advise her to go, he also declared that he would come too.

Louise wasn't at all sure she wanted that. William Herman Clinton-Baddeley was also a student at the Royal College of Music and everyone said how talented he was. He was a composer and musician and a brilliant pianist, but she wasn't in love with him; she just liked having the most promising student at the College mad about her.

About this time the Maxwell-Stuarts began to bombard Louise with requests that she return to Scotland at once. 'We absolutely forbid you to go on tour. You are our ward. And you are not yet eighteen.' At this point, William Clinton-Baddeley asked Louise to marry him. Once she had discovered that if she accepted she would be free to go on tour, Louise's interest was aroused.

She was not at all sure that she wanted to marry William. He was not a particularly handsome young man and he was inclined to be self-centred and morose, besides which her common sense warned her that he had not a penny to his name. On the other hand she admired him tremendously and everyone said he was a genius. She wanted to go on tour desperately and if it meant that the only way was to marry William . . . Before she ran away with him she wrote to the Maxwell-Stuarts: 'By the time you receive this letter William and I will be married. He is the most brilliant man I have ever met. One day he will be a great composer . . .'

After a successful tour with *The Mikado* she appeared in a musical play with Marie Tempest, and on the night that Marie Tempest was unwell Louise took her place. She did so well in the part that Marie Tempest made sure that Louise did not appear again.

And then, just as her career was taking wings, William decided that he had had enough of London and told Louise that he needed the peace and tranquility of the countryside to compose his new comic-opera. William was sure he could do better than Gilbert & Sullivan and he was to spend the rest of his life composing comic-operas.

Poor Louise was dismayed. She loved London and amusing people and there was nothing very amusing about William. He could be very moody and fell silent for hours at a time. He was quiet, serious and intense and when he was in a rage he could be frightening, but it was too late to change her mind about William now – she was pregnant.

They rented a farmhouse near the small town of Broseley, in Shropshire, and their first child was born. William was sure it was going to be a son; he was a man who wanted sons and didn't have a very high opinion of girls. Muriel my eldest sister was born, then came Ciggie, then Angela and then me. Four daughters! He was a disappointed man. He named me Hermione after the Greek god Hermes, the messenger of the gods and protector of travellers. In Greek legend Hermione was the daughter of Helen of Troy, but to my father I was just another disappointment.

The farmhouse was littered with musical scores – my father never stopped composing – but he never ever wrote a successful opera, comic or otherwise. There was no doubt he was brilliant, but he just didn't have the knack or the right touch, or whatever he needed to write a hit. I am sure he was before his time. Had he been around in the sixties, he might have written something like *Evita* and made a fortune. As it was, without my mother's private income we should have starved. She paid all the bills.

I think he did earn money now and then, for later on when my mother had left him he had to support himself. He had many talents and could speak seven languages. He read voraciously and the walls of his study were lined with books. When he wasn't composing, he was reading and when he wasn't reading he was stuffing his four daughters with education and discipline. We were taught to drill like soldiers on parade. He'd line us up and give commands like a sergeant-major and off the four tots would go, tottering back and forth. 'Left! Right! Left! Right! Atten – shun!' We'd been taught to jump to attention at the double, head up, legs apart, hands behind our backs. It probably did wonders for our deportment, but any daughter who fell out of step got whacked. He had a nasty little whip that stung the ankles. Drilling was not much fun. He used to get terribly cross if we told lies and I remember him saying to Angela: 'If you tell one lie a day, you'll have to tell twenty.'

When Daddy went off to London with his librettos and scores we all sighed with relief. We sang, we shouted and quarrelled with each other. A long time before my mother came to the conclusion that life was much more fun without my father, we children could have told her so.

I think one of the main reasons why my mother packed us up and left the farmhouse was money. Her funds were running out fast and, with four children to rear, she was apprehensive about the future. There were never ever any rows between them, but long silences between parents can be just as disturbing. The odd thing was that once they lived apart they got on quite well.

When we moved into Lancaster Gate Daddy was always showing interest in how we were getting on. He had taken apartments in Mandeville Place and a lady called Miss Wood who gave piano lessons took up residence with him. Miss Wood was rather nice looking with a pile of not very tidy reddish hair. The idea was that we should go round and have piano lessons from Miss Wood, but she wasn't a very good teacher and although we quite liked her she taught us very little. Mummie was much better – she could play anything she heard by ear, and Daddy could play any music that was put in front of him.

I used to dread lessons with Miss Wood in Mandeville Place. It was always a great relief when the music lesson was over and Daddy would read aloud to us. He used to read all the characters in different voices. By the time I was nine years old Daddy was reading us Dickens, Thomas Hardy, Walter Scott and Thackeray. We loved listening to him – he read so well and we were always agog to find out what would happen next. Although Daddy was not a good teacher by any means, he did teach us the value of literature, and I think we made him happy when we cried out for him to read us another chapter.

We four girls settled into our new way of life at the boarding house in Lancaster Gate very happily. I loved being in a house filled with people, I always have, and to this day I am happy to have lots of people around me. Mummy was naturally gregarious, as I am, and she made our paying guests feel more like friends than boarders. One of them was a nice young man called Stanley Pike with a marvellous sense of humour and great interest in the theatre. Whatever I did made him roar with laughter. I used to keep him doubled up with mirth by imitating everyone in the house. He especially liked my imitation of an elderly guest called Miss Farraday who used an ear trumpet, and he would beg me to do it time and time again. 'She's so tiny,' he kept saying, through bursts of hilarity. Angela, who wasn't much bigger than I was although she was three years older, entertained him too, though I was his firm favourite. He was always telling my mother that she should put us on the stage.

Angela and I had sung songs at our mother's knee, recited heroic poems and read aloud with Daddy ever since we could remember. We had parents who lived and breathed music, a mother who taught us every song from Gilbert & Sullivan. We had an inborn talent to amuse and we spent happy hours planning little entertainments and putting on shows for the paying guests. Muriel had no wish to entertain, but she was very clever with her needle, like Mummy, and made our costumes; we used to charge our audience a half-penny each to watch.

It was wanting to earn pennies for Christmas that prompted Angela and me to perform for the first and last time on the streets of London. On her way home from shopping one morning my mother was diverted by a small crowd of people. Two little urchins were singing and dancing; on the pavement was a cloth cap filled with pennies. One of the urchins wore a battered man's jacket and the other had a ragged black skirt and a flowered bonnet on the back of her head. A piercing high note from the urchin in the bonnet stopped my mother dead. She had recognized the treble of her youngest daughter. She was absolutely horrified and bundled us off home at the double. Our busking days were over.

Stanley Pike, however, kept urging my mother to have us trained professionally. There was, he told her, this remarkable woman called Margaret Morris who had opened a studio in Chelsea. He told her that this was nothing at all like the usual theatre school, but more like an arts centre. There was actually a real theatre in the studio where the children could put on plays.

The more she thought about it the more Mummy liked the idea. She had to give up the stage herself and had found happiness bringing up her four daughters, but she wanted Angela and me to have the chance she had missed. Greek dancing was taught at this school and Margaret Morris and Her Dancing Children were considered to be vastly superior to the Italia Conti children, for instance. Ordinary lessons were held as well, but the emphasis was decidedly on the children's artistic development.

The smallness of Angela and me and the fact that we looked years younger than our age appealed to everyone and Margaret Morris offered to take us at a reduced fee. Muriel could learn art and design at the school; Ciggie, thanks to the generosity of one of Mummy's rich friends was to be sent to boarding school.

It was finally agreed by all concerned that we should attend this rather avant-garde establishment. One of Mummy's paying guests was there, I remember, a Mr William Pye. He was a good-looking young man of whom we were all very fond. Uncle Pye, we were soon to call him. He thought the school was a delightful idea. Uncle Pye had a sweet character and as for us children, we found that a good-tempered uncle was a much better bet than a bad-tempered father. I suspect that Mummy and Uncle Pye began their devoted relationship that was to last for the rest of Mummy's life, long before we knew, but it was always carried on with the greatest discretion. Uncle Pye was there, part of our family, and we loved him.

I adored greek dancing at the Margaret Morris School, though I did rather hanker to learn ballet dancing instead. However, as soon as I entered the acting side I became much more interested in acting than dancing. I remember I was once to play the part of the Duke of Exeter in *Henry the Fifth*. By right I should have worn a suit of armour but I was too small, so someone suggested that I wear a balaclava helmet and a cloak instead. I would have none of it, and was adamant that I should have the proper costume. So I turned up at the dress rehearsal in a chain helmet that reached well down over my shoulders and the leg pieces of a suit of armour which nearly covered the rest of me. I played in this strange get-up with great satisfaction, even though I could hardly walk.

I don't think I was usually so fussy about my costume, but a certain amount of dressing up was always important to me. Stepping into a character's clothes immediately makes you feel different and helps you to get absorbed in the part you are to play. When I grew older, all I needed to transform me into a cheerful cockney bursting into song was a flat cap and a pipe.

Elsa Lanchester was another pupil at the Margaret Morris. Elsa wore only hand-woven Greek tunics and barefoot sandals even when the snow lay thick on the ground, and she was never without a *filet* around her brow. When they were older, Angela took a young actor called Charles Laughton to Elsa's club, the Cave of Harmony. It was rather a curious and risqué place, and Charles would never have gone there on his own. Angela introduced Charles and Elsa and eventually the two of them were married.

Once, we dressed up in our best clothes (Mummy could make

beautiful clothes out of reach-me-downs) and went off to visit a real agent. His office was off Piccadilly and we had to climb a long flight of rickety stairs. I've never forgotten this visit, for Angela and I walked into his office aged eight and ten and came out much older.

The agent seemed much more taken with our young and pretty mother than with us and declared that she was the one who should have been going on stage. Then he turned his attention to his two prospective clients: Angela recited one of her heroic poems and I sang a little song called *I was a good little girl till I met you*. He asked my mother how old we were and, when my mother told him, he pulled a long face. It seems that it was against the regulations to hire such young girls. The agent and my mother looked at each other: 'What a pity,' they both said. She smiled bewitchingly at the agent and then, with a stroke of his pen, Hermione and Angela Baddeley grew older before their time.

I think that although I grew older on paper I still looked too young, but he did offer Angela a part in *The Dawn Of Happiness*, a melodrama at the Dalston Theatre. She was to play a child and earn seven shillings and sixpence a week. We were all as wildly excited as if she'd signed a contract with Metro Goldwyn Mayer.

Some time later one of the patrons of the Margaret Morris School, the Baroness d'Erlanger, came round to the school with her friend Hugo Rumbold. Two little girls were to be chosen for a production at the Drury Lane Theatre. All the girls danced barefoot in front of our important visitors. After watching us for a while, Hugo Rumbold pointed out the two girls he had chosen. Angela stepped forward and then the girl standing next to me gave me a shove. Out of all the girls in the school, he had chosen us two sisters.

Angela and I didn't think this at all extraordinary. We had no spirit of competition, but we always gave of our best. Looking back, what was extraordinary was that neither Angela nor I ever did another audition in our lives. Another coincidence was that Hugo Rumbold had chosen us, and years later his nephew married my daughter.

I do think that Angela and I wouldn't have been quite so calm and collected if we had realized that we were going into a wonderful production of *The Marriage Of Figaro* at Drury Lane conducted by Sir Thomas Beecham. At the end of the first act when the curtain came down Angela and I came on as pages wearing little blue satin tunics. Every time we danced our minuet a great sigh of approval went up at the sight of two such tiny tots, and the applause was deafening.

I do remember the noise of the anti-aircraft guns that sometimes drowned out the music of the opera. It was the time of the Great War and once, when a Zeppelin flew over the theatre, the performance came to a halt and the whole company took shelter under the stage.

Daddy had joined the Intelligence Corps. We were never quite sure what he was up to, but we were very excited when we learned that he had become famous. He and another officer had tracked down a notorious German spy in the Channel Islands. Unfortunately, by the time they arrived on the scene the spy had hanged himself, but we were all very proud nonetheless.

Chapter Two

While we were still at the Margaret Morris School, we began to do tours of the towns and villages of England with a Travelling Theatre. We learned a lot about stagecraft and I learned a great deal about love.

Reginald Gosse and I had the whole of the Lake District as a backdrop for our love affair. We stood on the shores of Lake Windermere held hands and positively shook with passion, quoting Wordsworth to each other and exchanging tender kisses. I was completely innocent and had no idea what might follow, but Reginald was a perfect gentleman. It was absolute bliss and I sometimes gaze out at a lake and still remember Reginald. Then someone gave us away. It might have been young Charles Thomas, our stage manager. Charles was very keen on me, too, and gave me black looks if I as much as peeped at another man. I was told to report to Miss Eleanor Elder who wore long flowing draperies and ran the Travelling Theatre.

'Hermione,' said Miss Elder, tight-lipped and severe. 'I think you have something to tell me about Reginald Gosse.'

I thought it over and decided to play for time. For all the world as if we were having an everyday chat, I told Miss Elder that Reginald was distantly related to Edmund Gosse, and said what a coincidence it was that Edmund Gosse had once been an admirer of my mother.

Miss Elder's face went red. 'Reginald Gosse is thirty years old, and just how old are you, Hermione?'

She knew perfectly well that I would be fourteen that November. Miss Elder shook her head more in sorrow than in anger. 'If only you were more like your sister Angela.' Dear, serious Angela!

I longed to tell her that Angela was passionately in love with Stephen Thomas, the brother of Charles and that they were even talking of getting married, and I, even at thirteen and three-quarters knew that would be a disaster. However, I sensed that this was not the right time for such a revelation. One Baddeley at a time was enough.

The Travelling Theatre of the Arts League of Service was not at all a hot-bed of flaming passion. It was really quite a sedate affair, but I think that dear Miss Eleanor Elder was not worldly enough to understand that if you take young girl actors and young boy actors off to idyllic surroundings their emotions will be aroused both off and on the stage.

We went to Ilkley in Yorkshire and someone who saw us wrote: 'Two young sisters were in the Company and they danced, sang, took part in sketches and were ablaze with talent. They could do everything perfectly and "brought down the house" whenever they appeared. They were very young, but absolutely professional and had a magical quality which I recall vividly after a lapse of many years. Their names were Angela and Hermione Baddeley.'

The writer sent that to me quite recently and I remembered again our small company. There was Eleanor Elder, whose brain child the theatre was, Hugh Mackay, our Highland tenor whom she later married, and a small group of actors and actresses who performed one act plays (Reginald Gosse was one of these). But the only children in the company were Angela and myself. We danced little ballets and sang folk songs; Angela's hit song was called *The Lily-White Boys* and mine was *Jackie Boy, Master*.

The aim of our little company was to bring entertainment of a cultured kind to the villages of England. The first year we went with the Travelling Theatre was near the end of the war and Miss Elder wanted to give the troops live entertainment. Angela left us to do an important show in London after two seasons, but I spent several more summer holidays with the Travelling Theatre. The people in the villages always treated us with great hospitality, the doctor, the solicitor or sometimes the squire in his stately home. When I was thirteen we were touring Dorset and I was delighted to learn that I was to stay in the home of Mr and Mrs Thomas Hardy.

Thomas Hardy seemed a very old man to me, but he and his wife came to the theatre and sat in the front row. I remember I was doing a little butterfly dance wearing a yellow and orange gauze costume with wings. Afterwards he bought a picture postcard of me and told me that he'd loved my dance. 'I felt I was watching a butterfly,' he wrote to me after we had left.

Mrs Hardy told her husband that I had read all his books, though of course they had actually been read to me by my father. They were a sweet and charming couple and I loved my stay with them. Thomas Hardy and I used to have long talks. Even at my young age I could understand that he was a beautiful person and that I was in the presence of greatness; after my stay with Thomas Hardy everyone else seemed a bit ordinary. I had exactly the same feeling when years later I met Tennessee Williams. These two men were not ordinary beings, they had genius, and it was wonderful to be in their company. They saw things around them that no one else did, they had kept the wonder of childhood.

At Christmas Angela and I were always chosen to appear in a Christmas play or pantomime. The first one was at the Lyric Theatre in Hammersmith. We were in A. A. Milne's *Make Believe*. We were supposed to be battle-scarred pirates and we did a number called *Scissors and Paste*. We were a great success and got encored night after night. Angela, serious as ever, did a very careful make-up covering her face with realistic wounds and scars. I didn't want to make myself ugly in those days and just dabbed on an artistic wound or two. This annoyed Angela very much and one night she caught me and, in spite of my yells, covered my face with gruesome cuts and crosses. Strangely enough, later on I was the one who insisted on making myself ugly. I used any excuse to blacken my teeth or stick on a red nose.

It was in *Make Believe* that we met real theatrical children for the first time. The Margaret Morris School scorned such things as competitiveness – with them it was always art for arts sake. Now we were under the scrutiny of the sharp-eyed children from the Italia Conti School. They all had well-trained voices but they were very tough. Every second of applause was counted, every laugh was jealously guarded. They used to ask us pointed questions about the stage, hoping to show us up as not being very professional. They complained to the stage manager that we were trying to upstage them. Angela and I from our superior school where no one was ever beastly or mean if someone just happened to get a bit more applause were much too refined to answer back.

We really couldn't understand why they were so annoyed by us.

Some time later I appeared with another Italia Conti graduate, Noël Coward. We were in *The Knight Of The Burning Pestle* at the Lyric. I played a little boy in a velvet cap whose family had embarked on a series of disastrous travels. Everything I said, and quite a lot of everyone else's lines too, was punctuated with sniffs. For some reason, the critics rather took to this and it was mentioned in all the reviews. My little sniff became quite famous. Noël didn't get very good notices and sulked because of all the attention I was getting for such a small part, but I don't think he held it against me in the years that followed.

At home we were all growing up. Muriel, my eldest sister, was seventeen and she was now a teacher at the Margaret Morris School. Suddenly off she went and married Hugh Pearson Gee. Hugh was a talented designer who used to decorate the windows of the big London stores at Christmas. We were all to marry when we were very young, just as Mummy had. First there was Muriel who wed at seventeen, then Angela married at the same age, then there was me, and finally Ciggie who was only slightly older.

Uncle Pye was always with us, we couldn't imagine life without him, and of course we were young and so wrapped up in our own lives that we never questioned what was going on between the older generation. All I remember is the joy we all felt when Mummy went off to a nursing home during the war and came home with a little brother for us.

We had always longed for a brother and there he was, a little boy called William Pye-Baddeley, named after Daddy and Uncle Pye. We adored our little half-brother, but he was certainly like none of us. When he was about five or six, young Bill showed an unusual interest in religious matters. He loved saying grace and learning hymns and bible stories. We always said he would finish up as a Bishop, and he was in fact offered a Bishopric when he was a Dean of Brisbane.

By the time I was fifteen I had collected a coterie of boy-friends around me. My steady was Charles Thomas, who was still very keen on me. Angela was still in love with his elder brother Stephen Thomas, and soon after Nigel Playfair offered her a part in his production of *The Beggar's Opera*, she married Stephen who was stage manager of the show. Nigel Playfair's son, Giles, was one of my admirers and he always encouraged me greatly in everything I did.

The Thomas family played quite an important part in our young lives. They lived in Hampstead Garden Suburb and there were three sons. They were all very attractive: Charles, my admirer, had beautiful golden-red hair. Their parents were always putting on splendid pageants in their large garden, and all of us used to spend hours talking about everything and anything. Fond as I was of Charles, he wasn't the only boy in my life. Hugh Williams, who had just left Haileybury School and was thinking about becoming an actor, used to take me to little tea-shops and we'd walk round the park talking of our great future in the theatre.

About this time the Arts League of Service decided to show London theatregoers what the Travelling Theatre and the Margaret Morris School were achieving. The Royal Court Theatre in Sloane Square was taken over for a week and we gave the same kind of show with which we had entertained the rural areas of England. As one of the leading lights I was given some good parts; in particular I had a very dramatic sketch where I played a young girl not much older than I was. The show was a great success and we had splendid notices from the critics. The last matinée came round and afterwards Miss Elder appeared in the dressing room with a note for me; she handed it to me with a mysterious smile.

As soon as I could I dashed out to find Charles Thomas, who was our stage manager again, and thrust the note into his hands. Charles read the note. Then he said: 'It's from Basil Dean.' There was a note of awe in his voice: Basil Dean was one of the great managers of serious plays. 'He wants you to go and see him.'

'I know, I know.' I flung my arms around him. 'Isn't it exciting?' We clung together. I suddenly pulled away. I could hardly wait to get home and tell my mother.

Charles held on to my hand to hold me back and reached into his jacket pocket to bring out a small package wrapped in tissue paper. 'It's your birthday tomorrow. I was going to wait . . . but here it is.'

Inside the tissue paper was a box containing a little gold watch.

I was absolutely delighted and thanked him effusively – it seemed there could be no end to my good fortune that day. But Charles was looking rather thoughtful. He could see that Basil Dean might make me into a star, and had a vision of me as a haughty and unapproachable lady in the arms of some impossibly handsome actor. He made me promise that nothing would change between us.

But of course it did. I think that day probably heralded the end of my childhood.

Apart from the fact that Basil Dean was one of the leading producers of that time, there was another reason why I was so interested in his note. My great heroine Meggie Albanesi was his star actress. Mummy, Angela and I had sat in the upper circle of the St Martin's Theatre and watched her in a *Bill Of Divorcement*. She was small, waif-like, she was enchanting and she had captured the hearts of all her audience.

My mother was convinced that if Basil Dean could make a star of Meggie Albanesi, he could do the same for me. On the day of our appointment, we set off in a bus for the St Martin's Theatre. The nearer we got to the theatre the more apprehensive I became. I didn't know what kind of man I was going to meet and if I'd known that not everyone liked Basil Dean, that he was said to be an arrogant man with little charm and cold personality, I would have been terrified. If I'd heard that he had been Captain Basil Dean in the Great War and he still went around ordering people about as if they were soldiers I should have been more anxious still. As it happened, as soon as I met him I liked him. I always liked him and I think one of his difficulties was that he found it hard to show his emotions, to show warmth. The first thing he said after we had sat down in his office was that he had been looking for someone like me for months. He had seen my show at the Royal Court and declared himself astonished that anyone could get such a performance out of so young a girl. Then he gave me a play to take away and read, and Mummy and I laughed with delight and relief.

At the reading the following week I sat on the stage in the darkened theatre with just the working light overhead, I was sitting next to one of the most successful actresses on the London stage, Mary Clare. Mary was probably twenty years older than me, she was sophisticated, statuesque and completely sure of herself. The play we were to read was called *The Likes Of 'Er* by Charles McEvoy.

What seemed like hours later my mother and I emerged into the sunlight of Charing Cross Road. She caught my hand impulsively and said I had been wonderful and she was terribly proud. I wasn't quite so sure that I had been so very good and didn't want to get my hopes up too high – they still might not give me the part. My mother was always my very best fan. 'Do you know,' she said with some surprise that afternoon, 'I always thought you had so much comedy in you. I thought that you were going to be a comedienne, and yet this afternoon there was so much emotion and drama in your reading.'

I was so confident when I was fifteen years old. I was sure that I could do what I wanted with my career. The truth is that I've always been more proud of my dramatic parts than my comedy, but I have always been perfectly happy making people laugh, and that is where the money is.

Basil Dean asked me to sign a contract with his company. He and his partner, Alec Rea, had this company they called Reandean Management and they had put on some of the best productions of the twenties at the St Martin's Theatre. Basil Dean was a brilliant director; he had once been an actor himself but as a director and producer he'd had more success. As I was under sixteen my mother signed for me.

Basil Dean told me that I would be a permanent member of his company, what he called his 'perms'. There were only five or six of them.

My mother sat with her pen poised above the contract and then suddenly asked how much I was going to get paid. She always enjoyed a touch of off-stage drama. Eight pounds a week, Basil told her. But Hermione is to play a leading role, my mother responded.

'Ah,' said Basil Dean, 'but Hermione is very young and has a lot to learn.'

Eight pounds a week seemed a fortune to me even though quite rightly my mother sensed that it was not enough, and Basil Dean was getting a cut-price leading lady. However we both knew that the money would be a great help. Muriel and Angela had married and left home and Ciggie, I, and little Bill were the only children Mummy had to look after. A daughter earning a weekly salary would be a godsend.

When Basil Dean said that I had a lot to learn he was quite right. No one becomes a good dramatic actress overnight: some of the craft is experience, some of it is instinct, and some just hard grind.

The show went on and, as I have said, was a great success. The gossips were already predicting that, following the sad death of Meggie Albanesi, Basil Dean with his tendency towards small waif-like heroines would now promote my career as he had Meggie's.

Basil told me that his next presentation was to be *The Forest* written by John Galsworthy. The heroine was a voluptuous half-caste who knifes the hero in the final scene. The part was intended for Mary Clare, but Basil had changed his mind about Mary playing the part and decided that I was to play Amina.

I faltered. Mary was a good six inches taller and forty pounds heavier, and I wondered how I could possibly fit in; but what really bothered me was how Mary Clare would react when she learned that I was to take over her part. Basil, who was more interested in the takings at the box office than Mary's feelings, was adamant. *The Likes Of 'Er* was to come off and his new sixteen-year-old leading lady was going to star in *The Forest*.

He had thought up the most dramatic action for the final scene. I was to take a tremendous leap right across the stage, land on the back of Leslie Banks, and drive a knife into him. That at least would salve my conscience about Mary Clare. If that statuesque lady tried to leap on Leslie, they'd end up in an undignified heap on the stage. Instead of a curvacious half-caste, Amina would become a slim little Arab girl. As it happened Mary Clare, who knew Basil Dean only too well, was very nice about me taking her role and the show went ahead as planned.

Chapter Three

I took a flying leap across the stage, landed on the broad back of charming, suave Leslie Banks and drove a dagger straight between his shoulder blades. The little bag of blood squelched open and made a splendidly realistic crimson stain. Then Leslie, who had been carrying the white man's burden so nobly in Africa, sank to his knees and collapsed on the stage as dead as mutton. John Galsworthy's play, *The Forest,* came to a successful finale.

It wasn't a very strong play, in fact if it hadn't been for Basil Dean's gimmick about Amina the murderous Arab girl, the critics might have snapped their notebooks shut and made for the bar. As it happened they were thrilled: 'Hermione's leap to fame!' ran the headlines next day.

My mother read the notices with delight and pasted them into the bulging scrap-book, but she was not satisfied. Here was her daughter, leading lady in two of Basil Dean's plays and eight pounds a week was all the ungrateful man was paying her. She waited until the time was ripe and then descended on the unfortunate man's offices. Basil, who had years of experience in fobbing off zealous mothers, told her that he was training this young girl in her craft and besides, eight pounds was all he was prepared to pay. Upon which my mother played her trump card: she would remove her daughter to a manager with a more generous heart.

Basil smiled and mentioned the signed contract; the temperature in his office rose. There were cries of 'injustice' from my mother, and cries of 'ingratitude' from Basil. The dispute was brought to a close when Basil suggested that, if my mother insisted, he would farm me out to a producer who would increase my salary. He reminded her, however, that he would be entitled to a percentage of my salary, and warned her how hard it was to find parts for sixteen year olds. 'If you want to go where the money is,' he continued, 'it will have to be comedy.'

I wasn't consulted about my career taking another direction. At that time all I wanted to do was go on with my career as a dramatic actress and if I'd been asked I would have said that I preferred to stay with Basil Dean; although he was a difficult man I liked and trusted him.

There was an interesting footnote to my mother's quarrel with Basil Dean. Some time later Basil Dean took the play *The Likes Of 'Er* and turned it into a film with Gracie Fields, the music-hall star. Gracie played the part of the good woman, Sally, but I was not offered the part I had made famous of Florrie Small. Basil had a long memory: he never forgave my mother. As for the film, it fell flat as a pancake, in London but did well in the provinces.

I was sent where the money was, but by the time my next show opened I had fallen deeply in love. All the little love affairs I had had before, the ones with Reginald Gosse, Charles Thomas and Hugh Williams, seemed childish in comparison.

He was, of course, the mysterious and handsome stranger I had met a long time before when I went to my first big party at the house of Syrie Maugham.

Soon after that memorable night, a letter came for me. The writer mentioned Syrie Maugham's party and how much he had enjoyed meeting me. Would I care to have supper with him one evening after the show? His brother and another lady would make up the party. I showed the letter to my mother. I had danced with so many people that I couldn't remember any of their names, but there was a nice jolly man who kept saying he wanted to see me again. I thought it must be him. Nice though the jolly man had been, he hadn't made my heart miss a beat as the mysterious stranger had done. I turned the page and looked at the signature again. It was from a man called David Tennant. I wrote to him and accepted the invitation.

After the show on the appointed night, I waited in my dressing room for my escort and his party to arrive. A tap came on the door and in walked a very tall, extremely handsome young man. My heart missed a beat again.

'You can't be David Tennant,' I gasped.

But he was. The nice jolly man turned out to be Bill Astor, son of

the famous Lady Astor. My mysterious stranger was with his elder
brother, Christopher, who was Lord Glenconner. We had supper at
the Savoy and we danced. I was so small and David was so tall,
but despite the difference in size we were ideal partners. I was
sixteen and David was twenty-one. He was reading philosophy at
Cambridge. He explained philosophy to me by saying that it was
love of knowledge. I agreed. Whatever David told me I accepted
without question. He got me home on the stroke of midnight – that
was one of my mother's rules. I'd also promised her that I would not
touch alcohol, not even wine. I always kept my word and when I did
take my first drink, after my marriage, I realized how wise she had
been. Once you have had a few drinks, time can sometimes have no
meaning, and I would never have kept those midnight deadlines.

David asked me to tea, the accepted thing when courting a young
girl in those far off days of the twenties. It was romantic, yet
completely respectable; tea time was considered to be a safe time for
the young to hold hands. The place where David had asked me to
drink tea, however, wasn't quite so safe. I had been asked to the flat
he shared with his brother, Christopher.

In spite of the fact that I was helping to support my family and
that I was a leading lady in the West End with my name up in lights,
my mother's views about the protection of her innocent daughter
were unchanged. If I had told her that I was going to David's flat she
would have been outraged. So I didn't tell her. Instead I went off as
usual to my dancing lesson at the Margaret Morris School, changed
buses on the way and caught one to Sloane Square.

Sloane Street is a very long street and finding the right number
was just as difficult then as it is now. Time was going by and I was
getting late as I hurried up one side of the street then ran down the
other side. Eventually I found the number, climbed the stone steps
and pressed the bell. It wasn't David but Christopher who opened
the door. Two minutes later, David appeared and I breathed again.
We drank tea, ate buttered scones and strawberry jam and I looked
from one brother to the other. They both had lovely deep, resonant
voices, both were equally attractive in their different ways . . . and
then I caught David's eye and I knew which brother I was in love
with.

When I got home my mother remarked to me how radiant I
looked and how my eyes shone. She'd just arrived back from a

bridge party. Our life style had changed: my sisters had gone and so had most of the paying guests and only Uncle Pye was still with us. Mummy could now indulge herself in her favourite pastime, playing bridge. She had heard at this party that David Tennant came from a good Scottish family. She obviously approved of this information, for she often told us that the Bourdins and the Clinton-Baddeleys were very well connected and that although we did not have a great fortune, the blood of the Dauphins of France ran through our veins.

That Christmas, when I was seventeen, David gave me the most wonderful present I have ever had. A delivery man brought a huge box made of heavy white cardboard and tied with masses of pretty ribbons so that it looked like a gigantic chocolate box. We all carried it inside and lifted off the lid. It was breathtaking. Inside the box were compartments and nestling in each compartment amid the tissue paper was a gift. David told me later that he had gone to nearly every shop in Bond Street. There were pairs of gossamer-fine silk stockings, in another compartment a pair of grey doeskin gloves, handkerchiefs from the White House, dainty satin slippers from Pinet. There was a little gold mesh purse from Aspreys, chocolates from Charbonnel & Walker, a Christmas cake, a wonderful leather diary, a string of amber beads and, in the centre in a compartment of its own, a beautiful little sapphire and diamond brooch from Cartiers.

'He is *formidable* this young man of yours,' exclaimed my mother. She was very impressed.

From the beginning my mother trusted David to look after me. She knew that we just loved to be together. There was nothing else, no hanky-panky. Whenever he could, David came to the theatre to fetch me and we'd dash to the Savoy for supper and dancing. Neither of us drank. David had promised his mother, just as I had, that he wouldn't touch alcohol yet.

Christopher, David's elder brother whom David called Kit, joined us one night with a girl friend he introduced as Elizabeth Bowes-Lyon. She was small, like me, with lovely blue eyes and a sweet smile. Elizabeth's parents, the Strathmores and Christopher's family, the Glenconners, were friends – their homes, Glamis Castle and The Glen, were in Scotland and both families were Scottish.

Kit and David were intrigued to see that Elizabeth and I were equally tiny and made us stand back-to-back so they could see who had the edge. We took our shoes off obediently – both of us wore the high evening heels that were then in fashion – and the two brothers had a fine old time deciding who was taller. Eventually they decided there wasn't a whisker of difference.

When David was taking me home after the very happy evening we'd all spent having supper and dancing, David told me that Kit was very keen on Elizabeth. I said that they both seemed very keen on each other; we agreed that the sound of wedding bells was in the air.

The Tennant's family home in Scotland, called The Glen, was designed on the lines of Glamis Castle in Scottish baronial style. It was about fifty miles from Glasgow surrounded by great stretches of heather moorland. David told me that his great-grandfather had started off the family fortune with a chemical works in Glasgow. His son, Charles Tennant, had in turn amassed the fortune that made the Tennants so rich. He was known in the family as 'the terrible old grandfather' because he had twelve children by his first wife and then a lot more from a second marriage. The celebrated Margot Asquith and David's father had been two of the children from the terrible old Grandfather's first marriage. Then David's father, who was also very clever with money, had been elevated to the peerage and became Lord Glenconner.

I had been farmed out by Basil Dean to the impresario Archie de Beer. If that sounds like white slavery it wasn't at all: I was dropped head-first into the biggest thing in London at the time – a revue called *The Punchbowl*. I had been singing and dancing all my life just for the sheer joy of it and now I was being well paid into the bargain.

I shared a dressing room with the two headliners, the stars of the show, Gwen Farrar and Norah Blaney. To my eyes they were ladies of a certain age, frankly middle-aged, but they had a huge following. They were from the music hall and cabaret and they did the kind of act that has now been taken over by young men in drag. They sang naughty songs, did witty repartee that was sometimes risqué but never downright rude. We didn't get in each others way, for Gwen and Norah got into their evening dresses for their set act and had a sip of brandy or gin while they waited to go on. I was in and out all the time doing rapid changes – you have to be young and healthy for revue.

While they waited, a special friend would sometimes come in and have a drink and a chat with them. When this happened I would erect a screen in a corner and do my rapid changes behind it. One evening I dashed in, saw a male figure sitting in a corner, so I hurried behind my screen. While I was changing I took a peep over the top of the screen. There sat the heir to the throne, David, Prince of Wales – golden hair, tip-tilted nose and shy smile. He caught my round-eyed, astonished gaze and smiled. He didn't wink, but he looked as if he might. He used to come round quite a lot – something about Gwen and Norah must have appealed to him, made him feel relaxed and at ease. I suppose it could have been because of his liking for older, bossy women. The Prince of Wales was always a favourite of mine: if he hadn't been invited to Syrie Maugham's party, I should never have been allowed to go and so meet the man of my life, David Tennant.

Sonny Hale was my dancing partner in *Punchbowl*. He was a toothy young man, rather ordinary looking, who wore glasses because he was so short-sighted. But Sonny had enormous talent: he was a gifted comedian, a fabulous dancer and went straight to the top of his profession. He had a marvellous physique and was very athletic which meant that when we did our acrobatic dance together Sonny was as strong with the lifts and the catching as any ballet dancer. In spite of his ordinary looks there must have been a lot of sex-appeal there too. He was married to the beautiful Evelyn Laye and waiting in the wings when Evelyn divorced him for adultery was the alluring Jessie Matthews.

Sonny and I, the two juveniles, were given an acrobatic dance to the music of a song called 'Chilli Bon Bon'. The words of the song were fairly inane – something about how much we loved our Chilli Bon Bon – but it was a catchy tune, and in no time at all became the hit of the season. Sonny and I developed our number till we were very funny together and danced about the stage like electric things. We were young, carefree and had boundless energy; every time we came on the applause was terrific and the number was a riot. The two stars were not at all pleased – you can't blame them I suppose. But Sonny and I soon found that our number was being put in a different place almost every night to try and slow down the applause. 'Poor old ducks,' we'd whisper and pull faces behind their backs. We weren't deliberately trying to steal their laughs – that was unheard of on the English stage at the time – but we did inject fresh life into the show.

We had a comedian in *Punchbowl* called Alfred Lester, a great clown and the first professional to teach me about laughter. I owe so much to him: he taught me how to build up my laughs, how to increase my partner's laughs and how to wait for laughs. His timing was wonderful and he shared his years of experience with the little teenager who was new to the big business of comedy.

David came down from Cambridge about this time and because he was mad about cars he enrolled on a course in engineering. With his help I acquired a 'Baby Austin' – a little Austin Seven which was more or less a box on wheels with a canvas hood that fastened onto the windscreen. It was a wonderfully comical little runabout that always served me well. David suggested taking it to the reception held by Ramsay MacDonald when he was re-elected prime minister in 1929. Alongside all the huge shiny black limousines it looked just like a pedal car and I think all the waiting chauffeurs must have thought we'd come to the wrong place. Eyebrows were raised even further when they saw such a tall man as David unfolding himself from the front seat of such a tiny car. My Baby Austin proved to be extremely useful, for Mummy was longing to leave London and live in the country. We found her a little cottage on a hillside in Buckinghamshire. It was, in fact, the cottage where D. H. Lawrence had once lived. Mummy loved her cottage and garden – she had green fingers and very soon we were eating all our own vegetables.

Every night after the show, Ciggie would be waiting for me with the Baby Austin and we'd drive through empty roads into the country. Ciggie was the great driver of the family and she was so good that people used to ask her to give them driving lessons. In those days before the driving test all you had to do was pay five shillings for a driving licence and get behind the wheel. But if you didn't have a father or a husband or a brother to tell you what knobs to pull and pedals to press, Ciggie was ready and willing to give lessons.

I went home every night to the cottage unless there was a late party when I would stay with Angela or Muriel who had a studio flat. I usually spent my weekends in the cottage and on Monday

David would come round to my dressing room and we'd tell each other anything that had happened. After one week-end, I remember him saying: 'It's all off. Kit didn't go through with it.' I didn't know what on earth he meant, but it soon transpired that Christopher had been intending to pop the question to Elizabeth. He had armed himself with an engagement ring, but when the moment came said nothing. I was surprised. It was expected that Kit and Elizabeth would get engaged, but apparently Kit had unexpectedly been called on to do a tour of duty with the Navy.

Soon after, Elizabeth married the Duke of York. His elder brother, the Prince of Wales, became King Edward and then a year later abdicated to marry Mrs Simpson. And so the Duke and Duchess of York came to the throne, and Elizabeth Bowes-Lyon became the Queen of England.

Out of the blue, Archie de Beer told me that he wanted me to join another of his shows. I was dismayed – I couldn't understand his decision for I hadn't put a foot wrong. And then I realized what had happened. 'It's them . . . isn't it?' I said and Archie nodded. Sonny and I had been getting too much applause. This is one of the hazards of my profession – if you're too good you're going to make people jealous. Archie saw my downcast face and then told me the good news. He told me I was to join the most wonderful show, one which always played to packed houses. I would have to be very good indeed for they were an immensely talented company. I was itching to know what he was talking about. He winked at me: 'They're lovely people! All they'll give you is encouragement. Every one of them is a star and at the end of the season you'll know all there is to know about revue.' I could see he was enjoying the suspense, but at last he told me. I was to be a *Co-optimist*.

The show was called the *Co-optimists*. It might have started out as a pierrot show at the end of a seaside pier, but now it was the most popular variety show in London. It was really a typically English show – full of good humour and laughter – and the original idea had come from two of its stars, Stanley Holloway and Dave Burnaby. Every member of the company, which included Phyllis Monkman, Anita Elsom and Gilbert Childs, had put up a bit of money to put the show on the road. Based as it was on a pierrot show, the women wore tight little bodices with tarlatan pom-poms, short fluffy

On the left my daughter Pauline and me; on the right my sister Angela and her daughter Jane

My mother

My Sister Angela in her teens

Angela and me photographed at my home in California

The aristocracy marries the stage. [*David Tennant and me shortly before our wedding at Henrietta Street Registry Office*

The four sisters – from left to right, Angela, Muriel, Ciggie and me

David on right with Eric Dugdale
and his wife. They were to become
the parents of the notorious
Dr Rose Dugdale

My second marriage

My daughter Pauline

My son David

Tennessee Williams and me
photographed by Roloff Beny at Spoleto

Francis De Moleyns attempting to
teach me to shoot in the grounds
of his castle, Balnagowan in
Scotland

With my beloved Robin Maugham

△ Johnny Rebel

The two dogs in my life.
Above Lottie and left George

tarlatan skirts and little cone-shaped hats on the sides of their heads. The men wore satin suits and caps. Everything was in yellow and purple. They used very few props. That was a most useful lesson for me to learn, and I've done all my acts since then with the minimum of props. A red handkerchief and I can be a French *chanteuse*; a cap and a pipe and I'm a cockney dustman.

In spite of their brilliant success, every member of the *Co-optimists* was very kind to the young newcomer and I became the petted baby of the company. 'There she goes again, pinching all the applause,' Stanley Holloway would laugh. But I knew they were only teasing and that they actually liked it when I did well. Even better, in the easy-going happy atmosphere of the company I found that David could come round to my dressing room every night. He used to bring enormous boxes of chocolates for my dresser and hand the stage-door man large tips, so we were a popular couple all round. I knew I was learning a great deal from these generous people who never failed to give me good advice. They even tried to make Gilbert Childs cut down on the Guinness.

I did a sketch with Gilbert Childs called 'Missing The Bus'. We were supposed to be a cockney husband and wife waiting at a bus stop. We were on our way back from visiting our in-laws who had given a booze-up and to help the general chaos we had with us a portable gramaphone. That may not sound funny nowadays, but back in the twenties a portable gramophone was a huge and cumbersome affair with a winding handle and a great metal horn. Just getting to the bus stop half killed us. We argue and moan, then I discover that I've forgotten the gramophone needles. In no time at all, we start to have a collossal row. The upshot is that he goes off to look for a policeman and while he's away I sing a boozy version of a serious and sentimental music-hall song that was currently the hit of the season. It goes something like: 'What'll I do when you are far away, and I am blue, what'll I do?' This send-up always brought the house down. Eventually, however, it also began to be greeted with hoots of laughter when sung straight in the music halls and some legal gentlemen were wheeled in to put a stop to our irreverent antics.

It was a wonderfully funny sketch with this fantastic comedian. There was only one problem: at the end of the sketch, Gilbert and I sing our song then do a wild acrobatic dance. Gilbert was the worst butterfingers in the business and I hit the stage more times than I care to remember. Gilbert was fond of Guinness: most nights it was hard enough for him to catch me as I flew across the stage to his (hopefully) waiting arms, but on Saturday nights, when Gilbert had tanked up, it was mayhem. 'Gilbert!' the stage manager would yell, 'You'll kill the bloody girl. For God's sake stick to lemonade.'

There was a popular song at the time called, 'Everything's tops on Saturday nights'. On Saturday nights when Gilbert was full of Guinness it was a case of 'Everything drops on Saturday nights'. I'd learned acrobatic dancing well and I knew how to put my hands down if I was going to fall, but every time I went through Gilbert's nerveless fingers I got plenty of bruises. The audience absolutely loved it – they thought the fall was well rehearsed – but Gilbert was threatened with expulsion and worse time and time again. He'd stop the Guinness for a few nights, but there was something about that black frothy brew he couldn't resist.

I was with The *Co-optimists* for two seasons, their eighth and their ninth. I loved it all, the clowning, the jokes, the sheer good-temper and above all the brilliance of the performers. At the end of the ninth season, Mummy decided that I had been with them long enough. She agreed that they were very amusing, but got it into her head that they were frivolous, and not 'serious artistes'. I tried to explain to her that the reason why it all looked so easy and light-hearted was because they *were* great artistes, and that it took a lot of hard work and talent to appear frivolous. *'Tant pis!'* said Mummy, which was her way of saying 'so what!' My contract with Basil Dean had at last come to an end and the word was put out that I was ready to accept another offer. Mummy had decided that since I was a star, I should be paid like a star.

I knew what she had in mind. Mr Charles B. Cochran and his razzle-dazzle shows. Girls! Glamour! Glitter! One leading lady was never enough for a Cochran show, there had to be two or three. I didn't want to go into a Cochran show, but there was another producer I admired very much. I suggested that I should go to see André Charlot. His shows weren't as popular and successful as Cochran's, but he had a brilliant reputation. My practical mother, however, was not impressed.

Even so, when André Charlot asked me to go and see him, I went. He had heard that Cochran had made me an offer, and asked in his attractive and winning voice what it was. The offer, I told him, was for a three-year contract – £75 a week for the first year, £100 a week for the second year, and £200 a week for the third year. And would I accept this generous offer? I really hadn't made my mind up. And what would I say if he, Charlot, was to make me an offer?

I was sorely tempted. André Charlot's intimate revues were a cult in London. All the big names in revue had appeared in Charlot revues: Gertrude Lawrence, Beatrice Lillie, Jack Buchanan, Noël Coward – he created great artistes. He was different, his sets were simple even plain, but he was a brilliant director and producer. He demanded perfection and the impact of his work was breathtaking.

'And what would you say when I tell you that I can offer you only half the money that Cochran does?'

I hesitated. 'I think I might accept, if it were up to me.'

'But it is not up to you. Am I right?'

I nodded. 'I love your revues. I admire your work very much.'

Charlot sighed. 'I hear that your mother will advise you to go to Mr Cochran.' He raised his shoulders in a Gallic gesture of resignation. 'I regret, but I think this is how it will be.'

I signed with Cochran, and it was with regret.

Chapter Four

On With The Dance was my first Cochran show. Noël Coward had written it and it was also his introduction to the world of big, flashy revues with stunning sets and fabulous costumes.

We were rehearsing where Cochran always rehearsed his shows, in the Poland Rooms in Soho, and Noël and I felt rather swamped by the sheer extravagance of the production. The show girls, the chorus girls, the ballet dancers, the acrobats and the chorus boys milled around us. Cochran had to have the *most* of everything – it was his way of catching the headlines, ensuring that he got the maximum publicity. The girl Cochran had billed as 'the most beautiful girl in the world' walked past us wearing a huge head-dress and a wide crinoline.

'I suppose you know why the most beautiful girl in the world has to wear a crinoline, don't you?' demanded Noël.

'No, darling, why?'

'To hide her hideous legs, of course,' Noël replied.

C. B. Cochran himself came marching in with his hat stuck on the back of his head, a cigar between his teeth. He was a portly, round-faced man, generally good-tempered, but always in a hurry. He stopped in front of me and looked me up and down; I was in practice clothes so he could see a good deal of me. His face broadened into a smile. 'You've got very good legs, Hermione,' he said. 'Turn around!' I turned round obediently. 'They're good,' he said. 'Very good, and d'you know what? They're good all the way up. There are lots of beautiful legs around, but not many all the way up from the ankle to the top of the thigh.'

'What luck!' Noël's voice with its touch of acid floated to me. 'No crinoline for you, dear.' His tall thin figure disappeared into the crowd. As this was Noël's first revue for Cochran he was determined that it should be different. Full of the atmosphere of 1925:

flappers (large, colourful bows worn in the hair), syncopation, audacity, decadence and above all modernity, the *in* word. Noël, and the little group of brilliant people who were always with him, made sure of that. And Noël had written a marvellous song for me and Alice Delysia called 'Poor Little Rich Girl'.

But in spite of everything I knew that I resented being pushed into this great glittering revue. My sister Angie had said that Flora Robson was worried about me signing a contract with Cochran; a talented young actress should not throw everything away for the sake of a big salary, she warned. Flora was not going to let herself be pushed into anything – she had charted her own course – but it was different for me. My mother had done the pushing and she needed the money. She had been so magnificent bringing her four daughters up, sacrificing herself for us. I told myself that it was only for a while, then I could go back to doing what *I* wanted.

Mummy, at least, was now in seventh heaven, for everything she had wanted for herself was happening to me. She loved coming to rehearsals to 'look after' me, as she said; very soon she had taken the whole company under her wing. Everyone adored her, especially the chorus boys whom she mothered. She thought they all looked hungry, so she brought them slices of her pie to eat. After years of economies – and some of those years when we had had hardly a penny to bless ourselves with had been very tough – she now had a life of ease. And she deserved every part of it.

I wasn't at all unhappy, of course. In my private life I was blissfully contented. Sometimes David took me home with him to Wilsford for the weekend. Wilsford was a beautiful grey stone manor house in Wiltshire and the interior, decorated by David's mother, was unforgettable. Whenever I remember Wilsford I think of William Morris linen covers for the chairs, of wallpapers with exotic birds and of masses and masses of flowers everywhere. She had made it unique and wonderful.

Lady Grey, as she was now, had been a famous beauty in her youth, one of the three lovely Wyndham sisters. Sargent had painted a picture of them and called it *The Three Sisters*. I remember dropping a small brick when I asked her about it. Somehow I had imagined that the three sisters must have been wearing flimsy draperies and I enquired whether she hadn't felt cold when the artist painted her.

45

'Why should I feel cold?' asked Lady Grey, perplexed.

'Well you weren't wearing very much were you?'

'Dear Hermione,' smiled Lady Grey. 'I think you've got the wrong picture. It wasn't Rubens, it was Sargent, and he liked his models well covered.'

I believe the picture now hangs in an American museum.

Lady Grey was tall and statuesque, although nothing of a Rubens in bulk — she took great care of her figure. If anything she might have been like a Burne-Jones with a long neck, reddish blonde hair and lovely grey-green eyes. I think she was worried when she heard that David was spending a lot of time in the dressing room of a young actress, as most mothers would have been. But, as with the rest of her family, conventions did not rule her life and she always welcomed me warmly, although David did tell me once that his mother had said she wasn't at all sure that she wanted him to marry an actress. David had insisted that I was no ordinary actress.

There was a special bond between her and David. She had lost her beloved eldest son in the war and Christopher, the next son, was perfectly suited to the role of head of the family. I discovered later just how important was her influence on him and how much things changed for the worse when it was gone. Her greatest sadness, something that did change her life, had been the death of her son Edward, nicknamed Bimbo, who had been killed at the age of nineteen on the Somme. She could never get over it and she had turned to spiritualism for comfort. Conan Doyle and Sir Oliver Lodge, both spiritualists themselves, were two of her close friends.

Wilsford was full of old retainers, servants who had become friends during their long years of service. There was old Nanny Russler who had reared the four boys and whispered to me that she loved David best of all. 'Master David doesn't smile very often,' she said, 'but, oh, when he does, what a lovely smile!' Then there was the governess who had taught the little boys in the schoolroom at the top of the house. 'You're the one for David,' she told me. 'He needs someone to bring him out of his shell.' And of course there was the old cook, in her eighties by the time I met her, who still ruled supreme in the kitchen and whose speciality was her steak and oyster pie.

David's father, the first Lord Glenconner, had died in 1920 and two years later David's mother married Viscount Grey of Fallodon. Lord Grey was a marvellous man, quiet and unassuming but with his own dry wit and much charm. He was sometimes a long-suffering husband – Lady Grey was not renowned for her punctuality. She would flutter back and forth while he waited looking at his watch, ready to leave. 'I'm just going to be two minutes,' she would cry; then ten minutes later, 'Just another minute!' 'Darling,' Lord Grey would wearily say, 'I do wish you'd stop "justing" and get into the car.'

I remember that once, when they had finally climbed into the car, the chauffeur closed the door just a little too quickly and caught it right on Lord Grey's ankle. It must have been extremely painful, but instead of letting out a yell of displeasure as a lot of men would do, Lord Grey said quietly: 'Please, don't do that again.'

Christopher, as the eldest son after his brother died, had inherited a very large industrial and commercial empire as well as the family estate in Scotland. But no one ever talked about money. I suppose that's how it is: when you've got a lot you don't worry, but if you have nothing at all you talk about money constantly. Stephen, David's youngest brother, still lived at home and he was just as handsome as his two brothers. The whole family were so witty and had such a wicked sense of humour that it was a joy to stay at Wilsford.

Lady Grey did worry about David, particularly when he came down from Cambridge with a passion for racing cars and, as I have said, perhaps now and then she worried about David's growing involvement with an actress. Anyway, something did happen one day that made my mother and me wonder whether she might have enlisted the help of a friend of hers to try and put me off a bit. Out of the blue I had a telephone call. A male voice informed me that he was the secretary of Lord Beaverbrook and that His Lordship would like me to have luncheon with him. Max Beaverbrook owned the very popular newspapers, the *Sunday Express* and the *Daily Express*. It was common knowledge that a telephone call by the boss to one of his editors could ensure that a young actress was inundated with good publicity. I hadn't met the Canadian Lord and I was curious to know why he should invite me to lunch. I asked David what he thought and he told me to keep my wits about me because Lord Beaverbrook was a bit of a wolf and might well be after something.

On the appointed day I was picked up by his chauffeur-driven car and we drove through Chelsea to Fulham, which in those days was more of a slum than a desirable area. Then the car turned into a well-hidden drive and behind the tall trees was a lovely house. The chauffeur saw my surprised look and told me that His Lordship came here when he wanted to be quiet – and alone. My feeling of alarm mounted.

Lord Beaverbrook was short, squat and had a face rather like a garden gnome; as far as I could see he had no sinister motives in lunching with me alone. He was flirtatious, as most older men are with pretty young girls, in a slightly heavy-handed way, but nothing more. We began our lunch and the press baron produced a bottle of champagne. I politely declined a glass and his broad face split into a grin. He tried to insist, but I was sticking firmly to my mother's no-alcohol rule. Then he began to talk about my career, declaring that I was doing very well with Cochran and had a great future before me. I was beginning to wonder what he was working round to and I soon found out.

'And what about the young man who wants to interfere with that?' I smiled and said nothing. 'I want to give you some advice my dear. Marriage is not for a clever young actress like you. Spoil it all! You keep your mind right there on your career. Don't get married. D'you hear me?'

I told him that I hadn't planned to get married just yet, besides which, no one had offered. He picked up his fork and went on with his lunch as if to dismiss the subject. He didn't bring it up again – it was as if he'd done what he promised and now he was going to enjoy his lunch. In fact, we both enjoyed it. He had plenty of charm when he wanted and we always stayed good friends after that meal.

When I got home I repeated our conversation about David to my mother. She had guessed what the purpose of the luncheon would be and now we knew that she had been absolutely right about Lord Beaverbrook trying to warn me off. Lady Grey was a friend of Max Beaverbrook's, and I couldn't blame her for having a go, though I was disappointed that I wouldn't be all over the front page of the *Daily Express* next day!

We went to Liverpool for the try-out of *On With The Dance* –
Cochran always chose Manchester or Liverpool. It was generally
agreed that the show could not fail, but on the day of the dress
rehearsal none of us thought we would live to see the curtain go
up.

Getting the lighting right seemed impossible. There was hitch
after hitch, and if you're not properly lit you haven't got a show. We
went on rehearsing right through the night, grabbing five minutes
rest here and there. Cochran's young ladies curled up in corners, the
Massine Ballet lay about with limbs as limp as abandoned puppets.
Mummy was wonderful. She was the only one left with any energy
and she dashed in and out bringing jugs of coffee to the exhausted
company. At twelve mid-day, we were sent back to our hotel
bedrooms for a few hours rest and to get ready to face the first-night
audience. As 'they' never stop saying, 'it was all right on the night!'
The lights came on in the right places, the adrenalin flowed through
our veins and the audience roared their approval.

My big number was 'Poor Little Rich Girl!' Noël Coward's song
that was destined to become a classic, played on and on through the
years. It was one of the big hit songs of 1925 and every place I went
into where they had music, every restaurant and every nightclub,
greeted me with that song. Alice Delysia, who was very French and
very attractive, played a lady's maid preparing her young mistress
for yet another party. I was the wild girl whose life had become a
mess of drink and drugs and men. Alice sang the song to me and
then we did it together . . . *Poor little rich girl, don't drop a stitch
too soon* . . .

These poor little rich girls were part of the scene in 1925 and,
there were always some, with their doomed and mournful eyes, in
the society of Bright Young Things. I had seen many of them. What
I didn't know then was that one of these girls whose life was a mess
of drink and drugs and men would come into my life and try to
destroy it.

We had a huge and wonderful table for supper at the Adelphi
Hotel that night. We had the same table every night of the run, but
that night was especially glamorous. The champagne flowed and
everyone was happy, no one more so than Mummy – I had never
seen her so proud and delighted. It looked as if the party would go
on forever and I was tired so I whispered to Mummy that I was

49

going to slip away to the room we shared together. Upstairs in our room I undressed, slipped on a dressing gown and blew a kiss to the picture of David on my bedside table. David couldn't be with us as he was in Coventry with his engineering company, not enjoying it very much at all. He'd promised to get up to Liverpool as soon as he could. And then, just like in all the best movies, came a knock on my door. I opened it and there stood David.

We fell into each other's arms. The Adelphi was the only large hotel in Liverpool so he had found me easily. He noticed Mummy's things lying about the room. Where was I staying, he wondered. I told him that I was sharing the room with my mother.

'Come along and have a look at my room,' he said, a twinkle in his eye. We crept along the empty corridor. Hotels in those days, especially provincial ones, were very prim and proper and the Adelphi, even at the best of times, was a rather stuffy hotel. But once in David's room, we picked up where we had left off.

We were madly in love; we'd been separated and now we were together, alone in a hotel bedroom for the first time. Downstairs they were celebrating the triumphant first night of *On With The Dance*. My first night, my triumph, too . . . It had to happen and we didn't need champagne to light the fuse. Soon my dressing gown was on the carpet, my nightdress fell on top. And we were in bed.

Time went by. As far as we were concerned it could have been a week or a month of absolute bliss. It was probably an hour or two. Someone tapped on the door ever so gently. We ignored the scratching. What we had found was so new and so completely enchanting the roof could have fallen in for all we cared. But the tapping increased. The door suddenly burst open. A shrill scream: 'Oh, my God!'

We shot up in bed. Our eyes focused on Mummy. She stood there a hand pressed to her mouth, a picture of outraged motherhood. I jerked the sheet up to my eyes and peered at her over the top. A fraught silence descended. Then Mummy turned, the door closed behind her and she was gone.

'How awful,' said David. 'I forgot to lock the door.' We were both very new to the game. Subdued and expecting the worst, I crept back along the corridor. Mummy was sitting in a chair, bolt upright and facing the door.

'What was I to do?' she demanded. 'I thought you had been kidnapped. Then I had the good sense to go down to the desk and enquire. They told me that, yes, Mr David Tennant had arrived.'

'David says there's only one good hotel in the town, Mummy,' I said forlornly.

'Tonight of all nights,' she said, 'when I was so very happy.'

She sighed heavily and clasped her hands together. 'Until now,' she said, 'I have never worried about you. But now I am afraid. For the first time I must begin to worry about you.'

As it turned out, I'm afraid, she had every cause to worry.

David's interest in engineering didn't last all that long. He didn't like being in Coventry, so far away from London. He was going to throw the job aside, he told me, and come back to London and open a very *avant garde* club – a kind of nightclub, but also a club for struggling artists and poets. I was thrilled at the idea and convinced it would be a great success.

I had found out that David wasn't blessed with too much confidence – he was very sensitive and needed someone to spur him on, make him more extrovert. He didn't make friends easily – there was sometimes a touch of arrogance about him that was off-putting. When we danced at the Savoy, the floor would often empty to watch us. He used to lift me up in the corners and swing me round with professional skill, as if doing a kind of exhibition dance. But when the floor was crowded and there was little room, David would say that the time was ripe for us to open our own place. He meant it quite seriously.

Lady Grey was anxious that he get a permanent job and she had a word with her friend Lord Reith, head of the BBC. David was offered a job as announcer on the radio and in no time at all David became, so the newspapers said, 'the golden-voiced announcer. He is noted for his faultless enunciation and his effective delivery.' He received hundreds of fan letters. On Sundays he would sometimes read passages from the Scriptures.

But of course being an announcer was not a full-time job, so David continued to search for premises where he could open his club. He often spent hours in the company of a professor of philosophy named Matt Pritchard – he loved discussions. There was a lot of the guide and mentor in David and consciously or unconsciously he wanted to mould me into his own image. He enjoyed the concept of taking over the young Hermione and opening her mind to poetry, literature and art. He wanted to fill the gaps in my education, which, in spite of Daddy's enthusiastic readings, had been rather haphazard. The greatest difference between David and myself at that time was, I think, a sense of discipline. I was disciplined by the theatre – I loved my profession and worked hard at it. David's self-discipline, on the other hand, had ended when he left Eton. But in many ways, these were carefree years for both of us. When we got married, David became quite rigorous with himself, and used to get up soon after dawn every day for an hour or two of philosophical discussion with Matt Pritchard. Then I became the idle one, drifting away from the theatre and not really sure what to do with myself.

After *On With The Dance*, Cochran put me into a second edition of the same revue. The mixture was as before with a few additions and it was called *Still Dancing*. Then came *The 1926 Revue*, for which Cochran had a new gimmick – three leading ladies each from a different country: the French star, Spinelli, who had to be soothed and coaxed through her tantrums and bouts of temperament; the American star, Elizabeth Hyams; and the English star, Hermione Baddeley. I found a song sheet the other day from *The 1926 Revue* with our three faces on it splashed across it in oval frames, the way they used to do them.

David found the premises for his club in Soho. The house was in an alley off Dean Street and was reputed to have once belonged to Nell Gwynne. When he took me there to show me around, my first thought as I looked at the dingy exterior was: 'Poor old Nell. Couldn't King Charles have done a little better for you.' Inside, a tiny lift creaked up to the fourth floor. David helped me out into a scene of devastation – mounds of rubble and pieces of wood lying about and plaster falling off the walls. David was having it all done up and made into a bar, club offices and a restaurant. I was disappointed not to see a dance floor – David had promised there would be one. He pointed out an area marked out on the bare wooden floor. There was to be a staircase cut through there to the floor below, which was to be set aside entirely for dancing.

I heard the lift creak down, someone get in below, and the lift creak back up again. Ronnie Porter, one of David's friends from his

Cambridge days, got out and came over to join us. David called him 'm'tutor', as if he was still an undergraduate and Ronnie was his private guru. A man less likely than Ronnie to give good advice I could not imagine. I knew that he drank too much – long strange sessions on his own when he'd go off to Rosa Lewis's hotel, rent a room and drink himself into oblivion. He was well educated, he was clever, but there was something shifty about Ronnie. Twenty years later he'd have been called a wide-boy. An old Etonian wide-boy! I didn't like the way he flattered David, the way he could be so obsequious to his face and sometimes derogatory behind his back. The truth was, of course, that I just didn't like Ronnie at all.

He began to enthuse about all the marvellous things they were going to do – the staircase that would glitter with light, the walls covered in mirrors, the ceiling in gold. The restaurant would be one of the best in town and Ronnie and David would go to Bordeaux to select the finest wines. It was beginning to sound like a whore's boudoir. I learnt to my surprise that Ronnie was going to manage the club. 'He knows much more about it than I do,' David explained.

'But it all comes from you, David,' Ronnie insisted. 'It's entirely your idea.' The club was to be called the Gargoyle and it was, if possible, going to be a non-profit making club for hard up poets, writers and painters. Struggling artists and penniless musicians would use it as their own, but there would be another side: rich members (and the membership would include all the intellectuals of London) would subsidise the poor. That was the reason for the restaurant and the capacious dance floor. I began to wonder how my friends would fit into this great plan. David assured me that they would be guests, not members, by which I suppose he meant that he classed them as struggling artists rather than wealthy in-tellectuals!

That, in the end, was the way the Gargoyle operated. The highest in the land, the cleverest, the talented and some of the most extraordinary characters in London came to David's club. A lot of the leading lights in the literary world were members – writers like Arnold Bennett, Virginia Woolf and Cyril Connolly; poets like T. S. Eliot, W. H. Auden and John Betjeman; artists like Augustus John. The Gargoyle became the chic place for the Bright Young Things to have supper and dance and with some of my friends and some of

David's, the membership and guest list grew quickly into an exciting mixture of people. Everyone from the Prince of Wales to Tallulah Bankhead danced in our ballroom. Some of the very best parties were held at the Gargoyle. Every year we had a New Year's Eve party and a Gargoyle Birthday party with a celebration and a cabaret. I was always part of the cabaret and I took my work very seriously, just as if I was a paid entertainer.

I remember overhearing Thelma Furness, the current girl-friend of the Prince of Wales, saying to Emerald Cunard after my act: 'Very good cabaret artiste David has booked.'

'She ought to be,' said Emerald. 'She's David's wife and it doesn't cost him a dime.'

But this was long after. At the time the Gargoyle came into being, I was doing my best to get out of my Cochran contract. After three shows I felt I was being swallowed up by a gigantic carnival. C. B. Cochran was a wonderful showman, but I loathed being in the kind of shows he put on. In the end, I did manage to break the contract without any hard feeling; in fact we became great friends. I had always loved his wife Evelyn — everybody did — but in time I even loved Cockie.

My next musical show, *Ace Of Hearts*, was small and I was happy. The awful feeling of too much of everything was gone. I was given a wonderful dancing act and I worked really hard perfecting it. One evening after the show, while I was changing, I began to work things out in my head and realized something was up. David and I had been invited to supper at a house in Knightsbridge; he picked me up in his latest car, a racing Bugatti, and we drove off up Piccadilly and whirled round Hyde Park Corner. The exhaust was being pretty noisy, there was the usual 'vroom-vroom' of the engine, and we wore little leather helmets to keep our hair from blowing away — none of this made it any easier for me to say what I had to say.

'David!' I shouted to be heard over the din. 'David, can you hear me?'

'I can,' he shouted back. 'What is it?'

'David, guess what? I think I'm having a baby.'

At that moment an absolutely fantastic Italian car swirled along-side and overtook us. It was an Isotta-Fraschini racing car. 'My God,' cried David. 'That's the car I'm going to get.'

The Bugatti bumped suddenly and I put my hands over my stomach protectively. 'David! Didn't you hear what I said?'

'Oh yes,' he called back. 'What an awful bore!'

Chapter Five

In spite of this era of Bright Young Things, skirts above the knees and Marie Stopes' book on Birth Control (which I hadn't read) the twenties were filled with prudery and narrow-mindedness. To have a baby without being married wasn't just careless it was outrageous. David asked me to go into a nursing home with 'appendicitis'. He was used to me agreeing to everything he asked, but this time the answer was a flat 'no!'

My mother was the next person I told. She wasn't prudish or narrow-minded, but she was extremely annoyed. Furious! How could I throw my career away like this, she demanded to know. I thought she was being ridiculous. My career and my life were intertwined. The theatre was part of me – I could no more stop acting, dancing and singing than I could stop breathing. And besides, I liked the idea of having a baby. When she'd finished her little lecture on my lack of foresight, my mother's practical nature took over. Unlike David, she didn't suggest that I get rid of the child, but decided on a hush-hush approach. I could see an obvious problem with this plan arising in not very many months' time, but she looked me up and down and told me that since I was a dancer and my muscles were tight, it probably wouldn't show.

I told David of my decision. 'I suppose we could get married,' he suggested. It wasn't exactly the romantic proposal I was looking for, so I let it drop. In fact, I was more worried about what his mother would say when she found out.

'I expect she'll be annoyed, just like your mother,' said David.

That afternoon there was a matinée of *Ace Of Hearts*. I sat in front of my dressing table thinking it over. Slowly the seriousness of what would happen began to take form. The call boy tapped on my door: 'Half hour, Miss Baddeley.' I thought about David and his half-hearted 'I suppose we could get married.' I absolutely refused to marry a man who wasn't desperately anxious to marry me. And I refused to get married just because I was having a baby.

The call boy knocked again: 'Fifteen minutes!' By then I had decided that I was going to look after this baby. I had to work, so I might have to pay someone else to do it for me, but I wasn't a giddy little flapper without a care in the world. By the time the two-minute call came, I had made my plans. There was a get-out clause in my contract, so I could give notice without any one knowing the reason why. And that might have to be soon, because my dance routine in *Ace Of Hearts* was very strenuous.

My daughter was born in a nursing home. To me she was exquisite and unique, but what really surprised me was David's attitude – he was absolutely fascinated by her. We called her Pauline and although we were not married David took over all the responsibilities as her father. He used to pick her up out of her cot and say: 'If I had the choice of all the little girls in the world, I'd choose one just like you.' Of course she didn't understand a word, but it's the thought that counts! A nanny was employed to look after her and they lived down in Surrey. Every weekend we drove down to see her and exclaimed about the way she grew and how lovely she was.

I started rehearsals for a new farce called *Lord Babs* at the Vaudeville Theatre. It was all quite idyllic. There was little Pauline tucked away down in Surrey whom no one knew about. And then it all blew up – right in my face. David's mother, Lady Grey found out. She was very upset and decided to take David away on holiday with her. I didn't like the idea at all, but there was worse to come. Looking somewhat abashed, David announced: 'She's asked a girl I know to come with us. Her name's Merrod Guinness. She's one of these intellectual girls. My mother thinks I might find her interesting.'

'I've met Merrod Guinness,' I said coldly. 'She's quite pretty.'

'Well, my mother's quite upset, so I suppose I'd better go.' David was to some extent financially dependent on his mother.

I began to feel a bit upset myself, but there was yet another blow to come. 'By the way,' said David, 'you know how fond she is of babies. She asks if you'd like Pauline and her nanny to live at Wilsford?' I couldn't believe my ears. Not only was she trying to marry David off to some suitable girl, but she wanted my baby too. David told me I was taking it all much too seriously. I thought it was about the most serious thing that had ever happened to me, but I wasn't in a position to kick up a fuss.

The next three weeks were not the easiest of my life. I tried not to think too much of David and the intellectual Miss Guinness and Lady Grey trying to make a match. I tried not to wish too hard that one particular member of the happy trio might slip down one of the Swiss slopes and do herself an injury.

Three weeks later, while I was making up, David burst into my dressing room and plonked down on his knees before me. He didn't look sun-tanned and rested, he looked strained and bad-tempered. The first thing he said to me was: 'I hated every moment. It was the most ghastly mistake.'

'What about poor Merrod Guinness?'

'I hated her too. Darling,' said David earnestly, 'don't let's wait any longer. Let's get married at once before someone else tries to interfere and spoil things for us. Marry me, please.'

'Do you want to marry me desperately?'

'Of course,' said David. Now that was much more like it.

It was about the time that David asked me to marry him that Louis B. Mayer sent a talent scout to Europe to find two actresses and a leading man who could be groomed for stardom. Those were the days when Hollywood was changing from silent films to talkies and MGM wanted actresses trained in the theatre with good voices. They were having problems with their stars: Clara Bow had a Brooklyn squeak and Greta Garbo was having trouble being understood.

Metro Goldwyn Mayer had an office in a street near the St Martin's Theatre and my husband-to-be came with me to meet the talent scout. He wanted to hear what I was going to be offered and, like everyone else, he was interested to see how Hollywood worked. To our surprise, Mr Louis B. Mayer was there in person. I found him quite likeable – much more of a businessman than I had expected, he wore a well-fitting grey suit, and had a beaky nose and shrewd eyes behind his glasses. Later I heard that under that well-cut suit lurked a vendor of screen fantasy who wept easily when he couldn't get what he wanted.

My name was the first hurdle to overcome. 'Now how do you say that again?' he asked, 'Herm-ee-own-ee?'

'Try it this way,' I suggested, 'Herm-*eye*-on-ee!'

He knew that I could sing and dance and had SA, as he put it, so decided I was a natural for musicals and comedy. Then we got down to the fundamentals. Movies were a business and the film studio had to make money. If they were to invest a very great deal in making me an international star, Mr Mayer declared he had to have a guarantee that I was a good investment. I wondered what on earth that could mean but I loved the idea of MGM spending an enormous amount of dollars on me.

I was quite impressed by that first meeting and Louis B. Mayer's parting words that I'd have a powerful studio behind me. David wasn't so sure. He wanted to know just how many of those dollars I was likely to get. We went back for a second meeting. The question of a seven-year contract came up; David laughed and informed him that of course I couldn't accept such a long contract. Mr Mayer was astonished. Didn't he want me to be famous?

'Not particularly,' said David.

It was an uneasy meeting and at one point Mr Mayer nearly lost his temper. I remember he did raise his fist at David and groan: 'You're ruining this young girl's career.' But after all he was in the movie business and liked dramatic effects.

However we both accepted that the time had come for us to get professional advice. I needed an agent who understood the film world and David suggested Madeleine Carroll's cousin, Christopher Mann. This particular young man had asked me before if I'd like to take him on as my film agent. I wasn't so sure that he knew much about the movie business, but David said he was always writing articles about Madeleine Carroll in *Picturegoer's Weekly*.

Madeleine Carroll, who was just starting in British films had once been madly in love with David. She used to put her arms around his neck, catch my eye, and say, 'I'm going to weave my web around you.' It didn't bother me – any web that Madeleine could weave I could unravel quite easily. Christopher Mann was also just starting in show business – in fact, I could even say he was rather inexperienced. In the years that followed he must have learned a great deal for he opened a thriving show-business agency and did very well. Anyway, we told him to negotiate the contract with MGM.

Christopher kept running back to me with disturbing news. Apparently MGM didn't like the idea of my getting married at all, and would I postpone the wedding? I wondered how MGM would take to the idea of baby Pauline coming to Hollywood too. The next problem was that MGM weren't at all keen on a three-year contract. How long was I prepared to go for? I'd worked out that three years would work perfectly for David and me – just give David time not to get bored with Hollywood.

Christopher was getting in deeper and deeper, but wasn't doing any better than we had. In fact I'd say he was doing worse. David said: 'Are you sure you want to go? They might do terrible things to you out there. Change your name to Gloria or Betty-Lou and dye your hair pink and tear all your teeth out!' In those days I agreed with almost anything that David suggested. Negotiations in the hands of Christopher Mann ground to a dead stop. I think that in the end he may have sold Madeleine Carroll to them instead of me.

Still, when I look back it is often with a feeling of regret. I wonder what would have happened if I'd gone to Hollywood in those far off days. Would I have become a happy, carefree movie star with a few million dollars in real estate or would something awful have happened to me? Would I have become a hermit and cut myself off from the world or would I have married five or six pretty young men? Perhaps it was as well that I didn't go.

While I was nearly becoming a film star, my sister Angela was going through turmoil in her own life. Angela's career in the theatre was growing steadily. She had played Jenny Diver in *The Beggar's Opera* for five years, then went on to The Old Vic where she was very close to Laurence Olivier. In the old days, before my first big success in the theatre, they used to take me out with them occasionally. A young man called Jack Hawkins often tagged along, but I think I preferred Hugh Williams. Once I had done *The Likes Of 'Er*, I somehow left all of them behind and we went different ways. I went into musicals and revues and Angela stayed with the serious side of the theatre.

Angela's marriage to Stephen Thomas who was now an established stage director, had been very happy. Little did she know that he was being drawn away from her by her very greatest friend, who was already married to a very well-to-do young man. For a short time there was a kind of tug-of-love between Angela and Nadine over Stephen. Nadine was a rather tough and grabbing sort. She worked terribly hard, but wasn't much of an actress. Eventually things came to a head. Nadine got her way and poor Angela was left alone. We all suffered with her in her desperate unhappiness.

My wedding day in April 1928 was filled with rush and excitement. I was driving along the King's Road, Chelsea, towards the Registry Office where the ceremony was to take place, when I caught sight of a man hurrying along with a suitcase. It was Stephen Thomas. I thought to myself very sadly: 'Here I am getting married and it looks as if Angela's marriage is over.' It was true. Stephen left home on my wedding day and Angela was broken-hearted.

A small crowd of onlookers were waiting outside the Registry Office in Henrietta Street, just off the Strand. I recognized some of the company from the show, *Lord Babs,* which I had just left to get married and inside the door I saw Billy Merson, the star of the show. Wonderful Billy Merson was one of the greatest comedians England has ever seen, but he wasn't joking as he greeted me: 'Hermione! Did you know that you're an hour late?'

As it happened I did know that I was late, but it wasn't absolutely my fault. David had telephoned me just after eleven that morning and said, 'Darling, where are you? We're supposed to be getting married.'

'But you told me twelve o'clock,' I insisted. I never did find out who had made the mistake.

We had intended that it should be a quiet wedding with just our two families, but inside the Registry Office crowds of people were milling about. As I said, most of the company of *Lord Babs* had turned up, including Joan Barry, the pretty girl who was taking over from me and who became Mrs Tiarks, mother of the future Duchess of Bedford. Mummy was there, Ciggie and, of course, Tony Mackeson, our best man. David, who like me was under the impression that it was going to be a quiet wedding was dressed in a brown check lounge suit and a pullover. I was wearing a powder-blue frock under a grey squirrel cloak with a silver fox collar that David had given me. By comparison, the Glenconner family were charmingly dressed up for the occasion – my brothers in-law, Christopher and Stephen, in morning dress and Lady Grey in brown trimmed with fox with a feathered toque to match.

Even then things still went wrong. The registrar vanished and we had to wait another half an hour. Eventually we were married and the reception was held at the Gargoyle Club where I drank champagne for the first time in my life. My new mother-in-law and I embraced affectionately. We liked each other very much and she became the most wonderful mother-in-law. She was always on my side in any little tiff between David and myself.

There were crowds of people at the Gargoyle. As the champagne corks popped a very large lady pushed her way through the throng towards me. She was Mrs Pat Campbell, the famous actress who had once had a well-publicised affair with George Bernard Shaw. Mrs Pat was a friend of Lady Grey's and a fascinating woman. In her youth she was outstandingly beautiful, but when I knew her she had grown fat and rather creased.

'Oh dear,' murmured Mrs Pat, when she reached me. 'I haven't brought you a present. I didn't have time to buy you a wedding present.'

I patted her hand. 'You mustn't think of such a thing.'

'Oh, but I must.' She opened her petit-point handbag and rustled about inside. 'Let me see now . . .' Triumphantly she pulled something out. It was a rather grubby chiffon hankie. She shook it and a cloud of face powder floated over her dark dress. Inside the hankie was a rather grey looking swansdown powder-puff. She pressed it into my hand. 'Just a little remembrance, darling.'

We were given many beautiful wedding presents, including a jade and crystal brooch and a crystal and sapphire plaque from Christopher and Pamela his wife. We were given many lovely things, but the most useful at that moment was the grubby little powder puff, for when I went off to powder my nose I discovered that in the excitement of getting married I had left my own compact behind. Mrs Pat Campbell's present saved the day. I was just fishing it out of my handbag when in walked Lady Grey. She came over to me and pressed the most beautiful pearl, emerald and diamond ring into my hand. 'This is something very precious from me to you,' she said. 'The first man I ever loved gave it to me.' It was the best present of all – a romantic family heirloom with a touch of mystery about it.

Another present we were given was a book, from Bertrand Russell, entitled *How To Remain Happily Married*. I really feel that Bertrand should have studied it himself, for about six months after our marriage, he separated from his wife.

I thought of my broken-hearted sister Angela often on my

wedding day. Happily, something wonderful happened that later made her quite thankful that Stephen had run off with Nadine. One of Angela's charmed circle of talented theatrical people was Glen Byam Shaw, an absolutely marvellous man. He was in Australia when he heard what had happened to her; he cabled at once that he was returning to England and asked her to come down to the ship to meet him.

It was only a matter of time before Glen and Angela were in love. They married and she and Glen had the most perfect marriage I have ever seen. Their two careers ran together – Angela became one of the greatest actresses in London and Glen became a director at Sadler's Wells, then director of the Royal Shakespeare Company. But neither of them would ever allow their careers to come between them. If Angela had to go to America, Glen telephoned her each day. When Glen moved up to Stratford-upon-Avon with the Royal Shakespeare Company Angela went with him.

Theirs was the most beautiful marriage – it made us all so happy. Sometimes I would think how funny it is that people can break their hearts, but later someone else will come along and they will find the kind of happiness they had never dreamed was possible.

We went to Paris on the first stage of our honeymoon, then down to the South of France, and then we came back to Paris. We were sitting on the pavement outside the Café de la Paix drinking an aperitif – I was rapidly learning the joys of social drinking, learning to sip, never to gulp down a drink – when a voice behind me called out: 'Hermione! Haven't you heard. They've sent an SOS for you over the wireless.' Evidently the BBC had broadcast a message asking Miss Hermione Baddeley, who was believed to be in France, to get in touch with a certain theatrical manager at once. A new play was about to start rehearsals and the leading lady was lost.

David was not at all pleased to have our honeymoon interrupted – he had planned for us to stay away for another week – but I simply had to return to London. John Gielgud was appearing opposite me – he was a friend of Angela's and I knew that she would never forgive me if I let him and the rest of the company down. Not that John bothered very much, I found out later. He thought the play was an appalling concoction.

The play in question was a farce called *Holding Out The Apple* and it was the first time that John would have his name up in lights in the West End. The lady who had written the play was also providing the financial backing; I suspect that was the only way she could get her play on. It had some terrible lines. One I remember went like this: 'You've got a way of holding out the apple that gives me the pip.' The first-night audience also got the pip when they saw it and the playwright lost all her money. I think David and I also had to pay some money because I was late back to rehearsals, but whatever we all did, and we tried as one always tries with a play, nothing could save it.

As soon as we came back to London we took a flat in one of the most beautiful streets in London – Adelphi Terrace. In front of us flowed the River Thames; a short distance behind us was the Strand; and almost next door was the Savoy Hotel. George Bernard Shaw was one of our new neighbours. He had seen me act when I was about twelve years old and sent me a postcard saying that I acted twice as well as people twice my age and should change my name from Baddeley to Goodeley. My mother carried it around with her and showed it to everyone – she was so proud. When I grew up, GBS said that I reminded him of Mrs Pat Campbell. He thought we had the same mischievous ways on the stage; we did naughty things like winking at our partners. Mrs Pat had created the part of Eliza Doolittle the original 'My Fair Lady' in George Bernard Shaw's *Pygmalion* and once as I have said he had been very much in love with her.

Now that we were married, it didn't seem such a bad idea for Pauline to live at Wilsford with her nanny and most weekends we drove down there. I loved staying with my mother-in-law. Although I was so young I got on well with her circle of friends, especially one lady called Mrs Beedon. I felt they all approved and liked me. Once Mrs Beedon said: 'David and Hermione are inevitable to each other.'

My mother-in-law and I continued to be firm friends. I think she understood that the five years David and I had stayed together before we were married had resulted in a strong bond between us. Sometimes she talked about the loss of her eldest son Bimbo during the war, and she explained how spiritualism had helped her come to terms with it. She talked about her other sons, and once she warned me that David could be vulnerable to flattery by unworthy people. I

64

knew that she was trying to tell me to be on my guard. If anything happened to her, David would be a very rich man – an easy prey for flatterers and manipulators.

David's father, the first Lord Glenconner, had built Wilsford House and everywhere were reminders of David's childhood: the swing on the giant oak tree in the garden where he had once played; the stream from the River Avon where he used to fish for minnows; and the village blacksmith's shop where David had worked with the smithy and learned to work with his hands.

My mother-in-law had been a very beautiful woman and now, at fifty-six, she was still very good looking and took a great pride in her appearance. We had been married for about six months when she told me she was going off to some retreat in the country to be put on a starvation diet. When she came back from her cure she had lost a great deal of weight but she seemed to have become tired and to have lost her energy. I advised her not to try it again – it just didn't seem worth it for the sake of a pound or two.

Our life in London was as hectic as ever. Often, after the end of my show, David and I would go dancing at the Savoy – where the *maitre d'hotel,* Luigi, called me 'the little flappair' – and then we'd go on to the Gargoyle. If David was busy there I would call in after the show. When a performance ends at ten or eleven o'clock, an actress can't just go home have a cup of cocoa and go to bed. I myself am on a high and until that wears off I know that I can't go to bed and sleep.

David had gathered some excellent people around him at the Gargoyle. There was Miss O'Neill, the secretary, who was very popular and other members of the staff whom we trusted implicitly. Ronnie Porter had turned out to be a very good manager – he was efficient and always seemed to be there. David paid him £12 a week, which in those days was quite a good wage. I don't think he was given a percentage, but I'm quite sure that now and then Ronnie had a little bonus. There was, however, a very obvious change in Ronnie's life. He had a new girl-friend: her name was Brenda Dean Paul.

Brenda Dean Paul was going to be one of the most notorious women in England. She was perhaps the first woman in London that the media picked up and helped to destroy by splashing her picture across the front pages, and by hounding her every time she appeared in court. Not that Brenda needed much help in her path of self-destruction. She was hooked on drugs. When I first met her I thought she was fascinating. Not exactly beautiful but the kind of voluptuous girl who has plenty of sex appeal and lets every man within eye-catching distance get the message. Although she was not from an especially wealthy family she was the epitome of the girl in Noël Coward's song 'Poor little rich girl'. Her life would always be a mess of men, drink and drugs.

I called in at the Gargoyle one night after the show to find Brenda and Ronnie sitting at the bar. I went over to them and she offered me a cigarette out of a beautiful gold case. 'Look at it. Don't you think it's too divine?' she said. I took the case in my hands – it was solid gold and quite heavy with her initials marked out in tiny diamonds at one corner. Very beautiful . . . and very expensive. I looked from one to the other of them. Ronnie gave me one of his strange half smiles. He always reminded me of one of those dark secret men in a medieval painting, whispering in the ear of the Doge.

'It's a present from Ronnie.' She leant over and kissed him and then she smiled triumphantly at me. I could see that her pupils were dilated – she was full of cocaine.

That night at Adelphi Terrace I spoke to David. I asked him how Ronnie could afford such a present. He had no money of his own, and he couldn't buy gold cigarette cases like that on £12 a week. I was only trying to warn him, but David got angry and accused me of calling his friends dishonest. He was always ready to make excuses for Ronnie and this time he suggested Ronnie might have won a bet. It seemed pretty unlikely to me. The conversation was closed, but whenever Ronnie's name came up there was a coolness between us.

One Sunday we'd been to see friends in the country and it was a long drive back; we went straight to the Gargoyle to have an early supper. As usual the first person we met was Ronnie Porter. 'David,' he said, 'I'm afraid I have bad news. The butler telephoned from Wilsford. Lady Grey has been taken ill.'

David said slowly, 'Is she dead?'

Ronnie nodded.

With absolute certainty I knew that things would never be the same again.

Chapter Six

We got straight back into our car and drove to Wilsford. In those days with empty roads the journey to Wiltshire took something over two hours and we arrived late at night. Christopher met us and said that his mother had died very suddenly from a heart attack. She had not suffered at all. As we were taken up to her room I noticed that some of the maids were still weeping. Stephen was not there – he had motored off that afternoon saying he wouldn't be back for dinner.

We came downstairs afterwards and ate a quiet meal, then moved back to the drawing room. Christopher asked us to sit round a small circular table. We sat there the three of us without speaking, like three characters in a play. Suddenly Christopher reached into his pocket and drew out a splendid rope of pearls. The emeralds and diamonds of the clasp sparkled in the subdued lighting. 'These are for you, Hermione,' he said.

'No!' With an abrupt gesture David pushed them back across the table.

Christopher moved them back again towards me. 'She wanted Hermione to have them.'

I wondered how long this would go on. I drew off the ring I wore; it was the beautiful arrangement of pearls, emeralds and diamonds that my mother-in-law had given me on my wedding day. Both men looked at it. The pearls were part of the same set and there was no further argument about whether I should have them or not. I treasured those two pieces of jewellery – there was alway something about them.

The three of us sat up until after twelve hoping that Stephen would return; then, as we were all so tired and shaken, we went to bed. A room had been prepared for us on the other side of the landing from my mother-in-law's room. I must be honest and say that I felt quite uneasy. This was my first encounter with death and my dead mother-in-law lay only a few steps away across the landing. David told me to go in and kiss his mother good-night. He'd been brought up by his mother to accept and be quite calm about death. She had taught him about spiritualism and to a certain extent he had the same feelings as his mother about it.

I walked into the bedroom alone. I was very frightened at first. It was an over-furnished room by present day standards – a large bed, a chaise longue, chests of drawers, heavy curtains. But there were family photographs on the chests and pictures on the wall that I knew she had loved. She lay there calm and beautiful. She looked asleep and completely at peace. There was not a line to be seen on her face and her profile was noble. I stood beside her remembering her goodness to me, the way she used to laugh and throw back her head. Suddenly I wished I had brought her flowers, lots of flowers, the kind she loved. I bent down and kissed her and because I hadn't David's faith I whispered goodbye.

Neither of us could sleep for a while. I was much too troubled and shocked by what had happened. Eventually I knew from David's even breathing that he had fallen asleep. I closed my eyes, then the lights of a car coming down the drive made me open them again. Stephen had come home I thought. I began to doze off. And then I heard the door open gently. Someone came in and walked over to David's side of the bed. 'Is that you, Stephen?' I whispered.

No one answered. There was complete quietness in the room. I sat up terrified. No one was in the room. 'David,' I said hoarsely, 'someone's been in here.' My heart was thumping. 'There's some-one in the room.'

David roused himself. 'What are you saying? Someone's here?'

'They've gone,' I whispered. 'Whoever it was bent over you.'

David lay back. 'Don't worry, darling,' he said sleepily. 'It must have been Mummy coming to wish us goodnight.'

Soon afterwards, the lights of another car came up the drive and this time it really was Stephen. Later I learnt that the first car belonged to the head gardener. Stephen had been over to have dinner with Cecil Beaton who lived about twenty miles away. He was very shocked and upset by his mother's sudden death.

A long time later, I went with Stephen to a spiritualist meeting. Through the medium came a message for me. It was: 'Hermione, why were you upset when I came into the room? I just wanted to be closer to David.'

Next morning, to my utter surprise, Ronnie Porter and Brenda Dean Paul turned up at Wilsford. They said that they'd driven down to cheer us up. Perhaps strangers coming into the house was a good thing. We all sat round the breakfast table and while we were talking I mentioned the strange occurrence of the night before. In the newspapers next day there was a long story. 'Actress daughter-in-law of Lady Grey reveals her terrifying experience with the other world . . .' A highly exaggerated account of what I had related to Ronnie and Brenda followed. Stephen was very upset and wanted to know who had sold the story to the newspapers. I assured him that it wasn't me; I knew very well who it was, though. I said nothing to David. They were his friends and he was loyal to them.

My mother-in-law had died just six months after we were married. She was a great loss to us all and, as I rapidly found out, her death was greatly to my disadvantage. She was no longer there to act as a brake for some of David's excesses, no longer there to give me wise counsel.

David inherited a great deal of money and his mother left Wilsford House to him. I took it rather for granted that it would be our home but to my disappointment David said that he couldn't live there. He said it would be like wearing his mother's old clothes. He didn't sell it until some time later and then, rather than let it go to strangers, I suggested to David that his younger brother should buy it from him. Stephen lives there to this day.

Buying expensive racing cars became one of David's hobbies. He now had a Leyland Thomas, one of only three built by Parry Thomas, and he tried out a Mercedes Benz at Brooklands. Afterwards he said to his chauffeur: 'Tried and found wanting. Send it back to Germany!' Now in America they seem to think a Mercedes compares with a Rolls Royce, but I think David was right.

David could be both extremely generous and extremely mean. He often flew us to Paris in our own plane, a Gipsy Moth and bought me dresses at the grands couturiers. Once he went over to Paris with Ronnie Porter and they came home bearing three Matisse paintings for an amazingly low price – something around £600 for the lot.

On another occasion, we had arranged to fly to Paris with a great friend of ours, Martin Wilson. Martin used to love discussing clothes with me and was enormous fun to be with. We set off for Lympne Aerodrome, where we had to refuel before continuing on to Paris. Soon after landing at Lympne, we were accosted by an official who told us it was illegal to fly a Gipsy Moth across the channel with more than two people on board. David decided that rather than abandon the trip he would fly a shuttle service – take me over first and then come back for Martin. As we soared into the air, I looked down to see one of the funniest sights of my life: poor Martin sitting on the deserted runway, disconsolately dabbing his nose with an enormous powder puff! Martin's father, Sir Matthew Wilson – whom we called 'Scatters' – was a horseracing enthusiast. He once persuaded David to put £100 on one of his horses. Although he won £500 that day, he never got hooked on the races as many people would after such beginner's luck.

David's mean side emerged when I asked him to do something for my mother. I gave up working and left the theatre. It just happened. If you are married to a man with a lot of money you feel rather a fool tearing round trying to earn more. There just isn't the same incentive.

Angela did not approve. She was now at the Old Vic with Laurence Olivier and John Gielgud. They loved this old theatre where they devoloped their craft – it was like a wonderful repertory theatre for them – although none of them earned much money, £20 a week at most. Angela thought it was a terrible waste to give up acting after devoting so many years to the theatre. But I wanted to be a proper wife to David, to live a real life and have children. A more private thought was that I was the wife of a rich man and could have loads of fun. After all, I was only twenty-one years old.

Now that I had given up earning a large salary, David took over my responsibilities to my mother – to a certain extent. She certainly wasn't as well-off as when I had lived with her. I told David that we must make it up to her in some way, and asked if he couldn't buy her a little house, so at least she wouldn't have to pay rent. In the end he agreed that we might do this.

She chose quite a modest little house in the country and the three of us drove out to see it. I realised that something was wrong when we went inside to inspect it. David continually found fault with everything he saw. I could see that my mother was becoming uncomfortable. I took David aside and said that he might try and be more enthusiastic. He grumbled on, saying that the house was too large and that he would have to hire a man to look after the garden. He ended up by telling me fiercely that it was he who would have to foot all the bills. We both got into a fine old huff.

As we drove home, David continued to make remarks about the amount of money he was expected to lay out, until my poor mother spoke up from the back of the car. 'Please,' she said, 'I don't want the house. Let's leave it.' And that is what happened. My mother continued to rent a cottage in the country, and I helped her in all the ways I could. I felt very aggrieved over the way David had behaved. But rich people do sometimes develop strange ideas that one day they'll be paupers. Mummy took it very well, saying that as long as I was happy and David was good to me, it didn't matter.

I suppose that because I had known poverty myself I took nothing for granted. Angela was still hard-up with her meagre salary at the Old Vic, and to make some extra money she took a job dancing in the Midnight Follies at the Hotel Metropole. One evening, David and I had arranged to take his cousin, Michael Tennant to Mrs Meyrick's nightclub and we wanted a partner for him. Angela, who wasn't yet married to Glen, agreed to join us. We were waiting for her at the bar of the Berkeley Hotel when we received a message to say that Angela couldn't come but she was sending another girl from the Midnight Follies to take her place. A tall, slim, quite nice looking blonde arrived. Her name was Sylvia Hawkes. Her voice wasn't up to the rest of her, it was tinny and cockney with ladylike overtones. Before very long it was plain that Michael Tennant and Sylvia Hawkes were not going to make a twosome. 'She's a bit ropey,' he whispered to me.

Mrs Meyrick's nightclub was very dark, but in a corner, slumped in his seat and more than a little the worse for wear, was a friend of David's. 'Tony,' cried David with some relief, for Sylvia and Michael were becoming rather cool to each other. 'Come and join us.' And so Tony Ashley, the heir to the Earl of Shaftesbury, joined our party. Sylvia's feet were on the rungs of the ladder all right – a few months later she married him! The Earl and Countess of Shaftesbury did their best to stop the union, even making a last minute dash to persuade Sylvia to change her mind. The marriage hardly lasted any time at all – about two months I believe – but

Sylvia was now Lady Ashley and, in spite of a few more marriages in between, she remained Lady Ashley for the rest of her days.

Douglas Fairbanks was her next husband (after Mary Pickford had agreed to divorce him), then came Lord Stanley after Douglas's death. There seemed to be some misunderstanding here. Edward Stanley said afterwards, 'Oh, but I thought she had money!' Sylvia complained, 'I thought *he* had money.' Clark Gable was Sylvia's next husband and this lasted a very short time. Her last husband was a Russian princeling. Sylvia, alone again, died in a Californian nursing home a few years later. I sometimes wonder if all this would have happened if Angela hadn't sent Sylvia along on a blind date. I expect it would, for Sylvia obviously had a clever way with her.

We gave a lot of parties at Adelphi Terrace and one of our most famous ones was thought out upon a beach in Hawaii. I saw a poster with all these jolly looking South Sea islanders – girls in grass skirts and leis dancing the hula-hula. So I suggested to David that we go there. In those days almost all overseas travel was on ocean liners. We saw San Francisco from the ship's rails and adored it at first sight. We went ashore and then motored down to Los Angeles. I must say it looked rather nicer then for there were orange groves in Sunset Boulevard. But we didn't like Hollywood very much and didn't want to stay even though we had letters to the stars. I rather regretted that we didn't use the one addressed to Charlie Chaplin.

By the time we reached Hawaii, we were beginning to think of home. The girls dancing the hula-hula in grass skirts weren't gorgeous at all. Most of them suffered from a deficiency of iodine which produces swellings and lumps. The beaches were superb but we wanted to go home.

David and I decided on the beach that when we got back we should give a marvellous party, the kind of party that no one has given before. Something crazy and original. I loved fancy dress parties, and wanted to get the men out of their stiff evening dress, boiled shirts and stiff collars.

'And we'll get the girls out of their suspender belts and their silk stockings,' agreed David, warming to the idea.

'But we can't have a nudist camp,' I said, in spite of the fact that some bright sparks were already frolicking nude behind high wire

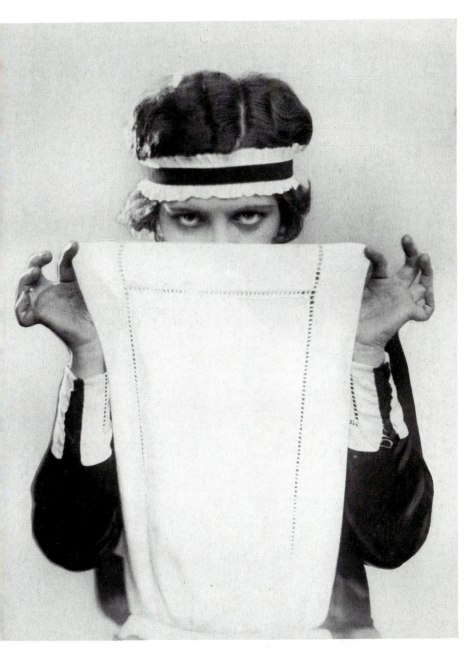

As Clare, in the farce Lord Babs *at the Vaudeville Theatre in 1938*

In John Galsworthy's play The Forest

Madame Fallover – send-up of Swan Lake
in one of the Nine Sharp Revues

The 200th performance of Nine Sharp, *with the stage hands*

The same occasion with the cast. Walter Crisham stands beside me at the centre of the back row

Arriving in Sicily with Leslie Henson's Gaieties E.N.S.A. party during the war. Walter Crisham and I are standing together in the middle with Leslie Henson on the extreme right

My send-up of Phyllis Dixey, at the Phoenix Theatre

With Hermione Gingold.
'Said Hermione B. to Hermione G.
I've admired and adored you since 190
Said Hermione G. to Hermione B.
I worshipped you, dear, playing
opposite Tree'

The two Hermiones appeared togethe
in a revival of Noel Coward's *Fallen
Angels* at the Ambassadors Theatre

Mrs Gwynn, Nell Gwynn's mother,
he play Nell *by Tony Hatch*

*h Moira O'Neil in Franklin
cey's play* Pagan in the Parlour

runk in Grand National
ht at the Apollo Theatre

△

*left is my take-off of Jayne
nsfield at a charity performance*
Night of a Hundred Stars

*With Vanessa Redgrave after a
performance as Mrs Peachum in Kurt
Weill's* Threepenny Opera

In The Killing of Sister George

fences. 'Most people look better with something on, even if it's only a feather.'

'Pyjamas!' said David. 'On the invitations we'll say, "come in your pyjamas!"'

Our guests took to the idea with joy, one might even say wild abandon. Although some of the costumes were pretty outré, the required pyjamas were worn by everyone. Striped winceyette, coloured poplin, check silk, orange organza, see-through pyjamas and grandma's pyjamas, beach pyjamas and pyjamas that have never been seen before or since. A three-piece band played jazz and the guests whooped it up. We had a wonderful time and the party was just as crazy and original as David had hoped. The Tennants pyjama party is still talked about to this day.

In the middle of all the high jinks with the noise floating up and down the River Thames, a small figure appeared outside our front door. He was not wearing pyjamas but we let him in just the same for he was our neighbour, Sir James Barrie. 'I haven't come to complain about the noise,' he said, 'or anything silly like that. But it sounds as if you're all having such fun I wondered if I could come too,' he asked wistfully. Of course we welcomed him. He was a tiny man, not much bigger than me, and he was enchanted with everything. He took a special shine to Greta, David's cousin from Sweden. She had her hair cut in a very short Eton crop. He told her she looked just like Peter Pan and his bright blue eyes twinkled with pleasure.

It was all over the newspapers the next day: 'The Tennants give a Pyjama Party'. It sounded very wicked and decadent – just the kind of party the outrageous Bright Young Things would throw. I don't think it was, not really.

I remember that I played 'little cupid' another time while we were living at Adelphi Terrace. David and I gave a party and there was Ian Howland, as he was in those days before he became the Duke of Bedford, sitting in a corner looking rather owl-like and not enjoying himself very much. Suddenly there was an *entrance*: a very slinky lady came in accompanied by three handsome young men. The slinky lady was not particularly attractive, but the effect her long, tight, slinky dress made could not have been bettered by Gertrude Lawrence.

They were gate-crashers, but no one made a fuss in those days for only the well-dressed and well-behaved were accepted as gate-crashers. The slinky lady was known by repute to most of the gentlemen present: her name was Brownie Holloway and she ran a rather questionable club in Soho. Brownie and Ian Howland were introduced to each other. He was rather a shy young man, but she obviously put him at his ease because they got on extremely well. We were all astonished, however, when Brownie and Ian got married. He was, after all, the heir to the Duke of Bedford and Brownie wasn't quite the usual kind of Duchess. But, like the best Somerset Maugham story, it was a very good marriage and there was no better wife than Brownie. Unfortunately she died in 1945 before her father-in-law died and she could become a Duchess.

After Brownie's death, Ian married someone of his own ilk and when, much later, they were divorced, he married the French film director, Madame Milinaire. As the Duke and Duchess of Bedford, their family house at Woburn became one of the foremost entertainment centres in England. I worked for Madame Milinaire once and I found her very high-powered and competent. I was with the costume designer once, looking for a dress to wear, and we weren't making very much headway for our thoughts and ideas of the character I was to play did not coincide.

Madame came in and understood the situation at once. 'Please let Miss Baddeley choose her own dress,' she insisted. 'She is an actress of such experience and high quality that she knows exactly what is right.'

Full marks for Madame Milinaire.

One winter, David and I decided that we must learn to ski. St Moritz in Switzerland was *the* place to go so we tried to make reservations at the Palace Hotel. Unfortunately it was full up as an international Winter Sports Championship was taking place and it was hard to find a hotel. However, determined as we were to master ski-ing, we got in at another hotel.

We discovered that a lot of the competitors were staying at our hotel and soon we became friendly with the English bobsleigh team. The leader of the team asked David whether he would like to do a run with them. David was a great success and he took to the sport with enthusiasm. As it happened, I was quite content to let him be the active one, for I was having trouble with my appendix and didn't feel like hurtling down the icy track. A few days later, there was consternation amongst the English team. Their big day had arrived and one of the team was ill. They asked David to help out.

With David tucked in behind them, the team won and David, along with the other members, was awarded a gold medal. A little later, the Belgian team was in trouble in a different bobsleigh event. One of their number had to drop out and David stepped in again. They won and David was awarded another gold medal. He was the lucky charm of the bobsleigh track that year. Yet another team asked him to join them and David won yet another gold medal. The last team he was asked to join came third and he won a bronze medal. I was pretty surprised that my husband had turned into an international winter sports champion almost overnight.

We went home from St Moritz with suntans, having had a lovely time. Lots of celebration parties, lots of mountain air, and stardom on the bobsleigh for David. Our only regret was that neither of us could ski – we hadn't had time to take a lesson. I had the medals made up into a pretty bracelet with a little gold charm between each one. We went out to supper at the Savoy and I wore my new bracelet for the first time. Noël Coward came over and his eyes rested on my wrist. 'What a beautiful bracelet,' he said leaning over to admire it. 'Medals! Did you win them?'

To tease him, I said: 'It's a medal for every lover I've had on my holiday.'

Noël fingered the bronze medal. 'Congratulations, darling, I see that you've had Paul Robeson.'

Being married to David gave me the chance to enjoy all sorts of pleasures I would never have dreamt of before. I loved the shooting parties in Scotland and the wonderful friends we made in the Highlands, friends who have stayed with me all my life. I loved the weekends in country houses; I remember meeting Lillie Langtry's grandson, Christopher de Bath, at one of those. He was outstandingly handsome and we used to call him 'the divine creature'.

I was received with open arms by the Bright Young Things when I married David. He was one of the leaders of this group but not by any means given to some of their weird and wonderful behaviour.

Perhaps the most sensational of the Bright Young Things was Nancy Cunard, but she soon banished herself to France. And David never joined in their excesses, for he had the Gargoyle Club to run. However, Nancy Cunard did sometimes invade the Gargoyle, bringing with her weird surrealistic painters lugging canvases filled with dream-like landscapes. Brian Howard was part of her group, but not Harold Acton or Clive Bell, though they were often at the Gargoyle.

If David was too busy at the Gargoyle, there was always some man or other who would escort me to parties or first nights. Christopher de Bath, 'the divine creature', was one and there were many others. David and the group around him had different moral values to mine. Promiscuity, so they said, did not worry them. Later, I was to find out that it wasn't quite true. David used to say to me, 'Marriage is not a strait jacket. Don't let's be dreary.' By this he meant that I was not to be jealous over him.

He encouraged me to play the game by these rules but when we were first married I wouldn't have dreamed of being unfaithful. The men who took me to parties were simply friends and admirers, but I wasn't always so sure about the women in David's life. There have always been plenty of women who look upon a good-looking and wealthy man as a challenge that must not be resisted. David liked the company of beautiful women, but he wasn't really a wolf. Ronnie Porter took a delight in pushing women in David's direction – only those, however, who would not be a danger to him, for Ronnie guarded his influence over David very jealously. He liked to be able to manipulate David and he didn't want another pair of eyes – that were often mine – watching what he was doing.

Although Brenda Dean Paul was accepted as his girl-friend, he encouraged her to hang around David. I didn't bother. She was too second-rate to be any kind of a threat. Brenda could be amusing and witty but she always worked too hard at drawing attention to herself and was often irritating to have around. As far as Brenda and David were concerned, I didn't bother. People on drugs, as Brenda was much of the time, are usually not very interested in sex. But Brenda was a troublemaker. Her little barbs were sometimes brought back to me by David. What started as a little tiff over one of her remarks one evening took on unexpected proportions. I retaliated by saying that I thought she was a bad influence.

David leapt to her defence immediately. Perhaps I would like to hear what Brenda thought of some of my friends? I couldn't have cared less what Brenda thought of my friends; besides which, most of them were David's friends too and he encouraged me to go out with them. Then the name of Christopher de Bath came up. I was astonished. It occurred to me that David and his charmed circle might be capable of strong human emotions after all. He might even be jealous. 'Christopher de Bath admires me,' I replied. 'And why shouldn't he? He is always at my first nights. He likes being with me. I like being with him. Just as I like being with my other friends.' I threw in a few more names like the Marquis of Donegal, Lord Hastings and others to tantalize David.' He immediately wanted to know if all these men were my lovers. It became a game. We each tried to score points. Our tempers flared. We said unkind things to each other. In fact we had quite a row.

Next day David rushed off and went to stay at the Savoy. Shortly after as I mentioned before I received a letter from my husband's solicitors informing me that David intended to sue for divorce and he was citing ten co-respondents! I read through the list with admiration. David had remembered every name I had flung at him, every one of my platonic admirers.

I was just as angry as he was. I was angry that he should allow a worthless woman like Brenda Dean Paul to interfere in our marriage. But I wasn't the type of woman to sit around and weep. Within a week I was back in the theatre, rehearsing a new play called *The Five O'Clock Girl*. Now I found out how much I had missed the fun and camaraderie of the theatre. The laughter and the hard work helped me forget my worries. I remember that Johnny Mills was a chorus boy in this show.

When we went off on tour, Mummy came with me. It was just like old times, we were back where we had started and it was great. Little Pauline was looked after by a very competent and loving nanny and at the back of my mind was the certain feeling that it was only a matter of time before David and I picked up our marriage again.

David telephoned me. 'I'm off to Canada,' he said. 'I'm going out to Vancouver to open a factory.'

'Oh!' I said, busily working out in my mind how soon I could go out and join him. 'What do I wish you? *Bon voyage*?'

'I'm sure it will be a good voyage,' he said and I thought I could hear something strange in his voice. 'By the way, I'm taking Brenda Dean Paul with me.'

Chapter Seven

I was in my dressing room making up for the evening performance of *The Five O'Clock Girl,* when the stage door man knocked on my door and told me there was a call for me. I was a bit late, but decided to answer the call anyway. It was Kit. He had just received a telegram from David saying could he please persuade Hermione to get a release from her show and come out to Canada with Pauline. It seems that David had sent Brenda Dean Paul home on the first available boat. In a way I had always known this would happen – he had asked her to go partly to infuriate me and partly because he had to have company. I loved David and didn't want this separation to go on, so I arranged the release next day and, after serving my three weeks' notice, set off with Pauline for Vancouver.

British Columbia was absolutely beautiful, and Vancouver on one side of the Puget Sound with Victoria Island on the other, was lovely. There was a little mountain that seemed right in the middle of it all called Eagle Mountain, and one could take trips up to the top where the view was splendid. The sun shone, winter and summer it blazed down on us.

As soon as I arrived we gave a party. I made two mistakes. The first one was to invite thirteen people to dinner and then discover that I had only twelve chairs; the second was to serve champagne cocktails. It was quite probable that none of our guests had tried a champagne cocktail before, but they soon made up for that. I think the lump of sugar soaked in curacao at the bottom of each glass was appealing.

That night it snowed. The pretty little house we had rented was covered with sparkling white snow and it lay deep in the roads outside. Some of our guests decided that they couldn't get home, so we all had another champagne cocktail and made up beds in the spare rooms and on sofas and chairs and the party went on until the early hours. Next morning some of our guests woke up with rather sore heads.

I'm a very slow drinker myself, but our guests had the transatlantic habit of downing a glass of wine in a couple of good swallows. To my young eyes, Canadian women seemed to have quite a lot of steel in their characters too – the pioneer spirit. They could, when they wanted, be just as tough as their menfolk and some of them could drink any man under the table. To prove that I was no sissy, I soon learned to pretend that I was a hard drinker too. I could weave round with a glass in my hand while in fact staying as sober as a judge.

David was starting up on his own with a factory that made steel containers. His brother Christopher had an interest in it, but it was mainly David's show. Our lives were very full in Vancouver, the steel factory prospered and at week-ends we went fishing in the Campbell river, deep-sea fishing and yacht racing in the lovely Pacific.

Everyone was very kind and made a great fuss of us; little Pauline, who had become a beautiful child, was terribly spoiled. After we'd been in Vancouver for some months Christopher came out to look around. I remember that I gave a party for him and the Canadian prime minister, Mackenzie King. We were really settling in.

While Christopher was with us, the first rumours of a world depression began to worry everyone. The New York stock markets were nervous and stories about people going bankrupt suddenly appeared in the press. The next few months were all bad news. David's steel factory began to lose money, but he pressed on as well as he could. The crash came with the most awful suddenness. One week everyone was looking forward to the weekend fishing and the next week there was no fishing because most of the factories had closed down.

David got in touch with Christopher and they decided the only thing to do was to cut the losses and close down the steel factory. I remember reading the banner headlines in the newspapers: 'Wall Street Crash. Thousands wiped out!' And it was happening in Canada just the same. I was terribly worried, feeling sure that we too had been caught up in the terrible disaster.

The crash upset David very much. He felt that in some way he should not have let the steel factory close down, but there was nothing he could have done. We had been in Vancouver for just over a year and now there was nothing to do but pack up and go home to England. When we arrived home we had to find a new flat to live in. David went on making a great fuss about what had happened in Canada.

I put the rope of lustrous pearls with the diamond and emerald clasp from David's mother into my handbag and went to find a pawnbroker. At last I found a place, went in and sadly laid them on the counter. The pawnbroker screwed a little glass into his eye and spent a long time examining the clasp. 'Eight hundred,' he said. 'There's a lot of jewellery about nowadays, you won't find a buyer.' I took the money. When I got home to David, I handed the money over to him in an envelope, saying I hoped it would help. He opened the envelope and immediately roared with laughter. When I told him that I had pawned my pearls to help us out of our financial crisis, he was first of all astonished and then he gave me a pitying look. It seems that we were very far from broke. Then why, I thought angrily, have you been making such a damned fuss. My gesture that I hoped would please him had turned out to be absolutely meaningless. What I had offered wasn't even a drop in the ocean . . .

I don't know why, but for some reason I didn't rush to get the pearls back. One day I was passing the pawnbroker's shop when I saw a large notice in the window: the pawnbroker had died and his stock was being sold off. In two or three days time the shop would be closed forever. Thank goodness I was in time and bought the pearls back. That was the last time I offered David money.

When we saw Christopher he took the crash in Vancouver quite calmly. The Glenconners as a family always clung together. I think that Christopher did cancel a new plane, but the crash was only a hiccup in the Glenconner empire.

We picked up our life where we had left off before we went to Canada. We found a delightful mews house in Canning Place off Palace Gate. Kensington Gardens was just a stone's throw away and Pauline was taken there every day. While we were in Canada, we had conceived another child – the discovery that I was pregnant was a happy but rather wearying thought. But at least I had my wonderful Gwen with me again and once she was in the house life always ran smoothly. Gwen was a lovely Welsh girl I had engaged as my maid when we lived in Adelphi Terrace. She was tall, slim and dark-haired with a soft Welsh voice and such an air of calm that you immediately felt that all was well with the world.

Our friends were around us once more. Nancy Mitford was one of our group. She wasn't married to Peter Rodd then and she hadn't published any of her witty books, but just listening to her was always entertaining. I remember spending a weekend at her house with her extraordinary family. Her young sister, Unity (the one who later fell in love with Hitler and caused such a scandal), stared at my hairdo – it was a new windswept bob. 'What on earth have you done to yourself?' she demanded. 'What a funny thing to do to your hair.' Unity and Hitler must have had quite a lot in common.

We used our own plane again and I began to take flying lessons. Through flying we met Amy Johnson and Jim Mollison, her husband, and they became great friends of ours. Although they had a few good years together, their marriage eventually broke down. It wasn't Amy's fault – she was a sweet, easy-going person – but Jim drank too much. At the time Amy was a great celebrity and was always having to appear in public at banquets and dinners. She worried about her appearance and thought she was quite plain. The truth was that she had lovely eyes and a good complexion; she was attractive enough, all she needed was a touch of glamour.

One day she asked me how I always managed to look so well turned out, so I decided to show her how to make herself up. I sat her down and made her up just as I did myself. I got to work with mascara and shadow to make her eyes look luminous, powder rouge to shape her face and lipstick for a highlight. When I'd finished she really looked very pretty. Such a simple routine, but it made all the difference to the way she looked. She was so grateful that she said if she ever had a daughter she would call it Hermione.

Poor Amy didn't get the baby she longed for. All in all I don't think she got a great deal of happiness out of her short life. When World War II came along she served her country by doing what she loved best – flying. Her plane came down in the River Thames and her body was never found. It was such a terrible waste of a fine woman.

The Gargoyle Club, in spite of David's prolonged absence, was still a money-maker, even though a lot of that money never found its way into David's bank account. Ronnie Porter was still manager, although the day would come when my judgement of him would be completely vindicated. That day arrived when David found out, through the faithful Miss O'Neill, the club secretary, that Ronnie was arranging with his cronies to vote David out of his own club at the next meeting. At that meeting, instead of David being absent as Ronnie had hoped, he turned up and saved the day for himself.

I'm not sure quite when David did eventually sell the Gargoyle, but I know it was much later, well after the war and even then I begged him not to. It always meant so much to him. For all these years when the Gargoyle belonged to David it was a part of my life, no matter what else might happen.

Rosa Lewis and the Cavendish Hotel were also part of my life for a time. The Cavendish Hotel was a perfect example of an Edwardian country house set down in the West End of London, between Jermyn Street and Duke Street. Rosa had originally been cook to David's great uncle, Lord Ribblesdale. King Edward VII used to dine there and always complimented David's great uncle on the excellent food served at his table, and as a result Rosa used to go and cook for the King when Lord Ribblesdale was away. Some scandal-mongers used to say that Rosa was not a cook at all, and that the King and Lord Ribblesdale were sharing the same mistress, but I don't believe it. At any rate, Rosa looked after Lord Ribblesdale and when he died he left her his London house, which she turned into the Cavendish. Because of her affection for David's uncle, she always had a soft spot for David and me. We were always made welcome in her hotel and it became a place of refuge for both of us. She was quite a character – every morning she would pull a large coat on over her nightdress and trail round the hotel, her little Cairn terrier yapping at her heels, to see what was new. Rosa would sometimes turn up at the Gargoyle, Cairn terrier in tow, pushing everyone aside, refusing to sign the guest book and declaiming loudly: 'I'm part of the family. I don't have to do nothing.'

I was never sure how much of Rosa's cockney accent and cockney grammatical mistakes were put on to please and amuse her clients. The odd thing was that Rosa wasn't at all funny or witty herself – it was the strange eccentric way she behaved that amused us. We laughed at her behind her back, of course, but it was always with affection. In times of trouble – and quite a few came my way – I could always turn to Rosa and she would find a room for me. I'd follow her up the stairs until she stopped at a door. 'I think this one's empty,' she'd say and turn the handle of the door. There might well be a muffled scream and someone would dive under the bedclothes. 'Can't have that one then.' She generally took her time about closing the door, making sure she got a good look at what was going on. 'Two busy little bees in there, right enough.' She had an acid tongue and could be very spiky, and if she didn't like you nothing on earth could persuade her to let you come into her hotel. 'Won't have that woman in my hotel,' she'd say of some titled lady. 'She's nothing but a tart.'

In Rosa's little parlour were hundreds of pictures and photographs of her favourites – David and me amongst them – and there was a copy of an oil painting of Lord Ribblesdale. Rosa had a special way of balancing her books. If she felt like a bottle of champagne – and Rosa was generous with champagne – the price of the bottle always found its way onto some unsuspecting customer's bill. If we dined at the Cavendish with friends, David used to laugh: 'Three of us will certainly get the same bill for this dinner sooner or later.' She knew they could all afford it, so let 'em pay up was her policy. But she was also very generous with us and often wouldn't let us pay a penny.

Daphne Fielding wrote a book about her and the Cavendish, and wanted to turn it into a musical play. She asked me to play Rosa; I turned it down at the time, but now I wish I had done it. If anyone could have brought her to life, I could. I knew her so well. Finally, a television serial was made about Rosa and her hotel, called *The Duchess Of Duke Street,* but it wasn't Rosa as she really was. She wasn't easy to capture and put on the television screen – she was such an odd mixture of cockney common sense, the refined lady and that little bit extra that no one else had got.

I have always loved parties. There's something about a room full of happily chattering people with a jazz band in full swing in the background and elegantly-dressed couples twirling round the dance floor that makes me tingle with excitement. At this time of my life there seemed to be more parties than days in the week. There were always the high spots of the season. A charming American lady called Mrs Wooly used to come over to London every year to give a party that was always talked about for weeks afterwards. Her parties had a theme. One year it was 'The Circus' and everybody came dressed as clowns, acrobats or strong men. Amongst other entertainments, she had hired an elephant. As soon as David saw the magnificent animal, he tried to leap on top of it – only to slide unceremoniously off the other side, losing the watch that his grandfather had given him in the process. We found it intact and the word went round that it had miraculously survived being trampled on by an elephant.

Another party I remember well was given by my great friend Barbara Redhead, whose sister Peggy married Lord Rothermere. She was anxious that it should be a glamorous evening and asked me to help her out. She told me that she knew exactly where to get the champagne, because she had recently met a certain Herr Ribbentrop who was busy promoting a very delicious champagne in this country. Everything went ahead, we took premises in Jermyn Street and hired a jazz band. I must say that when Herr Ribbentrop arrived with his wife he was extremely charming. I wonder what we would have thought if we had known that this man, whose champagne was frothing in our glasses, would one day be hanged as a war criminal.

That wasn't the only time I was asked to help at a party. Many years later, a great admirer of mine, Sir Alfred Beit, wanted me to play hostess at a large cocktail party he was giving. In fact, he had once asked me to marry him, but I had refused although I was always very fond of him. He wasn't at all a good socialiser and got very nervous as the appointed day approached. We set off for the party in good time, but on the way we were hauled in by a policeman for erratic driving. He made us get out of the car and asked us our names. Unfortunately for us, we all had either aristocratic titles or unusual names, which completely flummoxed the poor Bobby; amongst us were the Master of Glamis, the Countess of Seafield, Lord Stanley and the Honourable Mrs Cardiff. First of all he thought we were pulling his leg, then he kept repeating the names over and over in disbelief, and finally we each had to spell out our names to him one by one, titles and all. I think we may have been a little bit mischievous with him, but the upshot was that we were late for the party. When we arrived, poor Sir Alfred was holding fort as best he could, looking utterly panic-stricken. I dashed over to Margot Fonteyn and Emlyn Williams for comfort. They said it was perfectly alright.

Well-dressed gate-crashers were usually accepted at parties in those days, but not at Lady Elmsmere's. She kept a list of eligible people, including David and Stephen, and invited them and them alone. Soon after our marriage, David was invited to her annual party, but not me – I wasn't on the list. David was furious that his marriage had been overlooked and we didn't attend. Stephen decided he would take Cecil Beaton's sister with him, but she wasn't on the list either. At the door, she was sternly turned away, much to her embarrassment and Stephen's fury. Next day, it was all in the papers and 'Lady Elmsmere's list' became the laughing stock of London society. David insisted that on the invitations to our next party we put 'Gate-crashers Welcome'.

One of the most successful parties David and I gave was what we called 'the family party'. It was an excuse to meet the members of David's huge family, the progeny of the wicked old grandfather's two very fruitful marriages. My own family was quite small in comparison. The Clinton Baddeley's seemed to be dying out; there was my cousin Victor Clinton Baddeley, and my half-brother Bill Pye Baddeley, but they were the only two male Baddeleys left. At least now everyone had met all the members of our two families, and we knew each other when we met at weddings and christenings.

Perhaps the most splendid party we gave was the Mozart party. We invited about five hundred guests and told them to dress in costumes of the Mozart operas. We couldn't possibly get five hundred people into our house and the Gargoyle would be too much of a squeeze, so we hired the Suffolk Galleries in Bloomsbury. It was exactly the right atmosphere for such a party and we had a string orchestra to play for us while we dined.

We invited about thirty of our closest friends to dinner before the party. Served by candle-light, the flickering shadows gave an air of romance to the room. With the strings in the background, the crystal goblets filled with wine, the laughter and the gaiety, there was a touch of magic in the air and it seemed we were in Salzburg or Vienna in the eighteenth century. David was dressed as Don Giovanni and he looked magnificent, every inch a Don Juan. I wore a crinoline type of dress which might not have been exactly right for the period, but it did hide the nine months of my pregnancy. With a wig and a black beauty patch I think I called myself Donna Elena. After dinner the other guests arrived and we danced and enjoyed ourselves until dawn. There is something about dressing up in costume that gives an added excitement. I certainly forgot that I was about to give birth at any moment.

'Darling,' someone called to me as I danced by, 'what if the baby is born on the ballroom floor?'

'He's a Tennant,' I laughed. 'A Scot! He'd never do anything so rash.'

David, my son, was born a few days later. Whether it is the pre-natal influence or not, David likes a glass of wine. 'You can hardly blame me,' he says. 'After all I could so easily have been born right in the middle of a party.'

It was a very happy time of my life. I adored my baby son and I loved having a little daughter. I found myself becoming more and more involved with them. If anyone had asked me to go away and leave them I should have been appalled. But men with a lot of money and no settled job get bored and restless. David decided that he'd like to go a very long way away – to China.

In 1930 that wasn't all that easy. China was still the unknown continent and some areas were forbidden to Europeans; it was still the China of the Mandarins and oriental mystery. But that wasn't the difficult part for me, it was the distance. Getting to China meant a long journey across Europe and Asia. David wanted me to go with him. I think perhaps he was getting a little jealous of them. Little David was far too young for such a voyage and I really didn't want to leave him. I should have to stay away from my children for such a long time and China was such a long way off. I shook my head; if David was set on the idea, he would have to go alone.

Before he left David said he wished I was coming too. More than anything I felt like forgetting my responsibilities, packing a bag, and going with him, and as far as David was concerned that would have been perfectly in order. If he wanted to do something, he did it no matter what chaos he left behind. I had always accepted that David was like this. 'If you change your mind,' he added. 'Come out and join me.' A forlorn hope.

David didn't say, 'Now be sure to have a good time while I'm away,' because he didn't say things like that, but neither did he show any signs of worrying what I might get up to while he was in China. I missed him dreadfully at first, but still I carried on with the social round as usual. I went to parties, gave parties, went out to dinner with friends and I was certainly not bored.

Nina Seefield, the Countess of Seafield, one of my great friends had a home in London and a wonderful place in Scotland. While I was up there with her, she invited a young man called Freddy Childs, of whom she was very fond, to join the house party. Freddy had a little moustache and played the piano beautifully. Every woman in the party was charmed by his delightful manner and wonderful piano-playing. He was such a man about town, so kind and understanding. Everyone made a great fuss of him. I told him how popular he was and he touched his little moustache and said: 'And I'm after you, Hermione.'

When I got back to London I had a little party and Freddy came and played the piano and watched me all the time. He kept whispering that he couldn't understand how David could go off to China and leave such a desirable little creature behind. Every time I met Freddy, and that was nearly every day, he told me how rotten he thought David was to leave me. His Bentley stood outside my front door, his bottles of Moet & Chandon champagne filled my cellar. Freddy was manager of Moet & Chandon in England, and as I was beginning to have his interests at heart I used to get all my friends to order that brand of champagne. Freddy was not rolling in money by any means, but he had such a way with him.

David and I now rented a house in Sussex every summer. It was near Uckfield and called Tickeridge Mill. The house belonged to David's cousin and great friend Dick Wyndham, and he was always pleased to let us rent it because, as he said, 'Hermione looks after it so well.' In fact, when he was killed in Egypt during the war, I was asked if I would like to buy it for some marvellously low price. But by that time someone else was after my money and he advised me not to go ahead. I always regretted it, and quite some time after it was bought by Vivien Leigh.

I used to have weekend house parties down at Tickeridge Mill and Freddy always came down and rather took David's place, carving the joint on Sunday, walking the dogs and taking me to parties in the neighbourhood. He was very good with the children and, in his quiet way, he helped to fill the enormous gap left behind by my husband. David did not hurry back from China. He wrote what a long journey it had been, but how pleased he was to be there because there were going to be great changes.

Freddy, although not a very demonstrative man, did his best to make me forget my absent husband. One evening we were alone and he played the piano for me. We drank Moet & Chandon champagne and it was all so romantic. Later that evening I had to admit that Freddy had another accomplishment – he was a very good lover. Our gentle, undemanding affair began.

It wasn't until the night before David arrived home that I realized just what had happened. Freddy declared that he was madly in love with me and he couldn't bear the idea of my husband claiming me again. We had dinner together, a farewell dinner, or so I thought, at Pruniers, but Freddy only toyed with his oysters. He'd lost his appetite completely. We sat in the darkened corner of a night-club afterwards and held hands and felt very sad. He thought that David might not let me see him again and sighed. Poor Freddy was almost physically ill with the thought of what tomorrow would bring.

The front door sprang open next day and there was David kissing me, hugging me. He was absolutely delighted to see me. He told me how much he had missed me over and over again. David was still the best looking man in London and he was my very loving husband, just as he used to be. He was full of exciting stories about his travels and his trunks and suitcases bulged with presents for us. Those were the days when an English lady or gentleman travelled with real luggage, not a flimsy airline bag, and there were masses of willing porters at every station to move the baggage.

David had raided the treasures of China, delicate porcelain, beautiful embroidery from Peking, lengths of finest silk, intricate chains of jewels, little gowns and toys for the children. I have never seen such wonderful presents.

The telephone rang. It had been ringing all morning. 'David's home,' I told Freddy. 'I must say goodbye.'

Fifteen minutes later the telephone rang again. 'I need to hear your voice,' said Freddy.

David asked me who had called and I told him it was Freddy. He looked at the welcome home bottle of champagne we had opened. Moet & Chandon! 'Oh, Freddy, the champagne man!' We smiled at each other.

Next day Freddy continued with his relentless telephone calls. 'What's the matter with the man?' asked David.

'He thinks he's in love with me.'

'Oh, everybody's in love with you. Has he been a bore?'

I shook my head and told him that Freddy hadn't been a bore at all, but had been very kind and taken me everywhere. I told him how he used to come down to Tickeridge at weekends, how good he had been with the children . . . I knew then that if I didn't tell David, there was not a shadow of doubt that someone else would. We had been seen everywhere together, his Bentley had been a fixture outside my front door. I took a deep breath.

David said: 'You're not in love with him, are you?'

The words hovered on my lips, I bit them back. How could I say, 'I don't know, but if I am I'll try and get over it'. Why couldn't we have waited until David had been home for a time, until things had settled down, perhaps even faded away? I wondered just how much I should tell him. That I'd been unfaithful to him for the first time and it would never have happened if he hadn't gone away in such a carefree manner and left me alone for months and months? He may as well know the truth, I decided; hadn't he always said that marriage was not a strait-jacket, that life must be enjoyed to the full? Well I had enjoyed myself, just as he'd said I would. 'All right,' I said. 'It's better I tell you. Freddy is my lover.'

Chapter Eight

We should have had a tremendous row; we should have shouted and abused each other. David should have castigated me for taking a lover, probably even given me a slap or two, and I should have yelled at him: 'You've been unfaithful to me, and more than once.'

But we did none of these things. Instead, we faced each other and acted like two characters out of an early Noël Coward play.

'I'll get over it,' I said. 'Just give me a little time and I know I'll get over it.'

'It must stop,' insisted David. 'Find some way to tell him that it must stop.'

'I promise! Just give me a little time.'

'Very well.' David seemed quite calm. 'If that's what you want. Don't let's be dreary about it.'

But it soon became apparent that everything was not very well. In spite of David declaring that jealousy was so dreary, underneath jealousy festered. Discovering that I had taken Freddy as a lover was a great blow to David's self-confidence. His pride and male vanity were wounded. I don't think he ever forgave me. I did try to keep my promise, but wherever we went there, it seemed, was Freddy Childs hovering in the background. He and David always got on quite well and Freddy, at least in public, kept his adoration of me within bounds. But he was there, still in my life and I didn't try hard enough not to see him again. Much later I found out how this had affected David, but by then it was too late.

Because of the trouble over Freddy Childs when David came home from China, he decided that it would help us both if we looked for and bought a country house where the children could go in the summer and where we could spend weekends. We sometimes went back to Wilsford, which now belonged to Stephen, and we often went for little journeys in a horse-drawn caravan that David had built with the help of the village Smithy. It was quite a simple affair, made of wood, not ornate like a gypsy caravan but it had movable steps to the door at the back. Inside we kept tents and camping equipment, but if it was cold we used to sleep inside. We loved the simple life – for short periods – and we used to build fires and cook sausages and bacon and eggs.

It was so like David that the house he eventually set his heart on was very much like Wilsford, the house he had sold. We found this little village in a Wiltshire valley, a stream ran though it and in the middle of the village, set well back in its own grounds, was an enchanting grey stone house with its own little church. David and I were fascinated by the look of this house. Every time we went through the village, we would stop and admire it and discuss its finer points. He'd even found out that the people living there had once been tea-planters in Ceylon and had come home to retire. They hadn't a lot of money but they had no wish to sell. David urged the estate agent to try and change their minds, but to no avail.

One day the estate agent telephoned to ask if David and I would like to come to Teffont Manor, as the house was called, and have tea with them. We set off the day before in our caravan and camped that night on Salisbury Plain. Our intention was to rise before dawn to see the first rays of the sun strike the altar stone at Stonehenge where legend said human life had once been sacrificed. With us came a friend, Robin Mount, who rode his own horse.

As always, David was captivated when he saw Teffont Manor. It was a gorgeous place, but there was something strange about it, as if a siren were calling to us from within. Robin wasn't sure about it – he agreed with me that it was almost too perfect looking. As soon as we were inside the manor house, I shivered and felt cold even though it was a hot summer's day. I thought to myself that I didn't really mind if David bought this house or not. The interior was dull, almost gloomy. We passed one of the long windows and there was a shaft of light onto the green lawns outside. 'It needs light and green and yellow,' I thought to myself. 'The garden needs to be brought into the house.'

The tea-planter and his wife were waiting for us in the drawing room. I had never seen two people who looked so faded, as if the hot sun they had once lived in had bleached them. They had a transparent look like two grey ghosts, and their house had the same shadowy grey to it. The maid brought in tea and we listened to the tea-planters. They talked sombrely as if there'd been some tragedy. The tea-planter told us that they could not sell the house, it had to stay in the family. His wife asked me why I wanted to live at Teffont, and said that she didn't think I would like it. David caught my eye and I sensed that he didn't want me to reply. Instead, he told them that if we couldn't buy it, we would like to rent it.

It wasn't a very jolly party, and when we had left I turned to David and told him I didn't think we wanted the house even if they did decide to rent. What was the good of spending a lot of money if it could never be ours? But that house had a spell on David. He could see me doing wonderful things with it, transforming the interior into something light and cheerful, and he clearly thought that they might still be persuaded to sell it.

After a lot more gloomy discussion the tea-planter rented Teffont Manor to us. We did spend a lot of money on the house and changed it beyond recognition. A huge double drawing room was made into one and we covered the floors with a wonderful grass-green carpet that gave the impression we had brought the garden indoors. On the walls we had prints of brightly-coloured exotic birds. I found beautiful antique furniture and had all the curtains and upholstery done in light and airy colours. The gloom was banished and we had a beautiful home, but for some reason I was often uneasy and my first impression that Teffont was not a lucky house stayed with me.

It could have been the ghosts. The tea-planters had never been teased by ghosts – perhaps the spirits didn't care for them – but they were interested in us. The children and their nanny moved in as well as my mother-in-law's darling old cook, Winnie, a maid from the village, and Gwen, my own maid from Canning Place. When I arrived I asked Gwen how she liked the new house. Gwen shuddered and replied: 'Winnie and I go up to bed at night holding hands because of the ghost.'

'What ghost, Gwen?'

'We call her the Grey Lady.'

As the children grew up at Teffont, they often talked of the Grey Lady. A neighbour of ours said we would have to get the house exorcised. She assured us it was haunted. Augustus John, who lived nearby, was sitting with us one evening when we all heard noisy footsteps going up and down a staircase overhead. Yet we knew there was no one upstairs. Bedroom doors would fly open without warning and a gust of cold air would herald the arrival of one of our ghosts. We grew quite used to them.

Almost immediately after we moved in, David couldn't resist letting the whole village know just what we were like. Every single person was invited to a party, including the butcher, the baker and the owners of the local pub; and of course all our friends from London came down. We had wonderful weather, so David had the gardens lit with lanterns and naturally we had to have fireworks. A three-piece band played and everyone drank and danced until dawn. Some of the villagers still slept under the trees by the time the noon-day sun had risen.

In 1935, a great tragedy prevented me meeting one of the most fascinating and mysterious men of our times. While serving in the Middle East, David's cousin and great friend Captain Dick Wyndham had met T. E. Lawrence, the extraordinary man who inspired and led the Arab revolt against the Turks during the First World War. One day, Dick told us that Lawrence was coming to stay in a cottage on his estate. He had told Dick that he didn't want any entertainments laid on, but just peace and quiet, though he did want to meet Dick's family and close friends. So we arranged a small drinks party at Tickeridge and waited in some excitement for the day to arrive when we would meet the famous Lawrence of Arabia. Two days before the day fixed for the party, we heard on the wireless that Lawrence had met with a bad accident. He had been coming down Clouds Hill on his motorbike and had swerved to avoid a boy going up the hill on his bicycle. We were very upset by this news and hoped he would recover soon. We kept ringing up Dick to find out how he was, but his injuries turned out to be worse than had been feared; Lawrence died four days after the accident.

Teffont Manor did bring David and me together just as he had hoped it would. Being a frustrated interior decorator at heart, I could have gone on filling that house with beautiful old furniture forever. I loved the size of it, and the parties we gave that everyone enjoyed. I remember one Christmas when the house was filled with guests. One of them was Tony Gandarias, who had lived for some time in Hong Kong and had a very oriental way about him. Gwen, who was marvellous and could look after both our male and female guests – she used to act as David's valet as well as my personal maid – came to me. 'Madam,' she said. 'I've been unpacking for Mr Gandarias, what shall I do with the pipes?'

'Pipes!' I exclaimed. 'How romantic. I do hope he'll play for us'.

Gwen beckoned me to follow her. 'It's no musical instrument he's got with him, Madam.' They were opium pipes.

'Oh dear,' I said. 'Do you think it's legal?'

Gwen's eyes grew round. 'As long as he doesn't ask us to take a puff, Madam!'

At about this time, we were very friendly with Cynthia and Sir Oswald Mosley. At that time, Sir Oswald was extremely busy promoting the fascist party of which he was leader – there were meetings and rallies all over the country which attracted a lot of attention in the newspapers, although I took very little notice of their political views. What I did notice, however, was that David scrupulously avoided any reference to politics when we were with the Mosleys. Late one morning, when David was out for lunch, Cynthia rang me up and asked if she could possibly borrow a couple of our cars to help transport people to a rally they were organizing in the area. Not quite realizing what this rally might be, I readily agreed to lend them our Lagonda, and even David's cherished Isotta Fraschini, if they would be of any use. When David came back, I casually mentioned the arrangement to him. He was absolutely furious. 'I wouldn't dream of letting my motor cars be used for Mosley's ridiculous politics,' he raged. I received a long lecture on the politics of fascism and was told to ring up Cynthia immediately and tell her that she could not, after all, borrow our cars. I was so terrified that I asked David to ring Oswald instead. 'You know I won't discuss politics with him,' he said, so in the end I had to do it. It was an embarrassing episode.

Everyone seemed perfectly happy at Teffont, except perhaps me. We weren't there all the time – we went to London, there was the Gargoyle, weekends in Scotland, trips abroad. Yet although we led such busy lives and were always going somewhere, always doing something, I couldn't help feeling that my life was going by and I was wasting my time.

Someone else must have had the same thoughts. I was at a party given by two charming homosexual gentlemen, one of whom was Bunny Rogers. I've always had many friends who are that way inclined, and in those days they were much more readily accepted in the theatre than in other walks of life. These two particular friends of mine always gave good parties and this one was right up to standard. Music played, champagne flowed and everyone got rather tight. At the end of a very rollicking dance a group of us ended rolling on the floor. I found myself next to my two hosts we sat on the floor and congratulated each other on making everyone so happy. 'That's just it, Hermione,' said one of my hosts. 'You shouldn't really be here at all.' I thought he meant I shouldn't be sitting in an undignified heap on the floor and told him not to be so silly.

'No,' he said, 'I mean you shouldn't be making us laugh like this at parties, you should be back on stage. That's where you make people happy. You're an artiste, and you're wasting your talents.' His friend caught my hand. 'Go back to the theatre, Hermione. It's such a wicked waste.'

Their words stayed in my head. A few nights later I went to see my sister Angela in a new play. Just as I always did, I longed to be on the stage with the performers, up there under the lights with an audience to play to. After the show, when all the people who came in to congratulate Angela had gone, I sat alone with her. She was at her dressing table taking off her make-up. After some hesitation and a few restless sighs, I began to pour out my worries. I had done all the things I wanted to do, had children, given wonderful parties, travelled, enjoyed myself . . . Then why did I feel I was wasting my time, drifting from party to party, from long weekend to long weekend? My heart began to beat rapidly, and then I told her what had been nagging away at me: I desperately wanted to go back to the theatre.

She swung round and faced me. Angela's face was usually very composed, but she had the most beautiful smile that made her whole face look suddenly radiant. She was smiling then; she was absolutely delighted, for she had always hated the way I had walked away from the theatre. That smile made me so happy – it confirmed the decision I knew in my heart of hearts I must take.

As soon as I decided to return to the stage I felt quite different. All the slight, intangible feelings of dissatisfaction vanished. Even when no one came along with a wonderful offer I still felt good. The first person to approach me with a serious offer was Frank Vosper, the actor and playwright. He had been given permission to turn

Margaret Kennedy's novel, *Escape Me Never,* into a play and had decided while reading it that if I had any thoughts of returning to the stage, I should be the one to play Gemma. Of course I told him I would love to play the part, and asked him to send me the script as soon as he had finished it.

I put the telephone down and felt very happy. Having a great big success at the start of her career always worries an actress. Will she be able to cap it, or will it always be there to taunt her and make her long for the great part that always seems to elude her. I remember Doris Keane crying out: 'I'll never get another *Romance!*' Frank sent the script to me by instalments and I loved it. It could not help but be a great hit. The knowledge that there was this wonderful part waiting for me, a part that would even eclipse what I'd done in *The Likes Of 'Er* seemed too good to be true. Like so many things that have happened in my life that was exactly what it was. Too good to be true!

Frank Vosper rang me up one morning in despair. Someone else was planning to put on *Escape Me Never*. Margaret Kennedy had decided to dramatize the novel herself, and was handing it over to none other than C. B. Cochran. My heart sank, then I had a flash of hope. There was still a chance that I might play this wonderful role, for I had parted with C. B. Cochran on good terms.

Immediately Frank dashed my hopes. 'Even worse, he's engaged a German actress to play Gemma.'

The whole episode was a deep disappointment. I was full of anticipation and excitement about returning to the stage with this marvellous play and now that wily old showman had beaten me to it. Even sadder, it turned out to be the last chance I would have of working with Frank Vosper. A few years later he was on a boat returning from Africa and was lost overboard. No one ever found out what happened. It was a great loss for me and a tragedy for the theatre.

No actress worth her salt can sit around licking her wounds. There would be other plays, other roles, other shows. One of the strangest bearers of a very good part was Robert Newton. I was sitting on a high green bank at Teffont looking at the carpet of daffodils in front of me, when I noticed a figure staggering up the drive. A man who looked as if he'd slept in his clothes the night before came into view

– his thick black hair was tousled, his face flushed and his gait unsteady.

He yelled a greeting and immediately collapsed at the bottom of my bank. I slid down towards him. Robert Newton, who had obviously called at more than one pub on the way, grinned up at me. He managed to tell me that he had a play for me to read. I didn't take Bobby Newton too seriously – he was a man who needed a lot of drink to give him confidence. But he was a fine actor and at that time he hadn't reached the point where managements were afraid to employ him because of his problem with alcohol. He ran his own little theatre in Fulham, The Shilling Theatre because that's all you had to pay to get in. As he couldn't make much money this way, if he found a reasonable play he often got his friends to appear for nothing. And because Bobby Newton could be quite brilliant at choosing plays people did listen to him.

I listened to him now. The play he had found was called *The Greeks Had A Word For It,* and there were parts for both me and Angela. Robert planned to put it on at the Shilling Theatre. When he eventually left, in my hands he placed a dog-eared script. Although I didn't know it then, here lay the part that would take me back to the top of my profession. But before I did this play, I appeared in a musical show called *Ballyhoo* at the Comedy Theatre.

Freddy Ashton, who was the choreographer of the show, told me that I was going to dance with a young American called Walter Crisham. At the first rehearsal, a dark-haired young man sitting alone introduced himself as Wally Crisham. He had an Irish look and he told me that his father was a famous Irish baseball player in New York. Wally had a dry sense of humour and we became good friends. By the time the show opened, instead of the one number he'd been engaged to dance, Wally was doing eight. That gives a fair indication of his talent. He'd fallen in love with London and the London audiences fell in love with him. He stayed on for over twenty years.

There was another young man in *Ballyhoo* who was going to make it right to the top – George Sanders. He had a wonderful tenor voice, he was tall and good-looking, but he had no stage presence at all. He looked rather wooden on the stage, arms dangling like a gorilla at his side. No matter how hard the director tried to help, George couldn't get it right. When we opened, he sang from the wings, which was a terrible waste of such a good-looking and sexy man. He had this deliciously deep, rich voice, but on the stage he froze into something like a puppet in the hands of a weary puppeteer. I should have advised him to try the movies because it's often easier to act naturally in front of a camera than on stage. Someone else must have had the right idea, for once George was out in Hollywood everything fell into place, including those dangling arms.

George Sanders had a very attractive brother called Tom Conway. He had a lot of charm, perhaps even more than George. I think the brothers were partly Italian, partly Russian, a very appealing but also – as I was soon to discover – a very dangerous combination.

I'd been ill. I'd had a haemorrhage and my medical adviser had told me to stay in bed. George and his brother Tom came round one evening to visit the patient. They perched on the end of my bed and produced a huge flagon of Italian chianti. I told them that I was under doctor's orders not to drink, but not to let that stop them. It didn't. Gwen produced the glasses and as the chianti was drunk so their stories and laughter increased. 'Come on,' urged George, 'one little glass won't hurt you.'

'Good Italian wine, just like a blood transfusion,' agreed Tom as he poured me out a glass. After half a glass I must admit that I felt better, but by the time the bottle was empty I felt a strange floating sensation coming over me. Pretty soon, I had passed out.'

My life was probably saved by Gwen rushing in when the boys passed on the news to her. She took one look at me, telephoned the doctor, and I was soon in an ambulance being whisked off to hospital for an emergency blood transfusion.

By the time I recovered, George and Tom had left for America and fame and fortune on the silver screen.

Angela and I were delighted to be together in *The Greeks Had A Word For It*. We'd worked together often as children, but never as adults. I had this knack of making people laugh and Angela was the perfect foil. We had always worked like this when entertaining the residents at my mother's guest house.

Years before, in spite of the fact that neither she nor her two younger daughters had ever been on a tennis court or held a tennis racquet, Mummy accepted an invitation from one of her rich friends for Angela and me to go to a tennis party. Angela and I, because of Mummy's chronic lack of funds, had, in fact, never played any game that cost money. The only requirement for a game of tennis, as far as we knew, was to look the part, so we wore dashing bandeaux like Suzanne Lenglen. As soon as we walked down the marble steps into the picture postcard garden, we were handed tennis racquets and drawn into a mixed doubles. We tried whacking the ball as if using a fly swatter, but of course we were hopeless – we never got a ball across the net. But our partners were so doubled up with laughter that they weren't much better. With completely serious faces we clowned, we hammed it up and our comical efforts were a great success.

Angela and I were completely different characters. I am not the worrying kind, I live my life as if I've never heard of the proverbial rainy day, while Angela always took her responsibilities seriously. While we were rehearsing *The Greeks Had a Word For It*, Angela used to worry dreadfully, particularly for my sake, about whether the play would be a success. I was always assuring her that it was a brilliant play and would be snapped up by a West End theatre within weeks of opening.

That was exactly what happened. Almost as soon as we opened at The Shilling Theatre, we had an offer to transfer to the Duke of York's in St Martin's Lane. We had a good cast with Margaret Rawlings and Clive Morton, and the play ran in that theatre for over a year. Then, because the Duke of York's was booked for another play, we moved to the Cambridge Theatre. All in all, *The Greeks Had A Word For It* ran for three years. I couldn't have found a better vehicle for my come-back to the theatre. The cast was changed now and then, but Angela and I kept our roles.

Being in a hit play in the thirties was very gratifying – the theatre was very different fifty years ago. There were over forty theatres operating in London and most of the audience, especially if they sat in the more expensive seats, wore evening dress. Going to the theatre was treated as an occasion and supper in a nightclub afterwards was an added treat. London was a much more agreeable place, mainly because it was emptier. There were no pushing crowds in Oxford Street and Regent Street and there was less violence on the streets. No one was paid the astronomical salaries they get nowadays, but the quality of life was good.

All my family seemed contented. Mummy, I know, was happy in her pretty cottage in the country, with her gardening and her bridge and her four daughters and her son to fill her life with happenings and interest. Bill, our young half-brother, had gone to Australia and he was soon to become a Dean. Although Mummy had always been an ardent Catholic, none of us, except Bill, had taken religion very seriously. But Bill took after Mummy, he even had the same classical features. Uncle Pye sometimes came round to see her, and although Ciggie and Muriel were married with growing families and Angela and I were on the stage in London, we all called to see Mummy regularly. The evening of her life was filled with happiness.

At one time she did complain about severe indigestion and I begged her to see a doctor, but she said the discomfort came and went and really wasn't worth bothering about. One day I called to see her and she was in great pain. I insisted that she see my doctor at once. After tests and examinations he told me that Mummy had a growth in her stomach. He wasn't sure that surgery would be a good idea and suggested a course of radium treatment first.

We were about to have a holiday in the South of France, but we cancelled it and took her home to Canning Place to live with us. One of the best surgeons saw her and said he could operate, but he could not promise that she would recover. The best thing, we were told, was to keep her happy and comfortable and any pain could be controlled with medicine. This went on for months and months. When she became weaker and needed constant nursing, we had a family discussion and chose a nursing home in Sloane Square so that one of us could call in and see her every day.

She knew we had cancelled one holiday and she begged David and me not to cancel another one for her sake. So we decided to go to the South of France. Before we left, she made me promise one thing – to give up the flying lessons I was taking. She hated the idea of me piloting my own aeroplane; in fact, I don't think she trusted aeroplanes at all.

We hadn't been on holiday for much more than a week when a cable came from Uncle Pye to say that Mummy had died very peacefully. At the funeral we were all very upset, but in memory she always stayed with us. I will never forget all those tours with all those plays and all those shows she came on, times when she did everything for everybody. I think those theatrical tours might have been some of the happiest days of her life. She was part of the theatre and that was what she'd always wanted to be.

Chapter Nine

The New Year's Eve Party at the Gargoyle in 1935 was one of the best ever. A wonderful mixture of people arrived and we gave them balloons and funny hats and streamers. Wally Crisham and I did an adagio dance for the cabaret, one of those routines with plenty of action, during which I wound a long sash around my waist and he let me out and then pulled me back. As soon as the cabaret was over, Wally and I joined the large table at the back. More champagne was opened, people kept coming into the club from other parties hugging and kissing me and David and wishing us a happy new year.

We were full of hopes and dreams for the coming year. Hitler and Mussolini were still just a couple of noisy dictators in foreign countries and all the riveting talk was about the Prince of Wales and this new American woman called Mrs Simpson.

'Fruity' Metcalfe, the Prince's equerry, was telling us the latest gossip about the royal romance, when I suddenly realized that David wasn't listening. His eyes were on a couple who had just come in. The man I didn't know but the girl was familiar from a summer party we had held at Teffont. Her name was Virginia Parsons and I knew that her father Alan Parsons was a very good journalist and critic. Her hair still covered her face and she pushed it back as she approached our table. 'Here comes the Invisible Lady,' whispered Fruity.

David stood up to welcome them; he and Virginia kissed affectionately and wished each other a happy new year, then she turned to me. Lately David had said to me once or twice that he was taking out Virginia, but it could have been one of five other women. We accepted that we were both free to go out with other people. He would often say to me that it was me he had chosen to marry and no one else; as for me, there could never seriously be anyone else but David.

I remembered that the first time I'd met The Invisible Lady she had made a bee-line for David and they'd sat together talking for most of the evening. David had told me that she was the daughter of Viola Tree, the actress, who was the daughter of Herbert Beerbohm Tree . . . it could go on forever! Someone had telephoned once to say: 'You know that girl's after David, don't you?' Of course I had, but I never took it seriously. David flirted with lots of women: Poppet, the daughter of Augustus John, earthy and sexy, had been quite a number – for a time.

Late one evening, some months into the new year, David began talking about Freddy Childs, complaining that he still saw a lot of me. That was true. In a way I needed someone like Freddy always to be there when I wanted him. But he wasn't important to me any more, we weren't lovers, and I told David so.

'I heard a note in your voice when you spoke to him on the telephone once,' David replied. 'It was one I recognized. You used that note in your voice when you were in love with me. It upset me very much to hear you use it to another man.'

Why was he telling me this now, I wondered. If he had been so upset why hadn't he told me at the time? I knew that he'd always thought that he owned me, that he didn't think I'd ever fall in love with another man. That was why, in a way, I hadn't sent Freddy Childs away completely. As I'd grown more mature I didn't want to be owned by any man. I was a little sixteen-year-old when I'd fallen in love with David. Now I was a grown woman with two children and a career of my own. I reminded David that he had always wanted this kind of marriage, with nothing ever hidden between us.

'Perhaps I was wrong,' he said.

That was when I realized that the conversation about Freddy Childs was to justify something he was going to tell me, something I knew I didn't want to hear.

'Virginia thinks we should get married.'

So, someone else had flattered him, soothed this hurt pride he had never told me about, and now she wanted to take my place. It was an awful blow and instead of holding on and waiting to see if this affair would peter out as the others had done, I hurried off to see a solicitor. My solicitor loved socializing, he went to all the parties and he was delighted to be handed a society divorce. I wasn't so sure now that I wanted to go through with it, but my solicitor wasn't going to let this one slip through his fingers. He painted our marriage in very bleak colours and said he would find the quickest way to end it.

Now that I had gone to see a solicitor I discovered that David was in no hurry to leave me. I had moved to a flat in Elm Mews, Bayswater. It was a two-bedroom mews flat and Gwen was with me so there wasn't much room. But David moved in too. I told him that if he wanted us to divorce we would have to separate. My solicitor had warned me that living together would only complicate matters.

'I'm going to move – eventually,' said David. The arrangement was that he should move to the flat under the ballroom at the Gargoyle. The immediate problem was that he couldn't find his suitcases. I found it a very uncomfortable situation. If David was in love with another woman, I didn't want him clinging to me. If I had to start a new life on my own, then the sooner the better. I found his suitcases and Gwen filled them for him. I told him that I would be back at two o'clock that afternoon, and would he please have moved out by then.

I had lunch with a girl friend; afterwards we drove back to Elm Mews in her open sports car. I asked her in, feeling sure that David must have left. But no. There was David's head sticking out of an upstairs window. 'I can't find my binoculars,' he called. 'Any idea where they are?'

David's protracted move went on for weeks and weeks. I kept arranging for him to go, and I kept coming back to find him still in residence. One afternoon I found him removing all the paintings from the drawing room walls. I protested that they had been given to both of us. One was a beautiful oil painting given to us by an art-dealer friend. David declared that he would leave me the furniture instead, but I was beginning to feel that this was a very one-sided divorce. Just as I'd finished decorating and furnishing Teffont, so that everything was perfection – and a house takes years to get right – the Invisible Lady had appeared on the scene and our life together at the house was over. And now David couldn't let me alone in my little mews flat. Our farewell this time was cool.

A month later he wrote and asked if I would meet him in the park on the other side of the Bayswater Road. I enquired politely about Virginia and he enquired politely about Freddy, even though I hadn't seen my former lover for some time. We chatted about the children, about my solicitor and his solicitors, Russell & Russell, and then I discovered the reason for this invitation to meet on a park bench in Hyde Park. David was getting cold feet about the divorce. I decided to be noble. 'Look here,' I said severely. 'You've been dragging this young girl around, giving her expectations . . .' I knew I sounded like Jane Austen. 'Do you want to give her up?'

It transpired that he didn't want to give her up and he didn't want to give me up. He wanted both of us and couldn't make up his mind what to do about it. I had another letter from him about six weeks later. We met on the same park bench. Virginia had decided that they should get married in August and David didn't like the idea. August would be too hot, he thought, and there was no need to rush things.

'You're the first reluctant bridegroom I've met who uses the English climate as an excuse,' I said.

'You do understand, don't you, 'Mione?' He was even using the pet name he called me to get me on his side. 'No man in his right mind ever wants to get married.'

'I understand that you're not quite as anxious as you were.'

'What shall I do?'

David wanted me to make up his mind for him. I wouldn't and couldn't do it, although I must admit that several times over the years I've wanted to kick myself for being so noble.

However, we were divorced and I was given the custody of the children. That streak of meanness which I had noticed in David before reared its head again over the matter of the children's education. He told me that he couldn't pay their school fees. I was earning money in the theatre, he declared, I could afford to pay young David's fees at Eton. I was flabbergasted.

I missed David, I always did, but it didn't mean that we cut off all relations with each other. We still moved in the same circles and were bound to meet every now and again. Some years later, David and Virginia had a daughter called Georgia. I used to see quite a lot of Georgia during the school holidays and we grew very fond of one another. It sounds odd, but occasionally I would ring up Virginia and ask if I could borrow Georgia for the afternoon.

One day, David rang me up and asked if I would mind not coming to the Gargoyle any longer because it upset Virginia to see me there. I was so stunned that I simply said 'Of course,' and hung up. There were plenty of other clubs in London, so for the next few months my suitors gave me a chance to sample them. Before long, a message came from the Gargoyle: they had missed many of their former clients – people who had known David and me as a married couple – and requested me kindly to ignore Mr Tennant's demands. Divorce is bad enough without it getting banned from clubs, I thought to myself, so I took to going to the Gargoyle again and didn't care tuppence whether Virginia was embarrassed or not.

On the whole, though, David and I had a sympathetic divorce. When he and Virginia took a mill-house in Wiltshire I used to stay with them. I bought myself a little Ford car and thought I had weathered the storm of divorce quite well.

Earlier on, when *The Greeks Had A Word For It* closed, I confidently expected another dramatic play to come along. At the time, a formidable drama critic called Herbert Farjeon always used to give me beautiful notices for almost everything I appeared in. One day he called round and said he wanted to write a revue for me. He flattered me dreadfully, said there was no one to touch me in the field of revue and comedy, and eventually won me round. I had been hoping for a dramatic role, but I realised this would be a good way of keeping my hand in.

If anyone had told me then that *Nine Sharp*, as it was called, would run for three years, that I would become 'the queen of revue on the London stage', I would have been sure they were after something. But that's what happened, there were three series of the revue and each year new material was added, new people came in, new ideas. *Nine Sharp* became rather like a club, and some people came to see it two or three times a week.

Doing a revue in the thirties in London was fun, although I admit you had to be young and full of energy to keep up with all the changes. Artistes nowadays don't seem to have the light heartedness that it takes to send things up with such gay abandon. I am sure that this is because the situation in our world is so different now. It just isn't possible to be so carefree, and revue seems to have been laid to rest for a while. In America now, they start having nervous breakdowns when they're still collecting material. It's a new thing in the theatre to be so hypersensitive. Everything is so competitive and everyone is so critical of themselves. I do blame this partly on the critics. In my heyday, they used to act rather like talent-spotters, building people up and helping them make a career. Nowadays, they seem to be more intent on knocking things down.

Of course even in the thirties things could go wrong. Just before *Nine Sharp* opened, our leading man had to leave the show quite suddenly. Bertie Farjeon had heard Cyril Ritchard was available; he was a wonderful Australian dancer, but Bertie was worried that he wouldn't be sophisticated enough for London audiences. But in my experience Australians pick things up very quickly, and I recommended Bertie to take him on. I knew we would be good together: he is very tall and I am very small, and that's always a good start in revue. There was no question that Cyril might not be sophisticated enough for the West End, he fitted in beautifully and he had something extra – he had glamour. With every month that went by Cyril acquired more polish. He was indeed a beautiful dancer and together we created a dance that has become a classic – a send-up of *Swan Lake*.

Freddy Ashton, the great choreographer, started us off. He gave us the right positions for *Swan Lake* and we took it from there. I had never, to my regret, learned ballet, but I could stand on my tip-toes for ages and Cyril could do anything I asked of him. We started the dance absolutely seriously, dead-pan, exactly as Freddy Ashton had shown us. It looked as if we were going to do a nice little bit of ballet. We exchange proud looks. Then the first thing goes wrong and a flicker of irritation goes across Madame Allover's face; Cyril's wig shifts slightly. The dance is just a tiny bit off balance. The grimaces, the pained looks increase. Eye-balls start rolling as the two dancers realize that they are not getting it right. We invented every bit of that dance and added to it all the time. It became wildly funny as the two dancers grew more angry and struggle to save themselves, all the time trying to preserve some semblance of stage presence and keep their predicament from the audience. A bouquet is handed to Madame Allover at the end of the dance, they exit and when the curtain rises again Madame Allover is belting Cyril over the head with the flowers.

It was a number made to be stolen. I remember I once saw a man in the front row getting it all down in a note-book, noting every gesture, every little touch. Over the years I have found it quite uncanny to watch on television and on the stage the little pieces of business that Cyril and I invented being recreated. The last time I saw Madame Allover was on American television, when Sid Caesar and an American comedienne tried it. The lady just stomped around trying to be deliberately funny, which didn't work – as the aim of the dance was certainly not slapstick. Well, I suppose imitation is a compliment, and I do think the dance will go on forever.

Nine Sharp at the Little Theatre was a great success and everyone came to see it. Cyril and I on a percentage of the takings couldn't have been more pleased. However, the Little Theatre, true to its name was quite small. It had no boxes, so when important personages and visiting royalty came the management would take out the first two rows of seats so that the exalted ones would not be too near the stage. 'Bang goes our percentage again,' Cyril would groan.

My performance in *Nine Sharp* won me what must be the most obscure award in the history of the theatre. A great and imposing drama critic named Hannan Swaffer decided that he would like to institute his own award to be given to the actor or actress who had put in the finest performances during the course of a year. It was to be called the Golden Biscuit Award, I have no idea why. I won it first time round and I'm not sure who got it the second year, but there was no third award. Mr Swaffer died. Still, it's nice to think that I was the first proud holder of the Golden Biscuit Award, even though I didn't get a biscuit of any kind to go with it!

Nine Sharp was the hottest show in town and I had thrown myself into my work. I had plenty of admirers who were anxious to take me out, give me lunch, dinner, take me to parties and nightclubs, make sure that I was never alone. Freddy Childs was always at my beck and call with the latest model of Bentley. So I was divorced, so David had married The Invisible Lady – but I wasn't broken-hearted, was I? It hadn't hurt me. Then why, one afternoon, did it all collapse?

One matinée I was sitting in my dressing room making up my face. The call-boy had tapped on my door and given me the half-hour call – that good half hour before you do the show and the curtain goes up. I looked in the mirror and suddenly froze. What had I done? The face looking back at me wasn't mine. A clown, someone whose face was daubed with streaks of greasepaint leered back. I clutched the arms of my chair and shrank back. What had happened. Had *I* done that? A knock came at the door and Bertie Farjeon came in. I saw his face staring above mine in the lighted mirror. I saw his jaw drop, his look of shocked bewilderment. 'Bertie!' My voice started to tremble. 'Something's . . . wrong.'

He understood at once, picked me up and carried me over to a couch. 'Do you feel ill, darling?' he asked. I nodded slowly. It was so difficult to do or say anything, as if I was swimming in an enormous sea and making no headway. I heard the stage manager come in and a troubled conversation began.

'We'll need an understudy for Mrs Twiceover.' That was my old lady sketch.

'And the opera number.'

'And Madame Allover.'

'We're in trouble,' said Bertie. 'No one girl can do all these numbers.'

I tried to sit up and tell them that I was going to be all right and not to worry about an understudy, but an invisible hand seemed to hold me back. I closed my eyes. When I opened them again Freddy Childs was tucking me into the back seat of his car. He told me afterwards that I kept whispering: 'I can't bear it. I can't bear it.'

Later on I knew what I'd been trying to say. My break up with David had hit me at last and I couldn't bear it. I thought I had buried my loss under the showers of congratulations for my new show, under the attentions of eager admirers. But suddenly that afternoon I could no longer cope with the despair I felt because David and I had parted.

My breakdown lasted for six weeks. The newspapers were full of it. 'Revue star's mysterious illness!' Everyone was very kind and Freddy tried taking me out when I felt better. What I remember most about that time is the inside of Freddy's motor car.

Bertie Farjeon, who was a very kindly man and liked to give as many people as he could a chance, engaged five understudies to take over my numbers in the revue. It didn't work and when the management discovered that the takings at the box office were going down they got another star to replace me – Ivy St Helier. It was an awful time: nothing meant anything, I couldn't write, couldn't read, didn't even want to talk. Eventually I went back to *Nine Sharp* and everyone gave me a most wonderful reception. It helped me to realize that I would get better and that I could cope with life again.

Farjeon wrote a second edition of the revue and then a third edition – they were both tremendous successes. We now had the idea of having guest stars to join us. In 1939 Bertie and I went to a party where a relation of the people who were giving it did a very funny little turn. Her name was Joyce. When we went over to congratulate her we found she was very shy. She blushed bright red when we asked her what stage work she had done, and insisted she was only an amateur, doing work for friends and for charity. But she wrote all her own material and had managed to make a couple of hard-bitten revue people weep with laughter. I knew that Bertie had the same thought as myself. This dear shy lady was much too good to perform for the Mother's Union and indulgent friends. We asked her to join our revue and, after much cajoling and persuasion from us, a rather confused and bewildered Joyce Grenfell agreed.

A month later, fearful and trembling, she stood alone on the stage and did a little sketch about naughty children. The audience howled with laughter. Both the sketch and Joyce were unforgettable. Despite her subsequent success, she never changed; she remained the same sweet, rather shy lady she had always been.

In 1939, when I was thirty-one, Bertie told me that he was going to put the three editions of our revue together, taking out the best from each, and eventually transfer the show to New York. I was thrilled – every actress wants to cross the Atlantic and see if she can win on Broadway.

But in September 1939, any hopes of going to America, in fact any hopes of going anywhere unless you were a soldier, sailor or airman, were precluded. War was declared against Germany. A blackout descended on London and a government order closed all the theatres. There was a certain amount of anxiety about what would happen if Nazi bombs started to fall and anyone with children tried to get them out of London.

At that time one of my closest friends was a handsome young man called Johnny Bowes-Lyon. He was the nephew of Elizabeth, who had nearly married Christopher Glenconner and is now the Queen Mother. Johnny was tall and had lovely crinkly hair and the brightest blue eyes I have ever seen; our friendship was very soon a love affair. A friend of Johnny's who had been told about my worry over my children's safety came to my rescue. Mark Ogilvy Grant was going with his regiment to France. He had a beautiful house near Kew Gardens, which seemed a much safer place than Central London, and he offered to rent it to me. There was another reason why Kew Gardens was a good place to stay: it meant that I could get up to the West End quite easily for theatres were opening up again and the revised *Nine Sharp* was ready to start.

Johnny, who was living with his mother and brother Timothy up at Glamis, decided that he'd like a flat of his own in London when he came down to join his regiment and asked if he could rent my empty flat in Elm Mews. I was delighted, and before long Johnny and Timothy had settled in happily. I did wonder what my bank manager can have thought when Johnny paid a cheque into my account every month: 'Just another of those kept actresses,' I expect!

Our revue opened up again; it was now called *The Little Revue*. Because of the blackout and the need for people to travel home as early as they could, our performances now came on much earlier, but after the show there were always parties to go to, parties for the young men off to war. We were surrounded by wild young men determined not to worry about what tomorrow might bring, determined to enjoy themselves to the full before going off to fight.

I am sure that Johnny Bowes-Lyon was not an alcoholic, he was just part of the wild drinking that went on in wartime among soldiers on leave. Some of them could take it, but Johnny was one who could not. Sometimes he drank like a madman without care or thought of what it could do to him. We were very attached to each other, very much in love, but I knew that his drinking had to slow down. One night he kept ringing me up at Kew, protesting his love and saying we must get married at once. The calls went on until the early hours and each time he was more intoxicated. Then there was silence. I started to worry. I got up very early and went over to Elm Mews. I let myself in and found Johnny lying on a sofa, absolutely out for the count – I just couldn't wake him up. After a long time I managed to revive him, but I realised that his drinking had passed danger point. I was very firm with him and told him the drinking must stop. He sat up looking young and healthy and held out his hands for me to inspect. 'Look, I haven't got the shakes.'

The Queen, his aunt, who was very fond of him, found a certain Dr Brown who said he could stop Johnny drinking. Johnny went along to see him. Dr Brown was a serious-minded man. After giving

Johnny a lecture on the evils of drink, he said, 'Now here is a little rhyme you must say to yourself: *No more whisky, no more gin!*' Johnny repeated the words after him, and then he suddenly found them wildly funny. *No more whisky, no more gin!* he spluttered and started to laugh hysterically. He couldn't stop laughing. The doctor was not amused. Johnny was shown out of the consulting room in disgrace, and the report that went back to his aunt was doleful.

I think that Johnny's trouble was a wartime phenomenon, and that given time Johnny would have stopped his mad drinking. Unfortunately I shall never know. Johnny went off to France with his regiment in 1940 and was killed in an ambush. I shall always remember Johnny Bowes-Lyon with deep affection and sadly remember how before leaving for France we had said that we would get married on his first leave. I wasn't the only woman to lose my lover in 1940 by any means. It was a bad year for Britain – there was Dunkirk and the Battle of Britain. Later in the war, when I gave up being the revue queen of London and went off to entertain the troops in Italy, there was an incident that brought back all my memories of Johnny Bowes-Lyon.

Our company, formed by Leslie Henson, was doing a show in the ruins of a little Italian town near the front lines. It was just a hall, no stage, no seats, but the soldiers from the camps around were there en masse. Leslie and I were doing one of the hits from the show, what I called my crinoline number, when I saw a soldier push his way to the front of the crowd. A flushed face that I remembered so well looked at me – such a lovely flushed face, such a lovely man. It was Johnny's batman, Pearson, a real Scot – tough, hard, a real soldier. Afterwards we talked to each other about the man we had both loved. Pearson burst into tears. All he could say was: 'Och! He was so brave, so brave.'

'I've joined the paras,' he told me. 'I couldn't stay on with the old regiment.'

Back in 1940 we were just beginning to live through this war that was to last for five years. The bombing started in earnest and all the worry about the safety of my children came back. I was telling someone about my anxiety and he told me about an aunt of his who had a house in the country and loved children. He offered to ask her if Pauline and David might stay there. I looked with appreciation at this young man. Rosa Lewis, who took to the war like a duck takes to water, was giving a party at the Cavendish Hotel for the heroes of Dunkirk. This young man was a Major in the 12th Lancers who had been awarded the Military Cross for gallantry at Dunkirk.

Rosa came up to us. I told her about the young stranger's kind offer. 'Dozey's a good boy,' she said. 'He's very kind. You look after Hermione now, Dozey.' Dozey was the nickname Major J. H. Willis answered to. I never found out why he was called Dozey and I could never remember what the initials J. H. stood for. He was very tall and very good-looking and, as I found out, charming and kind. There was no reason why I should not have fallen in love with Dozey, for he had all the physical attributes of the type of man I liked. But somehow Dozey just wasn't for me; I never wanted to be too sure about my lover, and with Dozey I was completely sure.

Wartime marriages were more liable to fail than succeed. People were getting married because one of the bombs might have their number on it, because of the insecurity of life in London, the feeling of impermanence, or just because they felt it was cruel to refuse a soldier's proposal. I was having plenty of proposals, but nevertheless I turned them all down. When Dozey proposed I turned him down, too. Of course I liked him very much – you couldn't help but like Dozey. His aunt and my children had taken to each other and they were now living in the country with her. All Dozey's family were charming. His father had been governor of the island of Jersey and was a wonderful man; like Dozey, he was very keen that I become Mrs Willis. I couldn't help feeling guilty about not marrying him. He was a good sort and had had a rough time. The 12th Lancers were a crack regiment and one of Dozey's boys had won a double DSO when he blew up the last bridge at Dunkirk. Dozey had suffered a head wound himself and although he seemed to have recovered, he still had headaches and sometimes felt depressed.

My ex-husband saw a gossip item about Dozey and me in a newspaper and wrote me a letter at once. 'Don't for heaven's sake get married unless I say so,' he ordered. For some oblique reason of his own he ended the letter with: 'I'm looking through a glass darkly.' David had been keen for me to marry Johnny Bowes-Lyon, but really did not want me to marry at all.

During this time I acquired a black spaniel called Mr Baggs. I came to own the dog in a roundabout way by meeting an American officer called Captain Jocelyn at a luncheon given at the Savoy

Hotel. I sat next to him and I enjoyed getting the full blast of his charm, the cheeky American variety. He was dark, olive-skinned, dashing, and there was the touch of the brigand about him or the American movie gangster. He seemed to know everyone and he told me that he was working in some kind of hush-hush department. He worked so hard, he told me, that he never had time to look after his poor dog – take him out in the park, groom him properly and so on.

In no time at all I had said that, providing I liked him, I would let Mr Baggs move into Elm Mews as a lodger until Captain Jocelyn had more time to look after him. He grinned. 'I don't know who'll be the happier, Mr Baggs or me, for it'll mean that I get to see you everytime I come round to see my dog.'

Mr Baggs wasn't a young dog – he was about five years old – but he was a lovely animal and I fell for him at once. As Captain Jocelyn handed me the dog's lead he warned me rather diffidently that a woman might ring up and ask about him or Mr Baggs, but on no account was I to give her my address or tell her who I was. I thought this rather mysterious and asked him why not. He grinned conspiratorially and said that this woman had a thing about him and hoped that by getting hold of his dog she would get hold of him.

That sounded rather odd, but it was wartime and Captain Jocelyn had known so many people at the luncheon – it was probably all right. As it happened, a woman did ring up but Gwen told her that yes, Madam was looking after a dog for Captain Jocelyn, but no, Madam couldn't come to the phone because Madam was away. Captain Jocelyn often came round to Elm Mews to see how Mr Baggs was getting along. He was a very popular man and when he took me to parties, which he did quite a lot, I always enjoyed his company. He was a bit of a mystery man but I found that intriguing.

I went away for the weekend and came back to find Gwen in a great state of excitement. She produced a newspaper. 'You'll never believe it, Madam, but our Captain Jocelyn is in the news.' I read that a daring robbery had taken place at the home of a well-known man. He was, in fact, as rich as Croesus, and his had been one of the homes that Captain Jocelyn had taken me to. It appeared that a cocktail party had been held at the house and when the guests had departed jewellery worth a fortune was found to be missing. Gwen pointed to a paragraph lower down. One of the guests was believed to have some vital information. Captain Jocelyn, who was thought to belong to the American Armed Forces, had disappeared and the police wished to interview him.

'Our Captain Jocelyn,' said Gwen to Mr Baggs who sat beside us wagging his tail furiously, 'do you think he's an American gangster, then?'

Weeks went by and not a word from Captain Jocelyn. Gwen was on tenterhooks wondering whether the police would swoop on us and claim Mr Baggs. However, very early one morning, at about six o'clock, the door bell rang. Gwen struggled into a dressing gown and went to answer it. There stood Captain Jocelyn. He slid past her to the hall cupboard, opened it and took out a greatcoat he had left hanging there. We'd both forgotten all about it. Gwen stood watching open mouthed. Then he whispered to her 'Tell Miss Baddeley I'll be in touch,' and shot past her and out of our lives.

He never did get in touch, he never did claim Mr Baggs and we never did tell the police. Mr Baggs was quite unconcerned.

Chapter Ten

Dozey and I were married at Caxton Hall. Dozey looked very striking in uniform and I wore a halo hat, very much in vogue at the time, and a beautiful mink coat that David had chosen. When I put it on I remembered how David and I had taken months to decide whether to buy it from Bradleys or Revillon, what colour it should be, how it should be cut. It was a really luscious coat. I remembered how Dorothy Gish had admired it when she came to the Gargoyle and demanded to know where it came from. I remembered so much about David and my life with him that after the ceremony I couldn't remember that my name was no longer Mrs Tennant but Mrs Willis.

To this day I don't really know why I married Dozey. I didn't love him, I was very fond of him and I thought he was a darling, but I shouldn't have married him. In wartime one does crazy things; I know I was filled with gratitude for all these marvellous men who had risked everything for their country, and Dozey, after all, was a hero.

He'd just kept on asking me to marry him and I kept refusing. We weren't interested in the same things and I warned him that if we did marry I should probably have left him within a year. Dozey came from a military family and although he professed to love the bohemian life, I knew that underneath he hadn't the slightest idea about people who work in the theatre. But he kept on pleading and pleading and in the end I talked myself into thinking that marrying Dozey was something to do with the war effort. I should have known better.

We had the reception after the wedding at the Berkeley Hotel, one of my favourite places. However, while the wedding guests and the bride and groom had a lovely time, in another room nearby most of my wedding presents were being stolen. The thieves took everything that could be smuggled out of the hotel without being noticed – lovely clocks, beautiful silverware given to us by my friend Lady Phyllis Allen and a necklace of precious stones given to me by a dear friend Lord Farringdon. The only things left behind were too big to be smuggled out. I never felt quite the same way about the Berkeley Hotel after that.

Dozey chose rather a strange place for our honeymoon – the Isles of Scilly. It rained nearly every day and Dozey decided the best place to spend the holiday was the hotel bar. One morning when the rain had settled down to a gentle drizzle, I walked to the beach hoping that a ray of sunshine might come through. I love the sun and sunbathing. On the empty grey beach under a dark, sodden sky, I saw a lone figure sitting under an umbrella. I admired that sort of tenacity.

Later, in the bar, I recognized the brightly-coloured skirt of the lone sun-seeker and without the umbrella over her head I recognized her face. David and I had been at her wedding. It had been a very big affair and we had gone as friends of the groom and I hadn't seen much of the bride except to see that she was tall, slim, and had a charming face. Although we'd met at parties, we had never got to know each other well. Now here she was again, divorced from Michael Duff, and her name was now Lady Joan Assheton-Smith.

Joan had no time for pretence, she was as straight as a die and once she became your friend she gave you unswerving loyalty. We had such fun together during that holiday in the Isles of Scilly that we started to meet when we both got back to London. Joan had a flat in Westminster where she did her 'bit' by bringing together men serving in the war from every country. Men from the Free French army, the Poles, the Canadians, the Australians and the Americans. Her flat was the scene of some of the best parties I have ever been to. What neither of us realized was the importance of the friendship that began on the Isles of Scilly. Little did we know that we would become the greatest of friends. To this day I cannot imagine my life without Joan in the background, with her wonderful talent for turning up at exactly the right moment. At that time I had not learned that Joan is a completely selfless person – she gives all of herself, not only to me, but to all her friends. Nothing is ever too much trouble for her.

Chaos came to London because of the bombings, roads were up, gas mains broken and it was often a problem getting to the theatre. My two children were away at school in the country in safety. I missed them, especially Pauline, who before the war used to love watching my revues. She learned all my songs and was frightfully good. I had promised that when she grew older she could be trained for the stage.

So many things were changing because of the war. Gwen had to go home to look after her mother because her brothers had been called up. She wrote to me every week, but without her help I knew it would be easier if I found a small flat in central London. The flat was found for me by my friend Meg Armstrong Jones. It was found in Piccadilly, over a well known tobacconists called Salmon & Gluckstein, a landmark in Piccadilly for so long. It wasn't at all a luxurious building, quite the contrary; milk bottles were left out on each landing and a prostitute lived on one floor, a cabaret artiste on another. But it was wartime and one took a flat wherever one could find one. There were about one hundred steps up to the flat. I knew because I used to count them late at night, having a rest on each landing. And there wasn't much of a view when you reached the top – just the soot-stained building of Swan & Edgar, the department store.

While I was living above the tobacconists, I was the victim of a particularly cunning burglary. As I was leaving the theatre one day, I was jostled by a rather large and enthusiastic autograph-hunting crowd and I lost a beautiful fur hat. A few days later, someone telephoned me to say that they had found my hat and by making enquiries at the theatre, traced its owner. Would it be convenient if they dropped it round right away? I had a matinée that afternoon, so I had to say it wasn't, but we arranged another time for the man to call. I was very pleased that my hat had been found and impressed by the honesty of whoever had found it, for it was quite a valuable fur. When I got back from the theatre later that day, I noticed immediately that my fur coat, one that matched the lost hat, had disappeared. I soon realized what had happened. The man who had found my hat, far from being honest, had guessed that it would have a coat to match and found out from me when I would be out so that he could complete his set of furs at leisure.

My little flat had the great advantage that I could get to the theatre easily, walking the short distance if necessary. On the first

day Dozey and I moved into the flat we were invited to an important
dinner given at a hotel in Park Lane. Sir Sholto Douglas, the head of
the Air Force, had invited all the heroes of Dunkirk to celebrate their
safe return and I promised to get along just as soon as my show was
over. As I didn't want to be late, I hurried away from the theatre
without changing my theatrical make-up.

It was a very good party, a different wine with every course at
dinner and stirring speeches afterwards. A very delightful, dignified
evening – in complete contrast to the hair-raising incidents afterwards. When the time came for us to say goodbye, Lady Douglas
insisted that we use their car for the short drive home. Off we drove
to Piccadilly Circus. However, in the blackout the chauffeur wasn't
sure of the whereabouts of our flat. I told him not to worry – he
could drop us at the Circus and we would find our own way back.

Dozey and I and Mr Baggs, who went to the theatre with me every
night because I couldn't leave him alone if the bombs started to fall,
climbed out. All we had to do was find the tobacconists shop and we
would be home. Nothing was quite as black as the London blackout
at two o'clock in the morning. Dozey, for some wild reason of his
own, decided to tap briskly about him with his military cane. A
military cane is apparently used for drilling and popping under the
arm when one has to salute and Dozey was never without his. I
heard him swiping about in the darkness with his little stick and
bellowing: 'Where's that damned flat?'

'Dozey! Shut up!' I called. 'You'll break something.' There came
the most terrible shattering of glass as Dozey's side-swipe hit the
window of the tobacconist's shop. The noise was ear-splitting.
What happened next was unbelievable. Like mushrooms, shadowy
shapes sprang up around us. Torches shone on us, heavy hands
caught our arms. We were surrounded by what looked like a band
of storm troopers, but they turned out to be members of the London
police force. A torch shone full on my face, 'What's all this?'
shouted a stentorian voice. 'What's your game, eh?'

I drew back in alarm and blinked my false eyelashes. 'What do
you mean, "game"? I live here.'

A bellow of laughter. 'Tell us another one.'

'You are making a mistake, officer,' I declared. 'We have just been
to an important dinner . . .'

And then I remembered my theatrical make-up. If anyone could

*Richard Attenborough and me as Pinki Brown and Ida Arnold
in the film of* Brighton Rock

Cyril Ritchard and I appeared in
David Soskynd's Open Ends.
Here I am doing a take off of
Edith Sitwell

As Mrs Prohack with Cecil Parke
as my husband ▽

Again in Grand National Night

My send-up of Doris Day. A publicity photograph taken at the time I appeared in Midnight Lace

Laurence Harvey with Heather Angel in Room at the Top

...e 20th Century Fox film ...Not Disturb

... Disney's Mary Poppins, starring ...Andrews and Dick Van Dyke

As Mrs Naugatuck in Maude. *James Cromwell played the part of Alfie Valentino*

I appeared with Donald Pleasance in
The Good and Faithful Servant

Playing the part of Kiesier in
The Little House on the Prairie

be taken for a tart in full regalia at two o'clock in the morning, it was me. And just like the best French tarts, I even had a dog on a lead. This had to be explained at once. Dozey spoiled my little speech by starting to shout. A copper whistled and a Black Maria drew up as if by magic next to us. Mr Baggs, to my shame, tugged away from me and jumped into the front seat.

'Look at that dog,' exclaimed one of the policemen. 'Would you believe it? He's been in this van before. He knows all about it.'

'This is an outrage,' yelled Dozey, and waved his little stick in the air. Resisting arrest! We were bundled into the Black Maria to join the delighted Mr Baggs.

At the police station a woman police officer went through my bag. She drew out my purse and produced about thirty pounds, quite a sum of money in those days. The look she gave me told it all. I was a tart and doing quite well, thank you. Tomorrow's headlines flashed through my mind. 'Hermione Baddeley arrested in Piccadilly!' I could hear Dozey yelling and shouting somewhere down the corridor. I sighed. The policewoman gave me another look, then another. 'Haven't I seen you somewhere?' she asked. Then her face changed. 'You're Hermione Baddeley!' As my face was plastered on billboards all over London, she had taken her time about recognizing me. Once she had realized the mistake, she became most apologetic and asked me what I wanted to do about this terrible mix-up. I rang up Rosa at the Cavendish Hotel. I knew she never slept much at night and always got up at an ungodly hour. Like a good sport she had me and Mr Baggs bailed out. Dozey was kept in the cells because he was making such a racket.

Next morning he had to appear before the beak. At the station, a kind policeman with a sense of fun had it all worked out. Although I had to go in the dock as a witness I would not be recognized because they had changed my name on the charge sheet. I told the policeman that I couldn't stay long because I had a matinée that afternoon. He assured me I would be in and out and told me my courtroom name – Harriet Wilson. I wonder if he knew that the lady had been a well known prostitute in the eighteenth century!

I stood in the dock and gave my evidence. 'Well, you see, we had just moved into this new flat and we just couldn't find it. You know how it is in the blackout. My husband was looking . . . and looking, and that window . . .' As I spoke I saw the heads of two young barristers in the courtroom turn. Chins went up, eyes opened wide. I said no more, the Baddeley voice was a dead giveaway.

Dozey paid a fine for breaking the window and after that I was relieved when he rejoined his regiment in Suffolk. When *The Little Revue* finally closed, we took a house in Suffolk for a time and I became an army wife. I enjoyed it very much. The military environment was very lively, comings and goings, lots of social life and parties. Dozey was a very easy person to live with and I remember that little interlude as the best part of our marriage. But rehearsals for a new revue, *Rise Above It,* were due to start, so off I went back to Piccadilly.

Soon after I got back I invited a girl to come and live with me. A young man from Dozey's regiment introduced us and she told me that she hoped to become an actress and needed to live somewhere near the theatres. Maria Britneva was a tiny little person and my nickname for her, 'Little Brit', suited her perfectly. Her family had come over from Russia and she was delightfully bohemian. When she moved in, all her clothes and belongings were piled high in her arms – she didn't own a suitcase!

At that time she was doing little bits in various shows, the maid's part and things like that, but we always made arrangements to come home together in the blackout, shining our torches on the dark landings on the way up the stairs. Sometimes we'd knock over a milk bottle on the climb and watch with horror as it bounced all the way down the stairs to the bottom. We had great fun living together and I was very sorry when she had to go off and live with her grandmother. Later on she married Lord St Just, and even later she was instrumental in bringing Tennessee Williams and his play *The Rose Tattoo* into my life.

Jack de Leon was presenting *Rise Above It* and the revue had some excellent material in it written by a young man called Alan Melville. He'd started off by working with the BBC variety department and then gone into writing and directing. He'd just given it all up to join the Royal Air Force, but whenever he could get leave he came round to watch his material being rehearsed. We opened at The Q Theatre to good notices and then went on a six-week tour to polish up the show before the West End opening. All the company used to go back to London for weekends when they could and

Edward Cooper, our leading man, loved to plop into a large leather armchair at his favourite little club. Unfortunately, one weekend he had too many relaxing drinks and fell down the stairs at this club and injured himself quite badly. He had to withdraw from the show and in fact he never really recovered.

The loss of one of our leading men, the other was Henry Kendall, was a great blow – *Rise Above It* was so obviously going to be a hit when it came to London. That weekend I went up to London and arranged to call on Jack de Leon to talk about a replacement. There had been a terrible air-raid the night before and I was picking my way through the broken glass and debris that littered the Charing Cross Road when I was hailed by someone walking towards me. It was a BBC producer friend of mine called Brian Mickey; with him he had a lady he introduced as Miss Gingold and the two of them suggested I join them for a drink.

We found a nearby pub, settled ourselves at a table and of course all started to talk about ourselves. Miss Gingold's voice struck a chord in my memory. Her name was Hermione Gingold and I had seen her in a revue at the Gate Theatre. This show, called *The Gate Revue,* had been written by a talented writer and director called Norman Marshall and had been put on at the tiny Watergate Theatre under the Charing Cross tunnels. There had been talk that it bore a resemblance to Bertie Farjeon's show, *Nine Sharp,* and if perhaps there wasn't the same level of freshness and brilliance, *The Gate Revue* of 1940 to '41 had still done very well. As the tiny theatre wasn't much bigger than a large room it couldn't cope with large audiences, and later it was moved to the Ambassadors Theatre.

While it was still at the Watergate, my old admirer Sir Alfred Beit had taken Douglas Byng and me to see it. He had thought that Hermione Gingold was copying my act, and it was true this lady wore the same kind of crazy make-up that I did and used a similar tone of voice. But in other ways she was the exact opposite to me. In fact, Douglas Byng nudged me and whispered: 'I think it's me she's trying to be like.'

And now this lady and I sat together with Brian Mickey at a pub table. I asked her what she was doing and she pulled a face (she had a most unusual face). She too was doing a revue that had run into problems. I told her about *Rise Above It* and we sipped our drinks reflectively. So, Miss Gingold's revue was going to have starred Wally Crisham. I'd worked with Wally and he was a lovely dancer; and there was this lady who was undoubtedly very funny. It might work, I thought to myself. The idea floated around in the air and then we started to talk about the possibility of all joining up. Brian Mickey thought it was a wonderful idea and thought we could be together.

I telephoned Jack de Leon and he came over and joined us; negotiations went ahead at once. Hermione Gingold could see how taken we were with the idea, so she asked Jack for the same billing – and salary as me. The billing was easy – we wanted to have the two Hermiones side by side – but as far as money was concerned, a somewhat different arrangement was reached.

With Wally and Miss Gingold joining us and bringing a certain amount of songs and sketches with them, there was no doubt at all that the revue was strengthened and improved. Before opening in the West End, we did a short tour and opened first of all in Brighton. Some of Dozey's regiment were stationed near Brighton, so quite a few of Dozey's chums were in front. Naturally enough, they made a great fuss of me and everything I did was rather too heartily applauded. Also, it must be remembered that I'd been in the show for some time and had settled in. Miss Gingold seemed alarmed and down-hearted; she decided she did not have enough funny material and made sounds about leaving the show.

Jack de Leon was amazed. We really were very funny together and he couldn't bear the thought of losing this hysterical new partnership. I did an operatic sketch based on *Madame Butterfly* and it emerged that Miss Gingold wanted one too. We all jumped in with promises to find her good material and peace was restored. She was given a number based on Jeanette Macdonald, but it was eventually dropped. Miss G was no fool – two opera singers in one show was one too many. I did give her a skipping-rope number I was to do in the finale and we all concentrated on finding funny material for her. We then proceeded with a very enjoyable three-week tour.

Someone once wrote: 'Hermione Gingold can be a delightful person, but once she gets on the stage she seems to undergo a personality change. Rather like some people who get into a motor car and become raving lunatics behind the wheel, Hermione has to be watched with caution as soon as the curtain rises.' Henry

Kendall, who worked with us both in *Rise Above It* said, 'The two Hermiones are vastly different in technique. Gingold is single-minded, but Baddeley takes it easy and extemporises.'

Rise Above It ran for over a year and we had a wonderful run, in spite of some very nasty air-raids. Afterwards, Tom Arnold signed us to appear in a new revue called *Sky High*, written almost entirely by Alan Melville. Wally Crisham was engaged to produce as well as to appear in the show. Alan Melville's script was good and we thought that we couldn't miss. Tom Arnold chose the Phoenix Theatre for us. It had always been considered an unlucky place, but Tom Arnold thought that *Sky High* was a sure-fire winner and could break the spell. Opening night came, there was curtain call after curtain call and we were all well pleased. It was only when we went back to our dressing rooms that a sudden feeling of flatness seemed to sweep over us all. Had something gone wrong after all?

Alan Melville, who was on leave from the Air Force, spent opening night on a sofa in my flat. Next morning, I fished the newspaper out of the letterbox. They were pretty thin and small in wartime, but this had not stopped the theatre critic writing a couple of columns about the show. Alan and I spread the paper out in front of us ready to feast our eyes on the good news:

'. . . the script by Alan Melville failed to raise a laugh . . .'

We stared at each other in horror.

'What a disappointment!'

We read the next line and the next; as we went on it grew worse. Alan giggled nervously. I giggled too.

'Was it worth the effort?' another line ran.

'Was it?' I spluttered. 'The curse of the Phoenix strikes again!' We started to roar with laughter. We laughed so much that Alan fell off the sofa.

We were still breaking into fits of nervous laughter when we went to the restaurant where we had arranged to meet Gingold for lunch. Her face, staring at us from above a pile of newspapers stacked in front of her, was ashen. 'Have you read the notices?' Alan asked her. We had, by this time, and they were all, without exception, reserved in their appreciation of our show. Miss G nodded. Alan giggled. 'But they're so funny? Didn't you find them funny?' Miss G sighed. After a lunch where conversation was punctuated by sad silences from my namesake and hysterical giggles from Alan and myself, we went round to see Tom Arnold. He was quite cheerful and assured us he could extract a few good sentences from the awful notices to plaster outside the theatre. In spite of the critics, he was sure we had a hit.

Tom was quite right – *Sky High* ran for a very long time. We took it on a very hilarious tour that was profitable for all concerned. There was only one slight upset with Gingold, and it was not really my fault. It took place in our Mermaid sketch. We were two mermaids lamenting about our miserable life in the deep and resolving to surface, dress up, and go out to supper with that epitome of the entertaining companion, Noël Coward. At the end of the sketch we rose up from the briny depths and immediately I donned a silver fox fur, which always got a big laugh. One night I surfaced, donned my silver fox fur as usual, but instead of the big laugh I usually had, there came a half-hearted ripple of applause. We two mermaids went back to our respective dressing rooms. Almost at once I heard Gingold's door thrust open and Wally Crisham's voice coming over loud and clear. He was furious. 'What the hell made you do it?' he shouted. 'You killed the laugh stone dead.'

I soon learned that Gingold, off her own bat, had produced a feather boa as she surfaced. It hadn't come off. Two furs are not always better than one. Wally's temper exploded. It was most unlike him. 'What can I expect,' he yelled. 'All you've ever appeared in is a tunnel.'

The door banged shut. I looked in the mirror and saw my face. I was trying hard not to smile.

My marriage with Dozey was drifting along pleasantly. I suppose in reality we were drifting apart pleasantly. Dozey was with his regiment and I was living in the flat in Piccadilly and working in the theatre every night. When I went on tour and came back to London for the weekend, instead of going to an empty flat I sometimes stayed at the Cavendish with Rosa. The Cavendish was so much like a second home to me, and to many others. Rosa was enjoying the war and profiting by the presence of the American servicemen in London. It seemed to give her a new lease of life.

As she grew older I thought that Rosa became better looking. Some women are like that – not particularly pretty when they're young, but with age they come into their own. She always had a beautiful complexion and very nice eyes, and she was never pert or vulgar as she was in the television serial. Rosa was, in fact, rather dignified, except first thing in the morning with that overcoat over her nightdress. She could act the lady as well as anyone, and wives and mothers of her favourites often came to see Rosa when they visited London from the country. There was a very respectable side to the hotel, which seemed specially designed for occasions like these. There will never be another Rosa, nor another hotel like the Cavendish, I don't see how there could be.

Early one Sunday morning someone tapped on my door at the Cavendish and woke me up. A tall man walked in and sat on the edge of my bed.

'Hallo darling,' I said sleepily. 'How did you know that I was here?'

'Rosa told me,' said David Tennant. 'To be exact she said, "Aow! Fancy that. 'Ermione's upstairs in number five." '

David was in uniform and somehow he looked all wrong. The army and David were not, and never would be, adjusted to each other. It was not the cut or the fit of the uniform that was wrong, it was the man inside, determined to hate it all. David was on weekend leave. No Virginia, I noticed; no Dozey, David observed. Rosa came in, overcoat over her nightie, terrier yapping at her heels, a large grin on her face. 'Wot you two doing 'ere?' she demanded in mock severity. 'I thought this was all over and done with.' She kept coming in all the time she was so pleased to see us together. That was the weekend I became 'the other woman' in David's life.

David left the army soon after our weekend at the Cavendish. He was told that he did not fit in and they would rather not have him. Some people don't fit in the army because their eyesight is poor or they are not physically up to it, but David was just mentally incompatible with the forces. He would never accept or try to understand discipline and made no effort to conceal his boredom and irritation with military life. He had a very good brain and the many years he had spent discussing philosophy with Professor Matt Pritchard every morning had given him an intellectual outlook. David had been moulded by his time at Cambridge, and I think he would have liked to become an academic. He had many facets to his character, but he was never able to decide quite where he fitted in.

Perhaps the Gargoyle was the place where David fitted in best –

this club for the artistic, where his old friends from Cambridge could drink and talk endlessly. I remember I met Guy Burgess quite often there. Although he drank too much, he could on occasions be quite fun to be with. I met him not long before he defected to Moscow and he once said to me: 'You know, Hermione, your life is like a kaleidoscope.'

After *Rise Above It* it was assumed that I would go straight into another revue. Alan Melville had written one called *Sweet and Low* and it had all the hallmarks of a hit. Then I was approached by another management, Linnit & Dunfee, who told me that Graham Greene had turned his novel *Brighton Rock* into a play, and asked me if I would like to play the part of Ida, a brassy cockney girl with a big heart and a strong sense of justice. I read the script and the longing to return to the serious theatre made me accept the offer. Revue could wait awhile.

Richard Attenborough, a comparatively untried young actor, was to have his first big leading part as the young gangster and Dulcie Gray was to be his girl-friend. During rehearsals, Graham Greene left us completely alone, but when we were in Oxford on our tour before the West End opening, he gave us a small party and we met him for the first time. I found Graham Greene unusual. Instead of being confident, as such a successful novelist had every right to be, he was shy. Perhaps we extrovert theatre people overwhelmed him.

At the time, London was still being bombed, but the devastating blitz had quietened down. Opening night was all we'd hoped for. After our curtain calls, I led Dulcie Gray and Richard Attenborough forward and told the audience how marvellous I thought these two young people were. Then I turned to Richard: 'I think we've found a wonderful new star . . .' I began. At that precise moment the roof seemed to cave in. There was the loudest, most ghastly noise I have ever heard and for a split second I know we all thought this was it — The End. Everyone in the theatre thought we must have been hit; and then we realized we were all still alive and the bomb must have missed us. The audience got to their feet and the applause was tremendous. I think it was a mixture of admiration and great relief.

As it happened, the bomb had hit the Fifty Shilling Tailors, the men's clothing store along Charing Cross Road, where you could still buy a suit for two pounds ten, and completely wiped it off the face of the earth. We all felt very lucky, and Dickie Attenborough, instead of being blown up, went on to greater things.

Brighton Rock had a long and successful run and when they made the film of the play in 1947 I played my original role of Ida. This was one of the few times when the film world was kind to me. I've often been in a play that becomes a hit, but when the play is made into a film I don't get offered the part. In those days I was probably a little to blame. I'd got into the habit of saying publicly that I preferred acting in the more realistic atmosphere of the theatre. I can see how wrong I was to talk myself out of giving my work some permanence so often. When you make a film it is there on reels or tapes for a long, long time, while in the theatre its all over when the curtain comes down for the last performance.

Masses of people still think that I appeared in the *Sweet And Low* revues, but I didn't. Instead of going back to revue, I joined ENSA and went off to the war to entertain the troops.

I should have been in *Sweet And Low* – I'd signed the contract and was going to get a very large salary, but I gave it all up because I thought that if my country was at war and my countrymen were dying to save people like me, I shouldn't be cavorting on a stage in the West End of London earning a lot of money. I have always been glad that I did this. It had been in my mind for a long time, but I wouldn't have done a thing about it on my own. The man who showed me the way was a little comedian with bulgy eyes who looked rather like a very sweet frog. I love frogs and I have always loved Leslie Henson.

Leslie came round to my dressing room one night after the show. He gave me his wonderful wide-mouthed smile and asked me to go to the Middle East with him! He was no longer all that young and he'd just come back from doing a show in Egypt to entertain the troops. He had, however, the energy and drive of a man half his age. He knew all about entertaining the troops, for he'd done a great deal in the First World War too. In the twenties and thirties there had been no comedian to challenge Leslie Henson. Any musical comedy that starred him was a winner.

He warned me that I wouldn't earn more than £15 a week and that life would be tough. I told him that I was about to start rehearsing this splendid new revue, and would be paid a good deal more than £15 a week. Leslie's face fell.

'But darling,' I went on. 'Of course I'll come.'

I couldn't go just like that, however, there were things to do. First of all I had to talk about breaking my contract to appear in *Sweet And Low*. When that was arranged, I went along to see the man who had been my first boss in the London theatre, Basil Dean. He was one of the founders of ENSA and he ran this wartime entertainment association for the forces from his office in Drury Lane, and did so in his usual iron-fist-without-the-velvet-glove way. ENSA were not known for their generous ways. 'Uniform?' said Basil with surprise when I raised the subject. Apparently you didn't get a uniform, but wore your own old clothes. And they really were getting old, what with clothing coupons and utility reach-me-downs.

Leslie Henson was busy reforming a new company of his *Gaiety's* revue; apart from me there was going to be Prudence Glyn from the Ballet Russe, Decima Knight, a singer, four chorus girls, David Hutchinson and Gavin Gordon. And then I heard from Wally that he had decided to leave *Sweet And Low* and join us.

When I had left *Sweet And Low*, Alan Melville wrote a new song for Gingold. It was called, 'I do Miss Hermione Baddeley.' She held up a white handkerchief with a broad black border around it. 'I do miss Hermione badly,' she sang. 'I miss her taking my gin . . .' For the next two years, the West End of London had to learn to miss Hermione badly as well.

Chapter Eleven

We didn't get the flesh-pots of Egypt – none of those lovely parties in palaces by the Nile, not even Ali Khan playing polo at the Gezira Club. Instead we landed in a dust-storm in North Africa after a bumpy journey in an army transport, and discovered that our band parts had mysteriously vanished on the flight and we couldn't put on a show for days.

I was shown into a very nice room at the hotel in Algiers. While unpacking however, I was a teeny bit surprised to find a full general's uniform hanging in my wardrobe – red flashes, crowns and pips – most impressive. 'Am I sharing?' I thought to myself. The rest of the company crowded in to take a look. It turned out that I was the only one with a military room-mate.

Downstairs a group of rather wild young men were waiting for us. Some of Dozey's Lancers were stationed nearby and they wanted to welcome us in style. They were very sympathetic about the general and thought my confidence should be bolstered with a drink or two. Very soon our little gathering turned into a full-scale party as the rest of the hotel guests drifted our way and got themselves invited. One lady offered me a bed in her room, so she became an honoured guest. The hotel manager said that we were proving a disruptive influence as the party grew larger. When we were really swinging in the early hours of the morning, the general finally arrived. He joined us and was gallant enough to say that he was disappointed when I accepted the invitation of the lady with the spare bed.

Next day we settled down and prepared ourselves for what we had really come to do: entertain the troops. Leslie Henson, who was a wonderful old pro, knew exactly what they wanted. The boys were a wonderful audience, marvellous to play to, but you had to give them something that was right. When you did, the audience and the players seemed to be one and it was a perfect occasion, but if you got it wrong the troops showed their irritation.

Bea Lillie, who joined our show later, got it disastrously wrong at first. Her act was much too sophisticated, more the kind of act you'd put on at the Savoy than one likely to please a base camp filled with troops who had never eaten at the Savoy or seen Bea Lillie before. When she came off after her performance, she asked me why she couldn't get the boys going the way Leslie and I did. I knew what was wrong but how could I tell her to change her act? Then I remembered a number she had once done called 'Rhythm', where she shook her bosoms all over the stage, and I suggested she try that. Bea did, she shook her very low bosoms and everything else she possessed and the boys loved it. Sweet and low, that was how they liked it! At last she was being down-to-earth and doing something the boys understood.

Vivien Leigh made the same mistake when she did a show for the navy at Gibraltar. For some inexplicable reason, Vivien decided to recite 'Father William'. She began: 'I am old, Father William . . .' but the sailors were not ready for 'Father William' and Vivien was booed. She fled to her dressing room. Shortly afterwards, Noël Coward, who happened to be in the audience, came round to see her. 'Did you hear? They booed me!' Vivien wailed.

'I know,' said Noël. 'I started it.'

Leslie never made a mistake. We did several sketches together, one of them a cockney number that always brought the house down. Then there was the crinoline dance and a send-up of *The Merchant of Venice* where Leslie played the Merchant and I was Portia and we ended up doing a wild dance together. There was nothing highbrow about our material and we got nothing but applause from our audiences.

I remember that once I wept all through the Merchant sketch because my first letter from home had arrived in North Africa. Everyone who went through the war will know how important were letters from home. This letter was from Dozey and although we were no longer very close, Dozey was looking after Mr Baggs my spaniel for me, and he'd promised to write and let me know how the dog was settling down. After telling me a dozen little things about life around the station – Dozey's regiment was near Birmingham at the time – he finished the letter with the sentence: 'Mr Baggs wandered out onto a road late at night and was hit by a lorry. The brave old boy didn't die at once.' I minded about my poor little dog for a long time. I remembered how he had been brought to the airfield to see me off and had struggled to follow me onto the plane. I couldn't help but feel angry with Dozey for not taking more care of him. He had promised me that he wouldn't leave him and then had done so, for a whole weekend.

There was great excitement when Leslie had a wire telling the company to prepare to leave for Sicily, en route for Italy. The Italian campaign had started in September 1943; the British and American troops had landed, Naples had fallen and the armies were moving north, but were now held up at Cassino. We were to fly to Sicily, entertain the troops there, then travel to Bari, and then on to Naples. As the front lines were north of Naples and winter had settled in, it looked as if we might see some action.

Sicily was a good place to be after all the discomfort of wartime England and we were delighted to be among the Americans and their way of life – ice-cream and doughnuts and lots of food. And then to our joy they asked if we would like to be fitted with uniforms. They probably felt sorry for us in our thin clothes.

I went for a fitting and who should I find with a tape measure in her hands but the well-known British writer, Naomi Jacob. God knows how she had got there, but she was a very important creature indeed, probably a major-general at least. Naomi was a very large lady with well-known preferences and she took a long time over the fitting, but the result was wonderful. I had this beautiful uniform in the kind of olive green worsted that we hadn't seen in England for years. I never wanted to get out of it, and I flaunted myself everywhere.

There weren't enough seats in the American transport plane to Bari, so our party split up and Leslie and some of the company went on ahead to Naples. Wally Crisham, David Hutchinson, Molly Gay, one of the chorus girls, and I followed later. We flew to Bari in Southern Italy where we did one show and were then handed over to a pair of friendly American soldiers who were to drive us across Italy to join up with the others in Naples.

In wartime one never knows quite where the journey will end. I had not realized how very mountainous the middle of Italy was. The lorry climbed up the mountains and down the other side and as the day wore on black snow clouds formed overhead. We were all getting rather apprehensive, wondering what would be worse – meeting an enemy unit hidden in the mountains or getting stranded in a snowstorm. The snow came down and a blizzard had started when at last, on the other side of a mountain pass, we saw below us a small village.

We slithered into what might have been the village street and began to look for shelter! That had its problems. There was nothing but a tiny inn, very primitive, with a flag-stoned main room and great double doors barred by wooden crosspieces. The innkeeper said he could find a bed for Molly and me and might find food for us all, but that was the best he could do. An Italian family, a husband and wife with five children, said they would give up their matrimonial bed for Wally and David, and the soldiers, I believe, bunked down in their lorry. It was bitterly cold so we all huddled round the open wood fire and were grateful for a supper of fried eggs, bread and, of course, jugs of Italian wine. Afterwards one of the American soldiers produced a pack of cards: 'Anyone play poker?' he asked. We all brightened considerably and complimented the soldier on his foresight. It turned out that we all just loved poker.

Next morning it was still snowing. A beautiful sight, but not one that gladdened our hearts. Wally said that the snow was right up to his bedroom window. I noticed that he was scratching himself energetically and asked him what was up. On top of all our other problems, he told me the place was rife with bedbugs.

It turned out that the only people with any money at all were Wally and me, the others having squandered their wages on high living in Sicily, so we said we'd settle all the bills until we could move off. Breakfast was fried eggs, so was lunch, so was dinner. In between times we sat by the fire and played poker. Next morning, Wally tried for a change of menu. The innkeeper's wife was only too accommodating. They had run out of eggs and our diet for the day was to consist of goat's cheese. On hearing this news, David declared he would prefer to walk through the snow to Naples than live off goat's cheese. One of the Americans told him it was a fifty mile journey, but he wouldn't be deterred, even though it was still snowing. We dressed him up in all our spare gear and kissed him goodbye because we weren't at all sure that we should ever see him again. Then we stood back as the huge wooden crossbars were removed and David, like Scott of the Antarctic, walked out into the snowdrifts.

We rubbed our cold hands together, stamped our feet to keep warm then went back to our poker game. Our stomachs rumbled with hunger and the effects of the rough red wine. Before the day was out there was a great banging on the big doors. We rushed to open them and there stood two British soldiers and a jeep. They looked well-fed. 'Food!' cried Wally. 'Have you any food?'

Trust the British army: like all the best armies, it marches on its stomach and they had bread, corned beef, butter and everything for a brew up. As we munched the food and drank the hot tea, we asked them how they had found us. It turned out that there was a contingent of British soldiers nearby and they'd used their heavy equipment to clear a way down to the village. When they left they promised to return with more food, and in return we said we'd put on an impromptu concert for anyone who could make it to the inn. We really worked hard when we sang for our supper. Wally stole all Joyce Grenfell's songs and our small audience loved them.

Next morning, the sun was shining and the snow was melting. We hoped that David had been found on the road to Naples and now that we knew there were army units stationed in all the mountains we felt easier. Suddenly there was a terrible noise outside as an army transport came up the village street. We opened the doors and there was David Hutchinson, a bottle of gin in each hand, waving to us. He'd been picked up and looked after by another British unit on the way down. We congratulated him as if he'd been to the North Pole and back; it was, after all, a very brave thing to do.

When we finally reached Naples we didn't stay there long. The whole company moved off. We lived in some very strange billets and we did our shows in the oddest of places: the ruins of a church, a small dance hall with holes in the roof, a café in a village street. Conditions after the bombardments and the landings and the shelling were very rough, for troops and civilians alike, but there were some surprises. For instance, in Salerno there was a theatre still standing and we actually had dressing rooms. While we were performing there, we lived in a little pensione and at weekends the proprietor produced from somewhere or other a little three-piece band. On Wally Crisham's birthday we decided to give him a party after the show. One of the good things about Italy was the wine that was usually available if you looked hard enough. We stocked up with plenty of wine and Gavin Gordon asked the little band if they could play 'Happy Birthday To You' for Wally. They'd never heard of such a thing, so Gavin wrote down the top line of the melody and told them to play it over and over again. Wally came in, we all stood up, the band struck up and we all sang. We toasted Wally, gulped down some wine, and down we sat.

The little band was enthralled. They had no idea what the tune was, but they loved it. To them, it was the biggest hit of the year. They'd start off with some Italian tarantella, then smile to each other and strike up with 'Happy Birthday To You'. Up we'd get and toast Wally. This went on and on and very soon everyone was very drunk and heartily sick of singing the same song. But could we get the band to stop? No, we couldn't. They're probably still playing it down at the pensione in Salerno.

While we were in Salerno we gave shows for all the services, British and American alike. Two American GIs who became friendly asked if we'd like a little poker party one evening. Naturally we replied that there was nothing we would like more. While we did our daytime show, they set off into the hills to buy a vat of red wine. The Americans had everything except booze. Alcohol was forbidden on the assumption, no doubt, that if the GIs started drinking it might interfere with the war.

Heating was always a problem for us in the bleak Italian winter. However, the proprietor of the pensione, hearing about our little get-together, provided us with a charcoal brazier. Placed under the table where we played poker it warmed us all beautifully. We closed the doors, windows and draughty cracks tightly and we felt as snug as bugs in a rug as we played poker and sipped our way happily through the vat of wine. The glowing red coals of the charcoal sent up lovely clouds of warm air, but as time went by we started to feel sleepy. Everyone yawned and rubbed their eyes. Suddenly one of the players keeled over and slipped to the floor. With bleary eyes we stared down at him; then our eyes began to close too. 'Out!' yelled one of the GIs. 'Get out of here!' His words got through to us and we stumbled into the snow outside and discovered we were all gasping for breath. The senseless man was dragged after us. Unknowingly, we were slowly being poisoned by the fumes from the charcoal brazier. With no ventilation at all, the toxic fumes could not escape and unless the GI had got us out we might all have expired.

This didn't stop our poker parties and wherever we went someone had a pack of cards tucked into his pocket. The line of battle stretched north-west of Naples and we were often barely three miles from the front lines. We'd give our show in whatever place the army decided would hold the most men and then a bus and a driver would take us back to wherever we were staying. After our show, there was usually a little party for us in the mess – which might be a tent or the only building left standing in a rubble-strewn village street. One evening, Molly Gay and I missed the bus that was taking the rest of the company back. We were enjoying ourselves so much that we hadn't realized we'd been left behind. Still laughing and chatting, we were surprised by a great blast that suddenly rocked the little café and nearly blew us off our feet.

Apparently the Germans always started shelling about that time of night. It was the most alarming night I have ever spent, but we couldn't leave until the shelling was over and it wasn't until daybreak that we were driven back in a jeep. After that, we made sure we were on that bus after the show.

We had a famous American general in Naples one night. We were giving a show at the Opera House when Leslie Henson announced: 'We've got General 'Blood-and-Guts' Patton, in our audience tonight.' He persuaded General Patton to come up on stage and he did very well. In spite of all the bad publicity, General Patton seemed to attract a great deal of support. I found him the very type of the big, hearty American General and everyone in Naples was very fond of him.

We came back to London eventually and Leslie Henson gave us a break while he added new material and fresh talent to our company. On my first night out of uniform I had dinner at the Savoy with friends. Two well-known actresses were table-hopping. They reached our table. 'Darling,' said the first, condescendingly. 'Aren't you working?' The second commiserated. 'It's so *long* since we've seen you in a show.' I looked at them disdainfully. I felt I couldn't be bothered to reply. After what I'd seen in Italy, the bravery of the men, the pain and suffering I'd witnessed in the field hospitals, these two women weren't worth talking to.

'Hermione's been working abroad for the troops,' said one of my friends. 'Haven't you heard? There's a war on!' The two actresses hopped quickly on to the next table. We went off to Malta with a new company called *Africa Stars*. Graham Payne was the romantic leading man and we grew very fond of each other and always went round to each other's dressing room after the show. Later, when we were back in London with the same show, Noël Coward came backstage to see me. As usual, Graham was there and I introduced him to Noël. Afterwards, Noël was always around and I could see that he and Graham became great friends. 'Busy little cupid,' I thought to myself. Later, however, I learned that Graham had been in the chorus of one of Noël's shows, so they had probably already met. However, as Graham lived with Noël until his death, I like to think that their happy relationship was cemented in my dressing room.

While we were in Malta, Major-General Campbell Christie invited us to dinner. I'd heard that he and his wife wrote plays together. We got talking about the theatre and he said how glad he would be if I could appear in the play they were going to write after the war. And it really did happen. *Grand National Night* was one of the most successful plays I ever appeared in.

Later on we went to Holland and Belgium. In spite of the terrible devastation I loved Holland and I had a reason, of course. His name was Sir John Milbank, but we called him 'Buffles'. His aunt, Violet Wyndham was also my relation by marriage, so that gave us something in common to begin with. I had met Buffles in London many times. He was the most attractive of Englishmen – not too tall, not too short, blue eyes and a charming face. I'd also met his wife who was an adorable person, but he told me that they were having a trial separation.

We worked very hard in Holland, giving two shows a day, but after work I would go out with this fascinating man Buffles who was stationed with the army in the same town. I remember the night – we left Holland – we didn't know where we were going, everything was very secret – Buffles and I promised we'd manage to see each other somehow. After he'd gone I found a scarf he'd left behind. I held it to me and realized I was hooked all over again. We didn't manage to see each other again that time, but when I got back to London I persuaded ENSA to let me go back on another six week tour to Holland. That time we certainly met again. We made plans for after the war, just as all lovers do; I'd decided to tell Dozey that we must end our marriage legally.

After the last tour to Holland there was no chance of getting back to that country. Anyway, as the war progressed and victory grew nearer Buffles was always on the move with his regiment. We wrote to each other, letters that didn't always arrive, but I remember two came one morning and I was so happy. I was having lunch with Violet Wyndham. One of the reasons, of course, was that I wanted to be near someone who was near to Buffles so that we could talk about him. During our conversation Violet was talking about the brother of Buffles, of whom she was very fond. 'Oh, by the way,' she said, 'wasn't it sad about John?'

I stared at her.

'Didn't you know. He's just died. He caught some awful blood poisoning.'

The shock was unbearable. I started to talk uncontrollably. I told her all about my love affair with John in Holland, about how much I loved him and how much he loved me. I pulled his letters from my bag . . . And then I saw her eyes on me, the look of shocked surprise on her face. I had been married to her nephew, David Tennant, and now I was telling her of my love affair with another of her nephews.

'You think I'm promiscuous, don't you. I'm just alarmingly promiscuous, you think. But it wasn't like that. It wasn't like that at all.' It was an emotional moment.

Two people had met in a country ravaged by war and fallen in love. He had died, and the woman was left alone. It was happening all the time, countless times, to so many people, but the hurt was just as real and the pain just as hard to bear for a long time to come. But the war went on, life went on, and I went on tour again with ENSA. This time it was Belgium and the Battle of the Bulge was raging – the last battle before we knew that the war was nearly over.

Leslie Henson and his company finally packed up and went home for good. He had done a wonderful job bringing laughter and comfort to men going into battle and no words of praise could ever be too high for him. If ever a man should have been decorated for his brave and unstinting efforts in the war, it was Leslie Henson; but when the war was over I was shocked to see that he had been overlooked. I believe that George Robey was knighted on his death bed, but the powers that be let Leslie die without a word of thanks.

We did get medals, but they came from the American Government.

Another man found his world turned upside down when the war was over – Winston Churchill. I think he lost the general election of 1945 because he forgot the men who were in the forces in the Middle and Far East. They felt let down and neglected, and they used to say that when they got home they would put things right. Some time after Winston Churchill had lost that election and was no longer prime minister, I was at the Gargoyle with David and a few other people, drinking some of his lovely wine. One of our party was Raymond Blackburn, a Labour member of parliament. It was quite late, about half past one in the morning, and we were talking about Winston, when Raymond suggested we all drive down to see him. Churchill didn't sleep much and was used to late-night sessions with his advisers. Raymond telephoned Westerham and Churchill said that of course we must come down to see him straight away.

We hired a car and set off for Kent. David didn't come with Raymond Blackburn and me – he was furious afterwards. It was a lovely clear night; we came to Westerham, then turned up to Chartwell. We found him in his room in the little house he had had built for himself in the gardens of Chartwell. He was wearing the siren suit he had made famous and he looked at us over the top of his glasses, his eyes blue and bright like a wonderful beady-eyed parrot. He offered us champagne, which we gladly accepted, and said: 'Sometimes I think I deserve a little champagne.' We both agreed with him, and I thought of all the work that great mind had put into the long war.

We drank, we talked and laughed and enjoyed ourselves. Later he offered me a cigar – Raymond had told him that I sometimes smoked them in preference to cigarettes – and produced a wonderful long Romeo y Julietta for me. 'I'd better not smoke it now,' I said. 'May I take it home with me?'

After about an hour we took our leave. He came down with us and we walked down an avenue of very tall trees. He murmured a little song to himself that sounded like 'Ahumtitumtitum!'. As we neared the car he said: 'I hope I haven't said anything out of place.' Then he did a great high kick like a dancer. He was a most unusual man. He walked over to the car with us – the driver was still sitting in his seat. Churchill leaned in, looked at him and said: 'Well, I remember you.' The driver's eyes opened wide. Churchill went on: 'During the war you drove Averell Harriman and myself for two weeks.'

The driver said, 'That's right, sir. Never thought you'd remember that.'

All the way home the driver kept saying: 'My wife will never believe this. She'll never believe that I've talked to Churchill and that he remembered me.' So I leaned forward and gave him the cigar so that his wife would have to believe him.

I did rather regret my impulsive act afterwards. I should have liked to have kept that cigar as a souvenir of my meeting with one of the greatest men of our times.

When I came back to England I realized there was very little left of my marriage to Dozey. I didn't have to ask for a divorce – Dozey, as ever, behaved like a gentleman and gave me one. He was suffering more and more from the head wound he had received at Dunkirk. Our marriage had never really stood a chance. I married Dozey because I was sorry for him and that was the worst possible reason. I don't know exactly what happened to him in the years after we were divorced, but I was at a Savoy luncheon one day and a woman near me leant over and told me that he had died.

My two children were growing up. David was at Eton and Pauline was becoming a very beautiful girl. She was tall and blonde, more like David's mother than me. Soon she was to go to the Webber-Douglas School to study dramatic art, for her interest in the theatre, which had started when she was a little girl, had never wavered.

The first important play I did when I came back to the London stage was *Grand National Night,* written by the Major-General I had met when I was on the ENSA tour in Malta and his wife, Dorothy. In spite of the title, this play was not so much about the famous steeplechase as about a murder and a gambler who is playing for the highest possible stakes – how not to be convicted of that murder. Leslie Banks was to play this part and there were two female parts – two sisters, one of whom is a drunken creature who gets murdered, and the other is a good-hearted woman who tries to save the hero. I was to play the good sister. I remember saying to Angela that we should both be in this play, and that she should play the good sister while I played the sophisticated drunk. Angela agreed with me entirely!

I had a new man in my life called Francis de Moleyns. He read the play and told me I simply must play both parts. I knew, however, that Binkie Beaumont would never accept that. H. M. Tennent were putting on the play; Binkie ran that management and wanted to offer the evil part to another actress. It would have been possible for me to play both parts, though. The sisters didn't appear together and the bad sister got killed off in the curtain raiser. Francis was so set on the idea that I let him come with me when I went to see Binkie Beaumont. I tried to persuade him that I could do them both very well and that it would enhance the play, but Binkie was adamant.

Francis said: 'I'm sorry but that is what I would advise Hermione to do.' To my horror he got to his feet. 'So we must say goodbye.' He took my arm and marched me past Binkie's desk out into the hall and then to the lift. My knees suddenly grew weak. I was sure he had just talked me out of a very good part. Francis put a finger to his lips and rang for the lift.

Just as the lift arrived at our floor the office door was flung open and Binkie dashed out. 'Stop!' he cried. 'All right, we'll try it.' Francis would have made a very good agent – he was very tough. It was rather a pity he wasn't as tough with his own career.

He had come into my life at the Gargoyle Club. A kind friend had arranged a very jolly party for me; I remember that Rex Harrison's pretty first wife was there and, of course, David. Near us was a party of Air Force people celebrating the anniversary of the Normandy landings and making a good deal of noise. London was full of returning heroes, and a lot of them were having difficulty settling down to hum-drum civilian life. I looked over at them and my eyes met those of a very handsome man. His dark hair was going grey and he had silver wings brushed back at each side. He smiled at me and I knew without being told that he was Irish.

David, who could be very witty and entertaining, was keeping us all amused and everyone was having fun when I felt someone bringing a chair over and squashing himself next to me. It was the Irishman. David looked at him severely and demanded to know what he was doing. Francis, who I later discovered was as blind as a bat but extremely vain and never wore glasses, demanded in return: 'Who are you?'

'David Tennant.'

'Ah,' said Francis, 'just the man I wanted to meet!' Then he turned to me and smiled again. I looked at the stranger and decided that with his strong, wide face he was the best-looking man in the room, after David, of course. Francis insisted on buying everyone drinks.

Most people were fascinated by Francis, but some people loathed him and he and David always had a love-hate relationship. For myself, I was hypnotized from the word go. He took me home to my little flat far above the roof-tops of Piccadilly. He lay on my daybed with a drink in his hand and we talked and drank and talked. Eventually he laid down his glass, kissed my hand and left.

Next morning I woke up feeling bereft. This mad Irishman had pushed his way into my life and then walked straight out of it.

Chapter Twelve

The trouble with Francis was that he hadn't a bean. Although he was Irish through and through, he had been born in England and his family were aristocratic, but Francis was the second son, so that everything, the money and the title went to his elder brother. I seemed to have a leaning towards second sons – David was one. All this I learned when Francis called me the day after we met and took me to Wiltons for oysters. Afterwards we went back to my flat. This time we did not drink or talk, we made love.

Francis, however, was an incurable optimist. He'd come home from the war full of ideas on how to make a fortune and was convinced he would be a millionaire before he was fifty. I thought that quite likely, he had so much charm and energy, and, as he said, when he came up with a good idea his rich brother, Lord Ventry, might be prepared to finance him.

We soon knew everything about each other. His first wife, whom he had loved dearly, had died leaving him a daughter he adored called Valencia. He had married again, but the marriage had not been successful. I heard later from his Air Force friends that Francis de Moleyns was a war hero; he had been the man to plant the first British flag on French soil when the Normandy invasions began. His friend, who had covered him as he ran, had been killed.

I stayed hypnotized by the charm of Francis for a long time. I was always a very soft touch for him; I knew it and it made me happy. We used to go down to the sea and walk barefoot over the rocks and collect mussels. One day he suggested opening a sea-food bar. I was now making a large salary in the theatre and I could afford to become the chief investor. Francis found premises near the Rembrandt Hotel, not too far from Victoria Station, and a fan of mine called Jack Millet, who had once come to see me backstage and then became a good friend, agreed to run the bar. We opened with a great fan-fare of publicity.

The mussel and sea-food bar did very well, but after a while Jack Millet came to me and complained to me that he couldn't keep the books straight because Francis kept coming along and borrowing money from the till. As a result, the accounts were getting into a hopeless mess. Francis didn't take Jack's complaint seriously. He didn't see any point in running a profitable business if you couldn't spend the money. Francis had never heard the magic words *cash flow*. Then he said he thought the bar was rather a fiddly little place and what we needed was a whole string of them. As the chief investor who had to earn the money to balance the books, I didn't take up the suggestion. When the vogue for sea-food bars slackened, we turned it into a milk bar, and that did well.

We went on a long provincial tour with *Grand National Night* before opening in the West End. Our director, Claud Gurney, was rather an anxious man and sometimes he over-rehearsed us. Towards the end of the tour we were relieved when we heard that the Apollo theatre had been booked for the London opening, and we had just a week to go before we packed up and went home. And then we heard that Claud Gurney was coming down on the Monday morning and wanted us to spend it rehearsing with him. We all groaned. I didn't feel at all inclined to rehearse. My first scene with Leslie Banks as the curtain rises was very heavy, dramatic stuff where we quarrel violently and he kills me with a blow that knocks me to the floor. In the cold light of morning, it would be quite an emotional chore, especially as I had the actual performance to get through that night.

All the company were quite upset and we agreed that we should try to find some way of discouraging Claud. So, hoping to deter him but partly as a joke, I sent a card to his home in London saying: 'Is your "Gurney" really necessary?' This was an old wartime phrase. 'Is your journey . . .?' Anyway, the card didn't reach him in time, Claud Gurney came down and we all made the best of it and rehearsed all morning. Then we broke for lunch and went our different ways. Claud Gurney left the provincial theatre, crossed the road on his way to lunch, and was run over and killed by a lorry.

Sad thing was that my card arrived at his home after this tragedy and was read by his wife, to whom it must have seemed the cruellest of ironies. And even more sad was the fact that he didn't live to see the play transferred to the Apollo theatre where it had a huge success. *Grand National Night* had marvellous notices and my two parts won rave reviews.

At one of the digs we had stayed in on the *Grand National Night* tour, Francis and I met a curious old man who made dancing dolls. They were very quaint and could be made to do a kind of soft-shoe shuffle; you still see them in the shops occasionally. Francis was so taken with the dolls that he and an Air Force friend decided they would make their fortune selling them. In England at that time, toys were in short supply. They opened a factory to make the dolls and once again I became principal investor. Francis was always optimistic, never down-hearted. He wanted to make a lot of money with one thought in mind – to spend it. He loved spending money and having a good time, and he didn't always care who the money belonged to. The dancing doll venture was not a great success – I suppose they didn't promote them hard enough – and the factory had to be closed down.

Pauline was studying at the Webber-Douglas School and I was told that she was their best pupil. She was getting masses of offers and then she fell in love. She came to me and asked my permission to get married. Julian Pitt-Rivers was a charming young man and I liked him very much, but he was young and so was Pauline. I begged them to wait a bit. There was another drawback – Julian was tutor to the young King Faisal of Iraq. He had signed a seven-year contract, and he had three years to go. That meant that Pauline would have to go and live in the Middle East with her young husband. Still, nothing would make Pauline change her mind and off to Iraq they went. I think they were very happy at the beginning, but they were both so young. Their marriage lasted for about seven years.

I took a house in Chester Square; it was to be a home for my son David in his holidays and for Pauline whenever she came back to England. Francis was always talking about marriage. He wasn't divorced, but he was sure it could be arranged if he found his wife in a good mood. I wasn't at all sure that it would be a good idea. Anyway one morning I saw in the newspaper: 'The Honourable Mrs Francis de Moleyns is citing the actress Hermione Baddeley in her petition for divorce.' I was very shocked. Francis had no knowledge of what his wife was up to. Getting involved in another divorce depressed me; all the legal ins and outs upset me and I had to tell Francis to forget about marriage for the time being. With Francis, somehow there was never a great feeling of permanence. We got on extremely well and it seemed an ideal relationship, so I preferred to leave it like that.

He loved the theatre and he loved antiques and paintings, just as I did. When he had nothing much to do he would drive off into the country to the auction sale of some old house or other where the contents were being sold up. Once he went off in a thick fog to a sale in Hertfordshire and came back jubilant because the fog had kept the dealers away. He had bought three pictures, one of Napoleon, a landscape, and the third was a scene of a storm at sea which Francis was sure must be a Turner. We stood staring at it together and then I saw that tears were streaming down Francis's face. 'I can't help it,' he wept, 'it's so beautiful.' He gave it to me and I never did find out whether it was a genuine Turner, for it was removed from my house in the most awful circumstances.

Alan Melville wrote a delightful revue for me called *A La Carte*. We opened at the Savoy Theatre and in contrast to the unkind notices we had received for *Sky High,* this time the notices were ecstatic. Alan Melville was called the wittiest revue writer in London. One notice said, 'Hermione Baddeley's soft pussy-cat malice and the elegant wit of Henry Kendall (my leading man) make *A La Carte* a very tasty dish!' One of the young comedians featured in the show was Dickie Henderson.

It was in my dressing room at the Savoy that I unwittingly gave Francis a new idea to make his fortune. My dresser came in with a beautiful bouquet of flowers from someone. As she arranged them in a vase, she said what a pity it was that they would all be dead the next day. I suggested to Francis, half-jokingly, that he invent a magic powder to make flowers last longer. To my surprise, Francis and his ever-enthusiastic friend from the Air Force consulted a chemist in Scotland who took the idea quite seriously. For a long time he experimented and then he produced a powder that really did work. Samples were sent to Holland and the result was a deluge of orders. I had a little bottle designed, and filled with the magical powder and labelled *Flora Life*. It was a winner. It looked as if every florist's shop would be clamouring for *Flora Life* to dangle from their bouquets of cut flowers.

There was one obstacle standing between us and riches: without the support of the wholesale flower people in Covent Garden we might find ourselves boycotted everywhere. So we sent a sample off to them, sat back and awaited their congratulations. They didn't come. Of course, we should have realized that they would hate the idea of a magical powder that would prolong the life of flowers and cut their profits. The wholesalers said they wouldn't allow our little bottles to be marketed.

We were mugs at the game – we took it all seriously and didn't attempt to fight. And worst of all we forgot to take out a patent. Some years later Francis was in New York and went out to buy a bouquet of flowers. Hanging to the bouquet was the little vase I had designed and the label *Flora Life*. Some fiend had stolen our idea. Poor Francis, his schemes for making a fortune always withered and died. It was just as well I was earning money. While I was working in *A La Carte* I started to make films in the daytime. In those days it was the accepted thing – very hard work, but worth doing because the money was so good.

Richard Attenborough was making *Brighton Rock* for the cinema and he asked that I be given the role I'd played in the theatre – the part of Ida, the good-hearted tart, the sea-side pierrette. After that came *No Room At The Inn* and *It Always Rains On Sunday*, then *Quartet*, four short stories written by Somerset Maugham and put together, each with a different cast. The sequence I appeared in with Dirk Bogarde was called *The Kite*, and another sequence starred my sister Angela. I did another film with Dirk Bogarde, Cecil Parker and Glynis Johns, called *Dear Mr Prohack*. It was filmed in the winter and hurrying from the studios to get to the theatre every night in the snow and fog caused me plenty of anxiety. It was often touch and go getting to the theatre and I used to arrive breathless and exhausted with about five minutes to spare.

Filming during the day and appearing by night in a revue like *A La Carte*, where I had thirteen changes, was hard work, but it was the show that brought me into the public eye and these film offers were always made to me when I was appearing in the theatre. *A La Carte* was still drawing big audiences. On the 200th performance the management gave the cast a party. We all talked about another revue called *Slings and Arrows* that had just opened at the Comedy Theatre. My old friend from the ENSA tours, Wally Crisham, was in the show, as was the other Hermione. Evidently Gingold sent plenty of arrows winging our way in the revue, so to get a little publicity for our revue, Henry Kendall, my leading man, and I dressed up in full suits of armour complete with helmets and sat through a special performance put on for theatrical people. Gingold, it was said, was not amused.

The most gratifying moment of my stint in *A La Carte* came one evening when a note arrived after the show from that brilliant and influential comedian Jack Benny. He had come over to see his old friend Maurice Chevalier and had set a night aside to watch *A La Carte*. I was thrilled by his note – it said that mine was one of the best comic performances he had ever seen. I wrote back immediately, but by the time my letter was delivered he had returned to New York and I had missed my chance to meet him.

In spite of all the hard work and the anxieties I began to enjoy filming and realized I'd been a fool not to do it years ago. The film men always told me I would be in lots of films after this or that part, but they never offered me a contract – it was always a 'one-off', which was disappointing. Still, I needed to make as much money as I could. My life style with Francis was expensive. All these marvellous ideas he had so often just lost my hard-earned cash. He wasn't really to blame; some people are winners and some are losers and Francis usually slipped into the wrong category as far as money was concerned.

His latest venture looked as if it couldn't miss. Everybody wore them and everybody needed them – ties for men. But Francis's ties were, of course, going to be different. They were going to be exclusive silk ties made in Ireland. One of the designs he had in mind was a harp super-imposed over twin shamrocks against a background of orange and green stripes. Francis hoped it would do well in the Irish-American market in the States. He started going over to Dublin to look for workshops and get the business set up. While the Irish Tie Company slowly came into being, I was busy making films to keep the cash flowing. One of my favourites was *Passport To Pimlico*. The cast were wonderful, particularly Margaret Rutherford, who was exactly the same off stage as she was on stage. Such a funny, sweet and charming person. On her first day on the set she came on, was lead to a chair, but then refused to sit down unless a chair was found for me too. We became great friends.

Another member of the cast was Stanley Holloway whom I had known so well when I was a young girl in the *Co-optimists*. He was a very lovable man, but like a lot of comedians, in private life he had many anxieties. Just before he died in 1981, aged over ninety his son Julian asked him if he had any regrets. Stanley thought for a few moments, then he said with a sigh: 'Yes, there is. I wish I could have done the voice-over for the Kipling cake commercial.'

Way back in the late forties, none of us ever realized that a fortune lay in television commercials. Making *Passport To Pimlico* was enough of a challenge. We did some of the film on location in a corner of London and the weather was appalling – it never stopped raining. The film, which became a classic, was the story of a group of war-weary Londoners, fed up with restrictions and ration books and post-war shortages, who decide to make their London village, Pimlico, a free state. They opt out of England and assume the heritage of their ancestors from the province of Burgundy. It was a lovely film to make, full of charm and cockney wit and black-market enterprize made legal – very satisfying.

Only the weather was a bore. Without sunshine the location shots were held up. A tent was put up in the London square where we were filming so we could shelter when it poured down. 'Do you play poker?' asked Stanley during one of those damp interludes, giving me his contagious smile. We all played poker. Dark clouds gathered overhead, rain poured down and the cast sat in a lovely fug happily playing poker under canvas. Day after day the rain pelted down – no light at all for shooting. The poker school grew. We were all as thick as thieves. At the end of a week of solid rain a man lifted up the flap of the tent. A ray of sunshine had been spotted and we were wanted. Stanley lifted his head from a winning flush and gave the intruder a look of disgust, but we had to go. Stretching and yawning we crept out of the tent into a dull grey day. A tiny grain of sunshine peered down at us. Just enough to ruin our poker.

In 1949, two enthusiastic young men came round to my house in Chester Square with an exciting proposition to do a revival of *Fallen Angels*. Their names were Charles Russell and Lance Hamilton. They said that Noël Coward wanted me to play the part of Julia, the part Tallulah Bankhead had played back in 1924. *Fallen Angels* was not a successful play. In 1924, when it starred Tallulah and Edna

Best, it only ran for a few weeks. It was about two Mayfair ladies, who, while their husbands are away on a golfing weekend invite an old flame, a fascinating Frenchman, to call. As they wait, the ladies finish a bottle of champagne, tongues loosen and they reveal the indiscretions of their past. During their increasingly tipsy conversation they discover that the Frenchman seduced them both in turn.

The two young men looked at me. Would I do it? A lot depended on who was to play Jane. She had to be the right actress, the kind of person who would create the right atmosphere. They hadn't chosen anyone yet and a great and lengthy discussion ensued. Eventually we looked at each other and whispered: 'Gingold?'

The two Hermiones in a Noël Coward play – it was a sensational idea. There was a problem: Mother Gingold had gone off to America to seek fame and fortune. I had first called Gingold 'Mother' when we were in a pub and someone asked what we would drink. 'My mother will drink gin,' I said, and no one batted an eyelid. A cable was sent to Gingold in New York. Back came the answer: Gingold did not want to play Jane. She would only appear in the production if she played Julia. Noël Coward cabled straight back: 'Don't be silly, dear. Jane is the best part.' Gingold, reassured by the Master, booked her passage to London.

On a cold grey day we met at the Ambassadors Theatre for the first reading. Peter Daubeny had joined the management and was now to present the play. I sneezed; Gingold blew her nose: we both had heavy colds so it was a bad start. Over lunch we discussed the young actress, Diana Lincoln, chosen to play the part of the maid. Gingold thought she had over-acted and should be replaced. Diana had a vulnerable look and a large ladder in her stocking which endeared her to me. Diana was not replaced.

We went into rehearsal. It was felt, ever so slightly, that Gingold was giving a revue performance and over-burlesquing the scene where Julia and Jane drink too much champagne. 'If we over-do this scene,' said the director, oozing tact, 'might we not become a little boring?' 'Boring!' Gingold took umbrage. Gingold left the rehearsal. Next day Gingold was missing from rehearsal. Management tore round to the little house in Kinnerton Street and implored her to return. Gingold's health had suddenly changed for the worse. Management asked me to go round and see what I could do.

I went round to Kinnerton Street and sat in the drawing room amongst the beaded footstools and buttoned Victorian chairs. My namesake was still in bed, unable to receive visitors. I telephoned the management and Charles and Lance rushed round with flowers. The three of us were finally admitted to the sick room.

While Charles and Lance tried soothing phrases, I kept quiet. I was much too sensible in those days to say what I thought. Then Peter Daubeny rang up. We heard him loud and clear across the wires telling the recalcitrant Gingold that we had all been working much too hard and he was going to take us all out to lunch.

'Where?' demanded Gingold.

'The Caprice!' A not inappropriate venue.

Charles nudged me in the ribs, Lance pressed my foot surreptitiously, 'Darling,' I said, 'a little food will do you good. Cheer you up'.

Gingold was back and rehearsals began again. Sometimes I wondered what Noël Coward would think if he could see what was being done to his play. Coward is much harder to act than one would think, but I must admit that I was a little apprehensive about the way Noël's slick and sophisticated comedy was being turned into burlesque. However, Peter Daubeny said we had better leave it because that was the only way she could play it. As an actress I always did what the director thought best, so very soon I was having a marvellous time too, clowning, pulling faces and letting myself go. Not that we ever over-did it. We kept the light touch and did not over-act.

We played to packed houses on tour and then we heard that Noël Coward, who had been absent through rehearsals, was back in London and absolutely furious at the way his play was being burlesqued. He was coming down to the Palace Theatre in Plymouth to see for himself, we were told. A slight tremor of apprehension ran through management and cast.

Noël arrived. He took his seat in the stalls then our spies saw that after a while he could stand it no longer and began to pace back and forth at the back of the stalls. Peter Daubeny got the full force of the Coward fury when the curtain came down. We were using his play as a vehicle for our double-act and it was outrageous, sacrilegious even!

The two Hermiones tried their best to hang their heads in shame.

But no one took a blind bit of notice. As soon as his back was turned we were back at the burlesque. When we opened at the Ambassadors Theatre in the West End, all records at the box-office were broken. We were a smash hit and Noël had to agree that we knew best. On the first night a telegram arrived from Noel who was aboard a liner bound for the West Indies: 'Consider my criticisms incorrect. Please play as before. Best wishes to all and good luck'.

Fallen Angels had every seat booked for months ahead, which wasn't bad for a play that had once been a failure. We became a cult show. During the run we had three different romantic Frenchmen. It wasn't that we wore them out, but the two Hermiones had staying power. Just like *Charley's Aunt,* it looked as if the play would run forever, but eventually Gingold got the urge to go back to America – I think she'd left her little dogs behind. Although we were booked up far into the future, she went. Peter Daubeny asked Angela to take over, but she refused. My sister was not really a comic lady.

There was talk of taking the play to New York and all over again I heard that here was the play with which I was going to take America by storm. It didn't go to America, and once again I didn't appear in New York. An American impresario called Mr Barr did tell me that he watched the 'drunk' scene and thought he had never seen anything so funny; his one idea was to get it put on in New York. He did, but I wasn't invited to appear, he had an all American cast. I heard later that it was awful, quite unbelievably bad. The two women over-acted so much that one of them actually crawled up the curtains.

American and English humour was very different at this time. Television has changed a lot of this and now we understand each other's humour much more. The Americans have done some gloriously funny series, but I don't think they can do satire as we can – it is born in us. Nor do I think that *Fallen Angels* is a vehicle that should leave its native soil – it hasn't ever really worked in America. Much later, when I lived in California, I did play *Fallen Angels* with Joan Blondell, but we had so many problems, so much trouble, that it was not a success.

That 1949 production in London was loads of fun and I had a wonderful time. Francis got on very well with Gingold and was always taking her bouquets of flowers, but it is well known that Irish lovers are like that. Perhaps he should have tried a little harder to make her stay, for if *Fallen Angels* hadn't come off, if I hadn't agreed to do a certain film to make a quick bit of money, I might not have met Laurence Harvey.

Chapter Thirteen

Making films at Shepperton Studios at Walton-on-Thames was always agreeable – it is a pleasant place near the open country and the river Thames and not too far from London. In this particular film, called *There Is Another Sun,* I was playing a fortune-teller called Sarah. I always love fortune-teller parts, that hint of the unknown and the mysterious means I can let myself go.

I was trying on wigs for my role of Sarah in the studio hair-dressing department when I saw in the mirror a man standing outside watching me. The hairdresser, a new boy, asked how I liked the wig I had on. 'It suits you,' he said, 'Miss . . . er . . .' Quick as a flash, the man outside strode over to us. 'The lady's name is Miss Hermione Baddeley,' he admonished the boy. 'She is one of our most brilliant revue artistes.'

I had to smile at him. He was the male lead in the film, playing a fairground boxer. He was very good, in fact wasted in a B picture like this. I knew, just by looking at him, that he was on his way up and would become a star – it was written all over him. The way he looked, the way he held himself, he had that special mark. His name was Laurence Harvey. He held out a hand to me and asked me for a drink. Although he didn't know me very well, he behaved as he always did afterwards, catching my hand and marching me along beside him as if I was a tiny tot.

The cast of the film were very pleasant people: there was Leslie Dwyer, the comic, and pretty little Susan Shaw, the *ingénue.* I thought it more than likely that Susan and Laurence Harvey would be a twosome, but it didn't turn out like that. Leslie Dwyer was a great one for telling amusing stories and the older members of the cast would sit around roaring with laughter. More and more, Larry Harvey came over to join us. I thought it strange that he didn't stay with his own age group, but Leslie suggested he had a crush on me.

I didn't take it at all seriously. I found Larry very easy to be with and more sophisticated than most young men of his age, which I suppose was about twenty-four. He had a continental way with him and clearly his roots were in Europe. He had grown up in South Africa, but had been born in Lithuania and his family had emigrated to Johannesburg when he was a little boy.

One evening when I couldn't find my car or the driver, Larry gave me a lift home in his most cherished possession, a small Morris saloon car. He drove at a terrifying speed, talking and laughing all the time, but instead of being put off and closing my eyes as we went round corners on two wheels, I found his high spirits entertaining. Soon he got into the habit of picking me up in the mornings and driving me out to the studios. He told me about himself, how he'd come over from South Africa determined to make his way into the acting profession. He'd been accepted at RADA, which was a good start. I'd noticed that although this was a terrible film, he was trying to put in a good performance and I admired him for it. He stood head and shoulders above the usual 'B' picture leading man. He worked hard and didn't hold back and act as if it was all rather a bore.

This young man brought something new into my life. When he took me home at night we often had dinner together, sometimes we went out to a nightclub, but whatever we did it was always fun. Much later he told one of his wives that I was the first person in London to be kind to him. Well, I enjoyed being kind to him, it was rather like having another son. Young David was in the army at Pirbright at the time, and when he came home for the weekend, he sometimes met Larry and they got on well.

He was different to most men I'd known. His name wasn't even his own, he'd found it walking down Knightsbridge one day. He had been born Larushka Skikne, he told me, but had altered that to Laurence Skikne; but who could pronounce Skikne? Then he had passed by Harvey Nichols, the Knightsbridge shop, one day and thought to himself: 'Harvey. Anyone can remember Harvey.' He'd been Laurence Harvey ever since. Larry had joined the South African army as a kid during the war and been posted to an entertainment unit. He'd toured North Africa and Italy entertaining the South African troops, and had read about my performances for ENSA.

Once he was showing me some of his pictures and a family photograph fell out, one of the old-fashioned kind where the family sit in rigid positions. Amongst the group was this little boy in a sailor suit. I asked Larry if it was him. He looked over my shoulder and then suddenly snatched the photograph from my hands, mumbling that he didn't want me to look at it. I realized why. They looked to be a hard-working and poor family, and they didn't fit in with the image he had of a sophisticated young man about town.

One evening we had dinner together and went to a nightclub called Les Ambassadeurs. 'I've done a silly thing,' said Larry, 'locked myself out of my flat and I can't find my key.' He was living at the time in Shepherd's Market. I told him he was welcome to stay the night in my son's room if he wanted. Eventually we wound up with Robert Kee, the BBC commentator, and Natalie, Robert Newton's wife. Robert Kee had been very taken with my daughter Pauline before she married Julian Pitt-Rivers and Natalie, I could see, had her eye on Larry Harvey. We all went back to my house. Then after a while I told them I had to go to bed because I was getting up at the crack of dawn to get out to Shepperton Studios.

They were not in the mood to go home so they all followed me into my bedroom. I changed in the bathroom, came back and got into bed. The three of them sat around talking and laughing, and for a time I joined in. I remember looking at Robert Kee and thinking what a good-looking man he was and wondering idly . . .

I must have dropped off. I heard Robert and Natalie leave and I waved them goodbye. I closed my eyes again. Five minutes later, to my utter astonishment, Larry Harvey shot into my bed. I told him firmly that his bedroom was across the corridor, for this was not what I had envisaged for us at all. He nuzzled my neck and made it perfectly obvious that he had no intention of moving. 'But we're just good friends,' I murmured, conscious that I didn't sound very convincing. 'Darling, how can you say that,' whispered Larry, coming up for breath. I sighed. 'All right, but don't forget, this is just a bit of fun.'

I really didn't mind a bit when Larry Harvey moved into Chester Square. All my life I've been accustomed to people moving in and out of the places where I live and I like having people around me. Friends would frequently turn up for the weekend and then stay a month. Mine has always been an easy-going household – if I have empty bedrooms, I'm quite happy if someone moves in to fill them. In fact after a time, Larry asked if his stand-in, a very pleasant young man called Bob Porter, could move in too.

Larry was not at all a grasping sort of man. He moved into my bed and shared my house but he helped with the expenses as much as he could. It was fortunate in a way that all this happened when Francis, my Irish lover, was away in the Emerald Isle, setting up his Irish Tie Company. Word of what was happening did cross the Irish sea, eventually – I believe a well-known Irish actress passed on the news – but Francis had too much pride to come storming back. I heard about him from time to time, how he was drinking heavily and was short of funds. The Irish Tie Company wasn't doing all that well and his pompous elder brother, the millionaire Lord Ventry who was only interested in balloons, wouldn't lend him a penny. In the old days we had shared a secretary and she kept me informed. 'Poor Francis,' she told me. 'He's on hard times, he's down to eating lunch at Woolworths.'

One Sunday morning when I had friends to lunch, Francis returned. It was a disaster all round. Brian Desmond Hurst, the director, was there with some strange young men who wore long hair and necklaces – my first hippies. Larry Harvey and Bob Porter were also there and we were all sitting upstairs in the drawing room, drinking gin and tonics, when the door suddenly burst open and in marched Francis. He walked straight up to Larry Harvey and gave him a terrific punch that sent Larry staggering. As Francis was obviously very much the worse for drink, it was quite amazing that he was right on target. Larry got to his feet, Francis delivered another good blow but Bob Porter stepped smartly in front of Larry and was hit instead.

'Bravo!' cried Brian Desmond Hurst from his safe armchair. 'Soon we'll all need stand-ins.'

Whereupon Francis picked up a full bottle of whisky and went for Larry again. This time Larry prepared himself and floored Francis with a knock-out blow. He lay inert on the drawing room carpet, dead to the world. The young hippies gathered around, wringing their hands, then at my instructions carried him off to an empty bedroom to sleep it off.

Brian Desmond Hurst insisted that we all go over to his house. I went with the others, but I was so worried about Francis that I no longer enjoyed the party. I made all sorts of pledges to myself that I would help to get him back on his feet. I didn't think that he and Larry would ever get on, they had nothing in common. When we got back to Chester Square, Francis had departed. I was rather sad when I discovered that he'd taken all his family silver with him. It had been left with me for safe-keeping. But I knew quite well that this was only a temporary coolness in our friendship. Men like Francis just don't leave forever.

My way of life underwent a change. Larry's tall, slim silhouette had to be maintained on a strict diet. Out of the fridge went the goodies I adored: the chocolate layer cake, the trifle and the cartons of cream. Larry decreed that we were to eat chicken, fish, and burnt toast.

'Burnt toast?'

Larry assured me that I would learn to love it. I did not learn to love burnt toast, but I loved the new slim figure I acquired and I liked the dry white wine we now sipped instead of the more fattening beverages. Larry Harvey was the kind of man who picked things up quickly. He loved good food (when he wasn't dieting) and he loved wine, so he wanted to learn all about them. He worked towards acquiring all the good things in life, but he was by no means a dandy and didn't spend hours gazing into the mirror. One of the things that attracted me to him was the fact that unlike many actors he did not seem very conscious of himself. I admired a great deal about him. He was funny and witty and liked being with amusing people and, like me, he loved parties. The ambitious young actor and the older successful actress were hot news – a very popular pair in London and invited everywhere.

At first Larry used to suggest that we get married, but I always laughed at the idea and said it was ridiculous. I knew that Larry was going to do very well, his talent was so obvious, but by now I was too much of an individualist myself to take second place to any man. Besides we were having plenty of fun together. Larry was, after all, an actor, and no matter what strange situations he found himself in, he could always act his way out of them. For instance, I took him to stay at Megginch Castle, the home of my friends Violet and John Drummond. Larry made himself perfectly at home and one would have thought that his background was Eton and the Guards rather than Lithuania and Johannesburg.

I love castles. I love them when they are set about with turrets and spires in the fairy tale mould. I love them when they look like centuries old fortresses, and most of all I love them when they are in Scotland. I read once in the papers that 'Hermione Baddeley is touring castles this autumn'. The gossip columnist was having a go at one of my favourite pastimes. Instead of touring the provinces with the latest revue, I was visiting my friends in Scotland.

At Megginch Castle all went well until I heard John suggest that Larry join the grouse shoot. I wasn't at all sure if Larry Harvey had ever held a gun in his hands, except before a camera saving Burma from the reds or Africa from the fuzzy-wuzzies; and a grouse is not the easiest bird to hit. I asked him if he had ever been in the butts before and he cheerfully enquired what a butt was. My misgivings increased.

Next morning off went the shooting party and I heard volley after volley of shots in the distance. Panic rose inside me. If Larry didn't shoot his host he would probably get a beater or two. Or when he made one of his flamboyant gestures waving his gun, someone would probably get hit. However, that evening the party emerged through the Scottish mists absolutely loaded down with grouse.

'I've never seen anyone handle a gun like him before,' laughed John Drummond, our host, 'but he did surprisingly well.'

Thank God, I breathed to myself, and not a beater dropped.

Like so many film actors, Larry Harvey longed for a career in the theatre. He wanted desperately to be known as a good actor. One morning he read in the newspaper that Basil Dean was about to do a revival of a play he had produced very successfully in 1923, called *Hassan*. Larry decided he wanted a part. I reckoned I could arrange a private audition for him any time he wanted. After all, Basil had made me an overnight star when I was fifteen and he had never stopped telling me that he always regretted letting me go.

As soon as Basil Dean met Harvey I could see that he liked the look of him. It is always a bonus if a man can act well and be tall, young and very good-looking at the same time. Larry had memorized a good poetic piece of *Hassan* and after the audition Basil offered him two parts to choose from. Larry chose Rafi, and received very good notices.

Angela and her husband Glen Byam Shaw had heard about my

new young man and naturally were curious to meet him. Larry was anxious to meet them too, for he knew all about Glen's magnificent record at the Stratford-upon-Avon Memorial Theatre, where for years he'd been directing our greatest Shakespearean actors. Glen and Angela came to a performance of *Hassan* and afterwards we all went back to my little pink house in Chester Square. Glen took me on one side and told me he would like to have Larry at Stratford.

Larry was overjoyed. A season at Stratford. To have a brilliant director like Glen Byam Shaw offering to help was something any young actor would give his eye-teeth for. Angela reminded me afterwards that I had my own career to think of; she thought my young man was taking up too much of my time. That hadn't escaped me, but I enjoyed helping Larry. It wasn't that Larry used people, but he was the kind of man people wanted to help; and of course I did introduce him to people who did things for him.

It so happened that Romulus Films, owned by Jimmy and John Woolf, were promoting a film of theirs called *Treasure Hunt*. As a clever gimmick, the Woolf brothers organized a well-publicised treasure hunt. Celebrities were invited to hunt for the prize with a reporter so that everything they did would be in the leading newspapers next day – as well as the name of the film, of course. When I was invited, I asked if I could bring Laurence Harvey along because he was full of bright ideas. We joined up with a reporter from the *Daily Mirror* and the three of us were as keen as mustard. It wasn't easy by any means. I remember that one of the clues led to Tallulah Bankhead's house where we had to produce a hair from her head. We managed, got back to the winning post at the Caprice Restaurant and were pronounced victorious. Jimmy Woolf waiting with a jeroboam of champagne and massed photographers embraced us. We dined with Jimmy later and I sat back and watched how clever young men get to Hollywood.

I don't think I have ever seen anyone give such a brilliant unscripted performance as Larry Harvey gave that night for Jimmy Woolf. It was as if he'd flicked down a switch and gone into formula one, top-gear. His personality glowed, his charm warmed the cockles of our hearts. Stories poured out, dialects, jokes. Larry was magnetic and Jimmy Woolf was conquered. Jimmy was a homosexual and not at all a good-looking man. The friendship that began between them that night was gossiped about for years. Were Larry and Jimmy more than just friends? I don't think so. Larry had always had this effusive way with him. He'd kiss the *maître d'hotel* on both cheeks, he'd fling his arms around the manager, but that was his way – it amused him to tease onlookers.

Soon after the treasure hunt, came an invitation for us to attend the gala performance of *The African Queen* starring Katharine Hepburn and Humphrey Bogart – another Woolf production. It was a star-studded occasion and afterwards we were once more invited to have supper with Jimmy Woolf at the Caprice. As soon as we'd eaten the smoked salmon, Jimmy offered Larry a contract. Larry was naturally delighted. His salary at Associated British Pictures had been pretty small, about £35 a week I think, and he hadn't worked much since *Hassan*. However, his big chance in the theatre was coming up; he explained to Jimmy that he was about to do a season at Stratford. Jimmy Woolf scoffed: 'There's no money there.' With a touch of frost in my voice, I told him that actually the money was quite good, besides which it was a wonderful chance to work with Glen Byam Shaw.

Larry agreed that it was an opportunity he could not pass up. 'All right,' said Jimmy Woolf, 'tell you what I'll do. We'll draw up a contract and pay you something while you're at Stratford getting all that prestige. If a good vehicle for you turns up we'll hold on to it.' It was an astonishingly good offer and a bond formed immediately between the two men. Jimmy Woolf soon became Harvey's closest ally. He was the one who made Harvey a star and set him on the road to Hollywood. Jimmy was very kind to Harvey, he was always giving him presents, not small ones either, but little trinkets such as a new car. When the evening was over, Larry said I was like a lucky charm to him.

It was true. Suddenly his career was moving in the right direction. We went to first nights together, to nightclubs and parties. We were always having supper at the Caprice and I usually signed the bill – a lot of my troubles later stemmed from this habit I had of signing bills in a carefree way. But how could I worry about money when I had such a marvellous companion? I remember taking him to a dinner party at Beverley Nichols' one night. Beverley had rung me up specifically to ask me if I would bring along this brilliant young man he'd heard so much about. So we went together to this very chic and polite affair to which a rather stuffy selection of guests had been invited. After dinner, people started telling stories – of the genteel rather than the crude variety. I had noticed that Larry was getting rather more tipsy than was wise and my heart gave a gulp when he flashed a radiant smile at the assembled guests and began: 'I remember once . . .' Needless to say, the story was quite outrageous, unrepeatable. One by one, the guests marched stiffly from the room. Beverley Nichols came over to me with a scarlet face. 'You'd better take him away,' he said in an icy voice. 'Well, you did ask for him,' I replied. We left in disgrace. But I couldn't be cross with Larry for long – it had been a truly hilarious moment. 'Well,' he said to me in the car as we drove home, 'you may be able to fill the Café de Paris every night, but I can empty a dining room in three minutes flat!'

It was inevitable that the young, unspoiled Larry Harvey would change. I noticed that he was becoming more conceited, more interested in his appearance, buying new suits, silk shirts and Lobb shoes. Instead of rushing out without a thought for the way he looked, he spent more time choosing the right tie for the right suit. Most of the time he was still great fun to be with, witty, amusing and always concerned for my welfare – except, that is, when he drank too much brandy. Brandy and Laurence Harvey did not mix well. It brought out a side of him that was quite frightening; he could become filled with wild, unreasoning jealousy.

Driving home one night some sort of jealous scene erupted. I knew he'd had too much brandy and I was determined to get away from him as soon as we reached Chester Square. When the car turned into the driveway, I jumped out and hurried towards the back door. I put the key in the lock, then heard the sound of a car engine revving up behind me. I looked over my shoulder and saw the lights of the car coming straight at me. I hadn't time to turn the key, hadn't time to move. I was terrified. I shrank back against the door and saw through the windscreen Larry's face looming towards me set in an awful grimace. I closed my eyes, heard the squeal of brakes and I felt the car hit my legs.

I must have blacked out. The next thing I saw was Larry's face as he held me in his arms, tears pouring down his face. 'I thought you were going to kill me.' I whispered.

'I went mad,' he groaned. 'I didn't know what I was doing.'

I was badly bruised. The worst injuries were to my legs. Larry was filled with overwhelming remorse. I don't know which was hardest to bear, the pain from the bruises or Larry's remorse. One doctor was not enough – he called in two doctors to attend me after 'the accident'. He promised on everyone's head that never again would he be so insanely jealous.

Of course he didn't keep his promise. Every time I saw the brandy bottle near Larry I took shelter. We were at a party one night when I saw the danger signals start to flash. I noticed the amount of brandy he was drinking and the brusque gesture with which he interrupted a conversation I was having with a male friend. Unless I left the party in a hurry, the next thing would be a very unpleasant scene in front of everyone. I was quite controlled when I drove home, but underneath I was absolutely furious that he should get drunk and humiliate me like this. I wanted to hurt him in return. As I walked into the bedroom I knew exactly what to do. I took a suit he had just had made from the wardrobe, walked over to the window, opened it wide and dropped first the jacket then the trousers. They caught on the branches of the little tree in the middle of the garden below and for a moment they looked like dancing figures as they waved in the breeze.

I couldn't help laughing. I found another of his much loved suits and that fell in quite an artistic design on the lawn. I went over to get some more. A noise behind me made me turn. Larry, breathing hard, stood in the doorway. I beckoned him to the window. 'Come and have a look. Don't they look quaint.' My anger had quite evaporated. I was ready to laugh and make up. 'I've seen them.' His voice was cold and very angry. He came towards me and I saw the expression on his face – he was beside himself with rage. He lifted a hand and struck me a blow across the face, then another that sent me reeling back. Luckily I was agile and ducked under his arm. He chased me, grabbed hold of me and threw me onto the bed. He knelt above me and bashed me repeatedly in the face. 'I'm going to kill you for that.' His hands went for my throat. I could see his eyes glittering above me. 'This time I am going to kill you.'

I was quite sure that was exactly what he was going to do. His vanity saved my life. He was wearing one of his new, beautiful shirts, monogrammed with very expensive buttons. As he squeezed my throat, my hands went out and grabbed. They caught his shirt and I jerked for dear life, trying to rip the shirt apart. It worked. His hands let go of my throat. I was off the bed and I ran as I'd never run before. Fear gave me wings. I dashed down the stairs and into Bob Porter's room. He was in bed. 'Bob!' I screamed. 'He's trying to kill me.'

Bob jumped out of bed, caught hold of me and pushed me behind himself. At that moment Larry Harvey burst in and tried to grab me, but Bob was sober and in much better condition than Larry. In a few minutes he'd got him out of the room and he'd locked the door. For a long time Larry tried to break the door down. In the end Bob went out and remonstrated with him. He calmed him down and I spent the night in Bob's bed with the door firmly locked.

Next day we had the agonising remorse all over again. 'You don't understand what love is,' he whimpered. 'I go crazy with jealousy.' I understood very well. I don't think that subconsciously I ever forgave him for beating me up that night – women don't forgive men for hitting them – and this time the bruises were very visible. I knew then that Larry Harvey was probably incapable of making a woman happy for very long. This undoubted talent he had, had a black, dangerous side. Life with him was exciting and funny, but he was consumed with a hunger to have everything – fame, fortune, all the riches of life. It was as if he knew that there was only so much time allotted to him. That was the awful tragedy: when he had everything that he'd dreamed of, he discovered that he had cancer and he died in his early forties.

I looked at my face in the mirror next day and it was so bruised and swollen that I hardly recognized myself. In a few days time I was due at the studios to finish a film. I had to go. The director took one look at me and thanked God that it was a long shot and that I would be wearing a hat. He suggested a veil for good measure. The make-up man was so clever and kind and did such a restoration job on me that you'd think he'd been dealing with bashed-up women all his life.

But that wasn't the end of my troubles. I had a long-standing engagement to go to Jersey to appear at a Girl Guides' rally and the bruises were still there, under a heavy make-up. After my recent experiences with Larry Harvey, I probably wasn't the best person to hand out medals, but I had promised to go. When I got there I must admit that I did admire these young girl guides with their lanyards and whistles and badges for good behaviour and cooking. They made little fires, brewed tea in billycans and sang rousing songs. I was enchanted with the sweetness and innocence of it all.

Dennis Price, the actor, sat next to me at the prize-giving. He had sharp eyes for he whispered: 'Some of my boyfriends knock me about too.' Then he winked. 'I quite enjoy it.'

I did not wink back.

Chapter Fourteen

I made my entrance down the long staircase. I wore an elegant black velvet gown, stiletto heels and behind me I trailed yards of white fox fur. I thought to myself: 'I wouldn't have believed it if anyone had said two hours ago, "Tonight you're going to be the star of cabaret at the Café de Paris." '

Perhaps this was the only way to do it – finish another glass of *Cheval Blanc* and plunge right in. Larry Harvey and I were in the middle of dinner when the phone rang. Bea Lillie had lost her voice. Every table was full. Would I . . . It was right out of a thirties talkie, except that on the phone was Poulson, the manager of the Café de Paris. The tables were filled with a sophisticated West End audience used to stars like Noël Coward and Marlene Dietrich – only the very best for them. And this audience was already eating its dinner and waiting for the cabaret to begin.

And I didn't like cabaret. I never had. I felt like saying: 'Are you mad! At this late hour! Unprepared! Unrehearsed!', but of course I didn't. Larry Harvey, hovering at my shoulder with the bottle of wine in his hand, caught on quickly. 'Tell him you'll ring back in two minutes.' He had it all worked out. We would ring John Pritchett, my accompanist and get the beautiful new dress by Rahvis from my wardrobe. It was high time I was an international star in cabaret. 'But I hate it!' Larry poured me another glass of wine, while I rang Poulson back and accepted. I must have been mad.

The most important thing, we decided, was to make a dramatic entrance. A dozen telephone calls later we had half-a-dozen white fox furs to take round to the Café de Paris. There, I had them sewn together and soon after I was strutting on stage with a seemingly endless flow of glossy white fur trailing behind me. I made sure to drag it out as long as possible and the scene got me a big laugh. It was just the start I needed, and when they later took me on for a few months, this became my standard entrance.

I have to thank Larry Harvey for my success that night – he pushed me into accepting. But of course John Pritchett helped too, dashing round at a moment's notice and taking me through my favourite songs. When it was all over, the applause was deafening. It was most extraordinary. Nothing went wrong . Of course I hadn't had time to be nervous.

Bea Lillie's voice returned next day, but I was 'in' at the Café de Paris and I stopped hating cabaret quite so much. I still didn't like sitting around all day and having to prime myself to go on at midnight. It's no fun having to hold back and refuse drinks when everyone else is enjoying themselves, all because you still have a show to do. Nevertheless, as soon as Bea went back to America, I was asked back to the Café, and I kept returning. The Café de Paris was different. Old friends I hadn't seen for years sat in the audience; people who lived miles or continents away would have dinner at the Café and call round to see me. It was much more of a club than a place of work.

But cabaret is only part of theatre. I always hankered for the real thing, disasters and all. The play I did after *Fallen Angels* was a restoration comedy called *For Love Or Money*. On opening night there was a great deal of noise going on at the end of the performance. Quite confidently, I informed Henry Kendall, my leading man, that they were cheering us.

'No, darling. They're booing,' replied Henry.

When I was offered Tennessee Williams' *The Rose Tattoo*, I knew this was a great play and a marvellous chance for me. It happened because of Little Brit, the Russian girl who had once shared my flat in Piccadilly. At least it was Little Brit, who was now married and had become Lady St Just, who brought Tennessee Williams round to see me. The Maharajah of Cooch Behar was sitting outside my front door in his limousine waiting to take me to have a picnic lunch and watch the polo at Hurlingham. I knew that Maharajahs had good picnic lunches, so I was hurrying out when there was a knock on the door. Little Brit stood there with a smallish man with a smiling round face. In his hands he held a silver cocktail shaker and a rather worn script. He freed one hand and introduced himself as Tennessee Williams.

Photographed by Gregory Bernard at the time of
The Sunday Society Performances

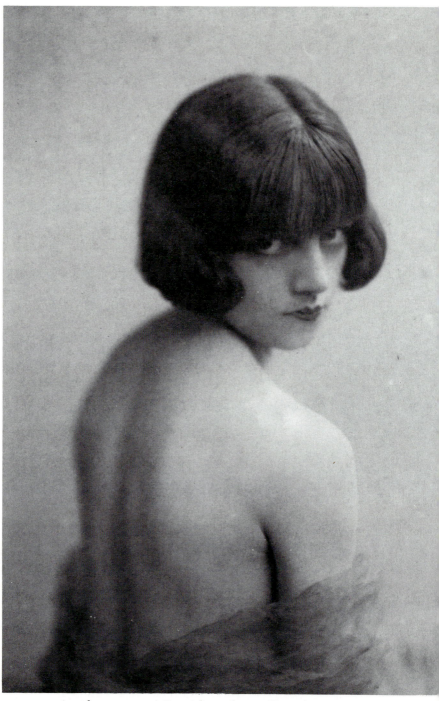

Aged seventeen. David used to call me his 'Pocket Venus'

portrait of me by Kanelba

the first of the
ne Sharp series of revues ▷

Specially photographed to appear in the paper London Life

Aged eighteen

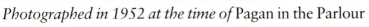
Photographed in 1952 at the time of Pagan in the Parlour

A photograph to send to fans

In Scotland at the lodge I rented on the Isle of Arran. Here I am with the gardener

Off the Isle of Arran. The photographer was determined to take a picture of me out fishing, rather against my will

This photograph was published with the caption; 'Hermione Baddeley, just returned to her Piccadilly flat from the remote Isle of Arran, is alarmed by the swirl of traffic and clings to an escort'. The escort is in fact the actress Elizabeth Ashley

At home in California with my beloved cat Lady Winifred who lived to be sixteen

Tennessee Williams, that most brilliant of playwrights, cocktails, and the Maharajah of Cooch Behar were soon joined together in my drawing room. Larry Harvey, who wasn't invited but came in wearing a new and pristine white silk shirt, joined the party that eventually drove off to Hurlingham. I must admit that my thoughts often strayed to that rather tattered script that Tennessee had left on one of my side tables. It was his play, *The Rose Tattoo*, and Little Brit had been kind enough to say that I was the only actress in England who should do it. Tennessee looked at me carefully with his pale blue eyes and said she was right.

Tennessee Williams was one of those rare people who make life seem constantly fresh and interesting. You want to be with them because when they're around life is more exciting, more stimulating. They are different, they enhance life. From the first time I met him, I was completely hooked by this extraordinary character. I felt he opened doors for me, showed me things about life which ordinary people simply missed. We all laughed a lot that afternoon – Tennessee had a fascinating way of throwing his head back when he laughed. But, as I discovered, quite suddenly he could have a change of mood. We were coming back in the Maharajah's car when he and Larry Harvey started to argue about something or other. Tennessee asked the chauffeur to stop the car. He got out and took a taxi home.

I read *The Rose Tattoo* over the weekend and I loved it. I rang Tennessee to say how enthusiastic I was about the play. He was waiting to hear from Binkie Beaumont whether they could put it on or not. Binkie Beaumont got in touch with me before Tennessee did. He agreed that it was a great play and said I would be perfect for it. Then came the bad news: he didn't think he could get it past the authorities. I couldn't understand it, for there was nothing obscene or shocking in the play.

'It's the religious angle,' he explained. 'I daren't do it.'

When I spoke to Tennessee I told him how awful I thought it was that the British censor might not pass *The Rose Tattoo*. It seemed such a waste, and I knew I might never get an opportunity like this again.

But I did. Tennessee Williams wrote a play for me.

When Larry Harvey went off to do his season at Stratford-upon-Avon, it was, I suppose the beginning of the end. He still came back at weekends and stayed at Chester Square and we still gave parties together. I remember at one of them, we arranged, so we thought, a romantic little twosome. There was a film actress, at that time, called Joan Collins who had a 'thing' about Larry. She thought she was in love with him, but he wanted to cool the situation and try and find someone else for Joan. We invited a young actor called Maxwell Reed to our party and he and Joan hit it off splendidly. We congratulated each other that everyone was happy again. Maxwell Reed became Joan Collins' first husband and I don't think the marriage could be rated very highly. But that, of course, was hardly our fault; we had meant it in the kindest possible way.

While Larry was up at Stratford, Angela looked after him. Not only did she look after Larry and her own husband, but she took care of all the members of the Royal Shakespeare Company. When any visiting star actor or actress came to appear in a play, she always arranged the accommodation for them.

As she told me, there were often surprises. A certain well-known theatrical knight arrived with his wife from London. They were renowned for the happiness of their marriage and the brilliance of their children. There was a pretty young man who tagged along with them, helping with the luggage, or so Angela thought. She showed them the luxurious suite she had reserved for them at a local hotel and pointed out the spacious bathroom and the splendid view over the river. 'Is it all right?' she asked.

'Well, darling,' replied the knight. 'It is and it isn't. This suite will be all right for me and Nigel.' he indicated the pretty young man, 'but where is my wife going to sleep?'

Angela could think of nothing to say, but she very soon found quarters for the knight's wife.

I went up to Stratford for the opening night of *As You Like It*. Larry Harvey was to play Orlando and Margaret Leighton was to be Rosalind. I drove up with Barbara Spencer – a great friend of mine with the best sense of humour this side of the Atlantic – and Noel Langley and we stayed at the Black Swan, called The Dirty Duck by the Royal Shakespeare Company.

On that first evening, Larry asked if I would mind if Margaret joined us for dinner. I had met Margaret Leighton before and admired her looks. But at the time I always found her rather too perfectly dressed, rather too coldly beautiful. She was married, so I heard, to a publisher called Max Reinhardt. I must say, we all wondered if perhaps Larry and Margaret were playing Orlando and Rosalind in private life, too, and much later, when it was obvious that they were, Glen complained to me that Margaret Leighton had fallen in love with him.

'But he'll only make her unhappy,' Glen said. 'He's not the kind of man women should marry.'

I could agree with that.

I went over to Ireland with Leslie Henson to do a show and who should turn up in my dressing room in Dublin but Francis de Moleyns. We fell into each others arms. Outside the stage door was an awful old car and Francis promised to drive me round in it. The first ride we took in this old banger was to a village outside Dublin. Whenever he could, Francis used to drive out to this spot just to look at an estate called Lughalore. It was the most perfect place. In the distance you could see the outline of what looked like a large rambling house.

I had to get back to the theatre for the evening show and on the way Francis showed me the broken down boarding house where he had a room. My heart bled for him. There was a telegram waiting for me in my dressing room. It was from a good friend of mine, Lady Oonagh Oranmore and Brown. 'You must come and stay with me while you're appearing in this show in Dublin,' ran the message. The address was Lughalore, the very estate we had visited that afternoon. I rang Oonagh immediately and she invited me to go there that evening. I accepted and said that I would get a friend to drive me out, but we might be a little late as we had a press party to attend. That was no problem, she replied; Michael, their faithful butler would take care of us both.

Francis could hardly get over the shock. He was a man transformed. Francis needed the gracious things of life as a flower needs water. Woolworths for lunch, splendid place as it is, was not for him. Before my eyes I saw the old Francis, the flag bearer at Dunkirk reappear.

At the press party was a dear little lady who came up and spent a lot of time talking to Francis and myself. Her name was Lady Ross, but she begged us to call her Joan. She was very petite and dainty with a sweet face. When I moved off to another group I saw how well Joan and Francis were doing together. Indeed the way she looked up at him made her look like a young girl. Francis soon found out that she was the rich widow of an American armaments manufacturer.

We drove through Oonagh's parkland quite late at night, but the butler showed us to lovely rooms. Next day we relaxed with our hostess, who was always lots of fun. I told her what a hit Francis had made with a certain Lady Ross the previous night.

'She says she can't wait until we meet again,' Francis admitted.

I was very pleased about this budding friendship. The Irish Tie Company was in its death throes and a little new blood might bring new life to the ailing company. Not mine, this time – I was having enough troubles of my own. The last year with Larry Harvey had been quite expensive.

I left with Leslie Henson and the show for our tour of the English mainland, waving Francis goodbye in Dublin and feeling in my bones that he was on the up again. Sure enough, I soon had a letter from him saying that he and Oonagh were now good friends and she had suggested he asked Lady Ross to Lughalore to stay another weekend. He ended the letter like this: 'Joan and I get along very well together. She says that she is madly in love with me and wants us to get married. What do you think?'

I thought it was a splendid idea. I should be delighted to see Francis safe in the arms of a good rich woman. I wrote back immediately advising Francis to make sure that he had got all the facts straight and that Lady Ross was as rich as people said she was. It wasn't that Francis was mercenary, but he was just incapable of making money himself and his next wife had to be able to keep him. He was a sweet man, and if Lady Ross was really so much in love, they'd be doing each other a favour. Francis sent me a wire shortly after saying that they had got married and were going to live at Joan's home, Balnagowan Castle in Scotland. We didn't have much to do with each other after that. We exchanged cards at Christmas and I hoped that Francis had found true love at last.

About three years later, there was a terrible story in the newspapers – Balnagowan Castle had caught fire. Francis had behaved just like a hero and saved all he could, but unfortunately a large part of the castle had been burned down. In time it was rebuilt and I went to stay up there, but that's another part of the story.

About the time that Francis was getting his love life straight again, my first husband was having a lot of trouble with his. The Invisible Lady had fallen in love with the Marquess of Bath, and she divorced David so that she could marry him. To marry Virginia, Henry had to divorce his first wife, Daphne, who was a friend of mine. Daphne and I sometimes exchanged little notes and I found one the other day that read:

Dear Daphne,
I hear that your name for Virginia is Mrs Mole. Very nice, my dear, but these days I find myself likening her to Lady Macbeth, (I hear she has strange nightmares). In future, I fear, we must refer to her as Lady Macbath.

David went off to Spain and started to have a villa built in what was then a primitive little village called Mijas, in the mountains behind Torremolinos. This was in the early fifties, long before the Costa del Sol became a package-tour playground. David begged me to come out to Spain and see it all for myself and I promised that I would.

But just about then, my financial problems became quite severe. One of the biggest problems for an actress is making sure she has enough capital put by to pay her income tax. I'd been working steadily for the past few years, both in the theatre and in films, but I hadn't saved any money. The madcap schemes of Francis had dug deep and then the last year with Laurence Harvey had been quite expensive. We'd had tremendous fun, but I'd signed bills as if there was no tomorrow.

In the theatre, if you're earning a flat salary and perhaps a percentage you can make a lot of money so long as the play is a hit and runs for a long time. But there's a lot of 'if' about the theatre. If the play is a flop you get nothing. A film, however, is usually much more rewarding. You either get a big dollop of cash or you can even be paid by the week. I had been contracted to make two films. The first was called *Pillar Of Ice* and I was naturally quite anxious for it to go into production. While I waited I took the odd cabaret booking. Suddenly, I was told that the financial backing for *Pillar Of Ice* had collapsed. The film would not be made and I would not be paid.

This blow made me realize that I should start getting my financial affairs in order. I had a very nice accountant called Mr Brown to whom I sent all those little buff coloured envelopes from His or Her Majesty's government. I never bothered to open them, for I knew that the clever Mr Brown would take care of them. And then I remembered that I hadn't heard from Mr Brown for a long time. I telephoned his office. A secretary told me that Mr Brown was no longer with the firm. Mr Brown was dead.

I expressed my dismay and offered my condolences and then I asked what about all those little buff coloured envelopes that must be mounting up somewhere. The secretary said she would look into it. The next buff coloured envelope that arrived I thought I had better open. Inside was a demand from the Inland Revenue for £7,000. It was a tremendous shock, for in those days £7,000 would probably be worth about £70,000 today. It must be a terrible mistake, I decided, and I had best get some good advice. I hurried off to see a solicitor who was a friend of mine.

I made the usual polite greetings before starting on my tale of woe, asking how he was and so forth.

'Not very well,' he replied. 'I've had a hunting accident and I fell on my head.'

I felt rather unnerved. 'Does it hurt?'

'Not much,' he answered, 'but it seems to have given me moods. Sometimes I feel extremely happy and sometimes I feel depressed.'

'How are you today?'

'Fairly happy,' he said.

I produced my grave letter from the Inspector of Taxes. He read it carefully. His mood changed instantly. 'My God, this is terrible,' he exclaimed. 'This is awful. They can turn very nasty, you know. You've got to pay up.' I told him I was broke. His face was grim. 'You must declare yourself bankrupt!'

This sounded absolutely horrible. Only people in the newspapers went bankrupt – spendthrift people like actors and actresses. My solicitor told me I would have to pay the Official Receiver back in instalments, there was nothing else for it.

As I found out later, my poor friend was in no condition to give me or anyone else advice. The fall on his head made him behave very oddly for a long time to come. When he did return to his senses, it was too late. I had become a bankrupt. It was a great mistake, perhaps the worst mistake of my life. I should have gone to my friends, gone to my family and borrowed the money to pay off my debts. Instead, I kept completely quiet and told no one. I know that I was ashamed of what I had done and hoped that it could be kept secret. The humiliation that followed was beyond belief. When you are a bankrupt, the authorities treat you as a worthless person. The bankruptcy soured my life and I wanted to run far away.

Two of my friends who lived in Cornwall, Angela Halliday and Gillian Carlyon did realize that something was wrong because I had become strange and depressed. They rushed up to London, scooped me up and took me back to Cornwall for a change of scene in the lovely house that Gillian had on Carlyon Bay. I came home feeling much better, but as I let myself in the front door at Chester Square, the scene that met my eyes was so horrible that I thought I was dreaming. The carpet had been ripped from the hall; all the furniture and pictures had gone; old pieces of newspaper lay crumpled in one corner; a length of curtain hung from a rail: it was the desecration of a home.

I went from room to room. It was as if some hideous, vengeful army had gone through the house ravaging and pillaging. The drawing room was bare, every picture and article of furniture taken, the carpets on the stairs ripped up. In my bedroom the light poured through bare windows and all that was left was my bed, turned upon it's side against a wall, and a cardboard laundry box lying in the middle of the room. It was very old and I'd used it to store little mementoes and keepsakes, theatre programmes and photographs. I knelt beside it. Was this all they'd left me? I had never felt so beaten in my life. I took off the lid and drew out a few photographs. And then the doorbell rang.

I groped my way down the stairs. I felt completely bewildered, unable to cope. Outside the door stood a young man, his hat on the back of his head. Down by the road stood a cluster of other men, some of them carried cameras.

'What do you want?' I muttered.

He slid inside the door and closed it behind him. 'It's all right I'm not press.' He jerked his thumb over his shoulder. 'I'm not one of those. I'm a freelance writer, I'm just one of your fans.' He looked round the desolate hall and told me, as if I needed to be told, that it looked as if the house had been struck by a bomb.

'They've taken everything,' I whispered.
'What's that?' he said, 'what you've got in your hand?'
I looked down. I still clutched the handful of photographs. That was all I had left after years and years of work.

Chapter Fifteen

The newspapers splashed the story all over their front pages next day. Hermione Baddeley was bankrupt. I hated having my personal and I thought shameful tragedy in the public eye like this so that everyone could see what a fool I had been, but at least it was now out in the open. I had been a fool in more ways than one, for what I'd done made no difference at all to my friends and family, and the people who loved me. Warmth and affection flowed in from every side. Christopher Glenconner chided me for not coming to him for help. It was hard to explain to them why I had kept silent. But I did know something: I was a changed person. To me it had been like going through fire. Never again would I take anything for granted. I was wiser.

I needed somewhere to live. Chester Square had been ransacked by the bailiffs and I felt I could never go back there. Lady Phyllis Allen, a good friend, at once asked me to stay with her and eventually she helped me find a very comfortable flat in Sloane Gardens. Invitations to stay with friends were plentiful. Violet and John Drummond sent an immediate invitation to stay with them at Megginch Castle for as long as I liked. Violet wrote: 'There's always a knife and fork for you at our table.' The Drummonds were a lovely family and when John grew older and had no son to hand over his castle to, he decided to leave it to his eldest daughter. Then John and Violet moved to the Isle of Man where they owned some land and a small hotel and pub. The funny thing was that their faithful butler, for whom they had found another position, refused to leave them and followed them to the Isle of Man. He was happily installed as landlord at the pub, where he occasionally bemused the guests by calling them 'M'Lord'. Violet and John's four lovely daughters were always part of my life, and no matter where I go, to any part of the world, one of the Drummond girls pops up.

Of course my troubles were by no means over. The Official Receiver seemed to have sold my cherished belongings completely at random. Maria Britneva came across two of my paintings in an antique shop in Chelsea. One, a portrait of myself by Kanelba, the other a watercolour by John Singer Sargent. She bought both pictures and gave my portrait to my sister Angela because she had always adored it. All the money I earned was now handed over to the Official Receiver. I was determined to pay off my debts as soon as possible and be free of this terrible label, 'Bankrupt'.

People were kind. I was offered some filming immediately and then I was asked to do a revue written by Alan Melville called *At The Lyric*. Working with me were two outstanding young people – Dora Bryan and Ian Carmichael. At that time neither of them had achieved stardom, but it was very obvious to me that they were on their way. The first time I saw this slim blonde girl perform a small part in a revue I went to the director afterwards and asked who she was. He told me that Dora came from Lancashire and had worked for ENSA during the war. Dora has since been very successful, but I don't think she has been looked after as she should have been. I feel about her career much as I do about my own. In England they're inclined – or they were inclined – to take their native-born stars for granted. Unless you go away and they can't find you for a while, they treat you rather like the paintings in the National Gallery. They think you're always hanging around.

I found Ian Carmichael's timing absolutely wonderful. In five minutes everything fell together quite naturally – link by link he had it all under control. In all my years in the theatre and TV there's only one other person I've ever found who can do this, and that's Bea Arthur, the American TV star. Both Dora Bryan and Ian Carmichael are brilliant performers and they were a joy to work with. I'd been away from revue for some time so I'd forgotten just how tough it was, just how much energy it takes to do all the changes. Although we were all completely exhausted by opening night, *At The Lyric* was a great hit. Every day the queue outside the theatre stretched right round the building. We stayed at the Lyric for a year and then transferred to the St Martins Theatre and the show was given a new name, *Going To Town*.

Everyone came to see us – royalty and visiting royalty were often there. At that time I had a dear little girl called Valerie living with me and acting as my secretary. She was a dark-haired, waif-like little creature who loved practical jokes. One of her favourites was to ring up and pretend to be someone very important. One morning I was in bed about ten – I never got up early when I was in revue – when she came in, shook me awake, and announced that Princess Marina Duchess of Kent was on the line. I told her to go away and stop being silly, but she insisted I answer the phone. Eventually, fully expecting one of her pranks, I picked up the telephone and wearily asked who was there. A rather taken-aback male voice identified himself as the Duchess of Kent's secretary. The Duchess had enjoyed my show enormously, he said, and wanted me to accompany her to a party the following week.

The party was given by Chips Channon who lived just round the corner and who was married to one of the Guinness girls. It was a lovely party and the Duchess of Kent was a friendly and delightful person. As happens at parties, people get up when they're asked to and tell a joke or sing a song. When Chips asked me, I said I'd love to but I wanted two props: a man's cloth cap and a pipe. I sang them a song that went: 'I changed my sex a week ago today, I don't know what my dressmaker will say . . .' The subject was extremely topical in the early fifties – sex-change operations were just being publicised. A Scottish peer had just become a lassie and a racing driver wearing a long blond wig was getting ready for the knife. But my son David was horrified when I told him about my song. A friend of his was about to lose his father and gain a second mother, and he would be mortified to know that I was singing ribald songs about this traumatic event.

Another of David's friends from Eton was young Tony Armstrong Jones. David asked if I'd give him a helping hand by going round to have my photograph taken. I was too lazy, but I sent round a girl who had a couple of beautiful children. Afterwards I regretted not being photographed by the future Lord Snowdon as I hear the results are extremely good.

While I was living at Sloane Gardens, I was rung up by the *Evening Standard* and asked if I would do an interview for them. I said that I would, and we arranged a time for a journalist to call. On the appointed day, I left the door open downstairs and waited in the drawing room for my interviewer to arrive. There came a knock at the door, so I went out on to the landing and called down the stairs:

'The door's open, come on up.' I went back in and sat down. He seemed to take an awful long time to climb the four flights of stairs to my flat, so after a while I went out onto the landing to see what had happened. The journalist was just arriving on my floor and he looked very hot and rather sad. Then I noticed that he was quite badly disabled – I later learnt that he had multiple sclerosis and could only walk with difficulty. I thought that gushing sympathy would probably not be welcome, so I simply showed him in and we got on with the interview.

His name was Quentin Crewe, and he turned out to be both charming and refreshingly direct in the way he asked questions. With his sweet smile and great natural curiosity, he soon made me forget completely that he was disabled and we went on chatting long after the interview was over. After that we became firm friends. We would arrange to meet at a restaurant or nightclub and his brother Colin would give him a piggy-back to the rendez-vous and pick him up at the end of the evening. Sometimes we would dance very happily together, and I counted him one of my very best companions for a night out: he was intelligent and amusing and not in the least helpless, despite his disability. Being in America so often, I have unfortunately lost touch with him, but I did learn that when his disability got worse, Lord Snowdon designed an ingenious electric wheelchair for him. Astonishingly, he is an inveterate traveller and has a particular liking for deserts – a remarkable man.

Both my children were now using the flat in Sloane Gardens when they came to town. Poor Valerie was always having to answer the doorbell to someone or other. A very funny, eccentric man whom I had known for years had recently become an admirer. At seven-thirty one morning, he came to call and Valerie, much against her will, answered the door; there stood a very large stout man carrying a huge bouquet of flowers and a massive basket of fruit. She tried to stop him but he brushed past her and made straight for my bedroom. The noise outside woke me up. I watched this very big man thunder into the room, stumble down on one knee at my bedside, and puff out a proposal of marriage. He only lived a minute's walk away and I was sure I detected a pyjama leg emerging from below his trouser cuff; he really should have married Rosa Lewis!

At seven thirty in the morning I would have turned down Crown

Prince Rainier or Prince Ali Khan. 'Campbell,' I murmured. 'Can I ring you later?'

Sir Campbell Mitchell Cotts heaved himself to his feet and huffed and puffed out of the flat.

Valerie, who had been lurking outside, came in. She went over to the basket of fruit and selected a peach. She remarked thoughtfully what a darling old thing he was. It was true, but not first thing in the morning, not forever. Sir Campbell Mitchell Cotts later had a beautiful house in Onslow Square where he gave enormous parties. He mixed everyone up together, all the personalities in London at the time, and he made it work. It was quite expensive, of course, and he went through a fortune every year.

During the war he went into the Scots Guards. For some reason he was very nervous about going on parade for the first time. So he used to practise in the back yard of his house. Passers-by would stop in amazement and watch him stomping up and down doing sword drill, practising drawing his sword then shoving it back in its scabbard without looking, his large stomach always getting in the way. He was very lovable, but I couldn't take his proposal seriously. The trouble was that I'd fallen for a younger friend of his – and Campbell had introduced me to him. He had invited me one weekend to stay at Barmore Castle in Northumberland with a friend of his called Bill Sitwell. He was rather like a Father Confessor to Bill and there were no secrets between them.

Barmore Castle was quite beautiful and very lonely, surrounded as it was by wild uninhabited Northumberland moorland. Bill Sitwell was very charming. He had been a naval captain during the war and I think he had been the youngest captain in the navy. He was one of those men who fall in love with their ship and are never completely happy ashore; perhaps he should have stayed at sea and become an admiral. Bill had a rather extraordinary marriage. He had a little Scandinavian wife, but they seemed to live most of the time apart, the Scandinavian wife staying down in Brighton with her young son. Campbell, in his role as Father Confessor, told me that they weren't getting on very well. As time went by Bill and I grew fond of each other and Bill went to Campbell, as he always did, to tell him how devoted he was to me. Campbell was furious.

When the period of coolness between us all had passed, Campbell came to me and said that he had been having nervous spells. His doctor had told him that he was a frustrated actor and that a spell on the stage would work wonders. It sounded a most unlikely cure for nervousness, but I asked Leslie Henson what he thought. I did want Campbell to be happy and he could be very funny. A music hall comic was leaving Leslie's show and Campbell might be able to fill in. We all went on tour together. We had a grapefruit sketch involving two north-country couples on an outing; the women want to try a fruit they've never tasted before. The comedy started with the way grapefruit was pronounced in a Lancashire accent. Campbell turned out to be a natural comic. He had no stage nerves at all and in costume this big fat man was a riot. I had to keep turning round because I couldn't keep a straight face. When we came back from tour and opened in London, Binkie Beaumont came to see the show and offered Campbell a part in *The Heiress* with Katharine Hepburn. Immediately he turned from comic to character actor and did several more shows before he decided to retire. He never had another nervous spell, which just goes to show – doctor knows best!

I don't think he ever quite forgave me for turning down his proposal and forming this very happy relationship with Bill Sitwell. It was very good to have the support of a kind lover again. My former lovers weren't doing so well with their own love lives. Margaret Leighton had obtained a divorce and she and Laurence Harvey had married. Just as everyone had predicted, it was a disaster. Larry, not very gallantly, said he'd married Margaret because she'd left her husband for him, which wasn't a good start. The marriage went downhill all the way. Poor Margaret used to spend a lot of her time going round in a taxi poking her head out and calling to the doormen of restaurants and nightclubs: 'Is he there?' Their marriage didn't last long and after they were divorced I became very fond of Margaret. As she grew older she became a much warmer, sweeter person. Her next marriage to Michael Wilding was a good one. I'd known Michael from the old days. He was a man who should never have become an actor because his nerves were so terrible that every appearance was an ordeal. He spent his life battling with those nerves, but he did put in some classically good performances, particularly in partnership with Anna Neagle. Later in life, when he and Margaret lived in Hollywood, he worked with an artiste's agency and he asked me to join them. He did find me a job or two. Poor Margaret and Michael – the dice were always loaded against them. Margaret died much too soon of a dreadful nervous disease and Michael died soon after.

Francis de Molyns had a tragedy in his life. He went with his wife Joan to America and while she was over there she caught some illness or other and died. Francis inherited Balnagowan Castle, but not a lot of money to run it with. But it had been rebuilt following the fire and was an interesting castle – just the right place for Francis to live.

Ever since I was made bankrupt, I had never stopped working in an effort to get my debts paid off as soon as possible. I remember that one of the plays I did was directed by Terence Rattigan and called *The Pink Room*. It didn't run long because the critics did a hatchet job on it, saying that the theme was too realistic and the language obscene. This was predictable: when I first read the script, I told Terence that I was sure it would flop because it sent up a famous critic something rotten and the language did go much too far. I agreed to do the try-out because it was written by a friend of his, but I refused to do the London opening. Years later, I sat through another play and thought how very much like *The Pink Room* it was. It had the same bad language and the same kind of powerful drama, but this play was called *Who's Afraid Of Virginia Woolf* and it was a smash hit.

Terence Rattigan always promised that one day he'd write a play for me. We often talked about this elusive play. He kept saying how versatile I was, how difficult it was to decide what part would suit me best. Eventually I suggested that he write a play where I could play two parts, or better still turn the play into two separate pieces. And that's exactly what he did. He called it *Separate Tables* and the lead part was given to Margaret Leighton. But that's life!

One day, one of Angela's friends rang me up and said she had just returned from India, where she'd done a huge circuit of the continent, had a marvellous time and been very well paid. She was sure they would love to have me and suggested I do a tour. So I went, and stayed there for about three months, earning enough money to discharge myself from bankruptcy once and for all. Apart from the money, it was wonderful working in India. I worked in big hotels under huge whirling fans that kept everything cool without freezing the guests. My cabaret act was a hit and in the daytime I took in the sights and enjoyed myself. There was a big race-course in the Maidan in Calcutta, where I met many old friends from England and Ireland: owners, trainers and jockeys.

I could have stayed longer but I missed Bill Sitwell. When I came home he persuaded me to go up and stay at Barmore Castle. I loved my time up there. I have always had the good sense to cut my private life off from my public life when I think I need a change. My debts were paid, my career could wait and I spent months up in Northumberland. I had time to do all the things I revelled in – walking the dogs, calling in at little country pubs, living the life of a country-woman.

When I eventually got back to London, television was taking over. I accepted an offer to do a television series and I found it opened up a whole new way of life. No longer was it imperative to live near the theatre, no longer did you have to get up at crack of dawn to get to the film studios and spend hours on take after take. Television was quick, there was no time to waste, and it was almost like working office hours. A week's rehearsal, then wham – the big day when it went out live. Then a rest before another week's rehearsal. It was even easier when everything was recorded on tape.

I'd given up the flat in Sloane Gardens so I had to find somewhere new to live and it occurred to me that I need not stay in London, but could find some fresh air. I chose Brighton and found a flat in Arundel Terrace. Laurence Olivier heard me talking about my new way of life and became interested in Brighton himself. A house was up for sale in Royal Crescent and Olivier, who had by now married Joan Plowright and become the father of two small children, moved to Brighton. Larry had always been a great friend, although we tended to move in different circles, but I had always been closer to his second wife, Vivien Leigh.

Vivien was the most fascinating creature. She never took any notice of fashion, but knew exactly what suited her. She never bothered whether skirts went up or down, whether hats were fashionable or not. She always wore a turban that suited her classical features. Poor Viv, she had the most extraordinary nerves and was always terribly unsure of herself. When she first went to Hollywood to make *Gone With The Wind,* she thought that the other members of the cast didn't want her, resented the fact that she'd won the role. When she came back to England she told me of her unhappiness with tears in her lovely grey eyes. But Clark Gable had stood by her and insisted that she play Scarlett O'Hara.

Olivier gave her the most gorgeous parts to play, but his attitude never helped those soul-destroying nerves. He is a stern man, and occasionally behaved like some terrible bank manager. But there are always two sides to a broken marriage: Olivier went through hell and he had every reason to want a quiet, peaceful life. Vivien loved the social whirl and he didn't. In spite of all her wild infidelities, Vivien loved Larry dearly and was filled with misery when their marriage broke up. She wrote to me in despair: 'I have been made unhappy for so long but once Puss [Olivier] makes up his mind there seems to be nothing to do but let him have his way. God knows I have been fiercely reluctant, but now it seems inevitable . . .'

David was now living in Spain and asking me to come over and see him. Anyone who visits Spain today for the first time cannot realize how different it all was thirty years ago. Fuengirola, in those days, was an odorous little fishing village while Mijas, up in the mountains behind where David lived, was positively primitive.

David's villa was beautiful; it had verandahs and balconies with overhanging red geraniums and long views that looked over the Mediterranean. He seemed much happier living there, in fact we got on splendidly and he kept suggesting that we marry again. But I was much too fond of Bill Sitwell to think of leaving him, and I wasn't the kind of person to give everything up and live in Spain.

Pauline once warned me, quite sensibly, not to marry David again, saying he was much too selfish. Sometimes I worried about him over in Spain, worried about the strange stories of remittance men and women in search of a meal ticket. There was too much alcohol around, too much cheap Spanish wine and brandy, and David was surrounded by people he would not have given the time of day to in England. There was something in the air down there – a touch of amateur evil. David rang me up in Brighton one day and in an abrupt way he asked me to come to Spain and throw some girl out of his villa. It seemed an odd request. The girl's name, apparently, was Jilly, and David had already had to get rid of her mother who had moved in first. He wheedled and cajoled me into flying to Spain and dealing with Jilly.

I got off the plane at Malaga. There was no one to meet me but I didn't bother too much, I knew the ropes. The taxi drove me out to Mijas, but I found the villa in darkness. Typical, I thought to myself. David drags me out here to do him a good turn and what do I get? The villa was, of course, wide open. In those days, before the hordes of tourists arrived, complete and perfect honesty prevailed; no good Spanish peasant would have stolen as much as an orange from a tree.

As I mounted the stairs, I saw a glimmer of light and then I heard the sound of music. Someone was playing one of my favourite Paul Anka songs. I pushed the door wide open and fug of proportions that would not have disgraced Los Angeles enveloped me. The room was thick with the mingled smoke of tobacco and marijuana. I could just make out a girl lying on a bed of cushions in the middle of the room. She put out a languid hand, reached for a bottle of wine and re-filled her glass, then asked me if I had come to throw her out. I sat down on the floor – there didn't seem anywhere else to sit – and asked her for a glass of wine.

She sighed and got to her feet. She was a very frail-looking girl wearing what was to become the uniform of the western world, blue jeans and a tee-shirt. She had untidy fair hair that fell in little scrappy pieces round her neck and large eyes smudged with mascara. She looked pretty ordinary; an ordinary, unhappy girl. I smiled at her when I took the glass and said I liked her taste in music.

She wanted to know how long I was staying and told me in a melancholy voice not to try and throw her out – she wasn't going to leave. I thought we had better have it out. Didn't she want to go? Wasn't it rather pointless hanging around when she knew that David didn't want her? She refused to accept this and seemed to think that in time David would fall in love with her. We weren't getting anywhere. A good friend of David's and mine, called Tim Willoughby, had a villa only just down the road, and on the way up in the taxi I had heard the sounds of revelry from within. I thought that perhaps David was there and suggested to Jilly that we go down and have a look. So I took the girl I was supposed to be throwing out to a party at Tim Willoughby's! Not a very good start.

Next morning, David was furious. According to him, Jilly was a fiend who was trying to get me on her side. All in all, there was an uneasy feeling in the villa. I noticed things I hadn't seen before. David had changed: he had always loved good wine and interesting company, but now he couldn't carry his drink and his temper was erratic. I noticed something else, hard to define at first. I wondered if David was on drugs.

On my last night in Mijas, Jilly went out on her own. She came back in the middle of the night, when David had deliberately locked every door, and climbed in through my bedroom window giving me a terrific fright. I awoke to find her standing at the side of my bed, looking down at me. She looked a mess, her eyes, as ever, smudged with mascara. 'I wish you'd stay,' she said. 'It's better when you're here.'

'I've got a job waiting for me at home.' I didn't add that I wanted to get away from the heavy atmosphere. I tried to persuade her one last time that she would be much happier away from David. Unexpectedly she began to weep. Something about this strange girl always worried me. I left Mijas in an anxious mood and on my return I begged the children to go out to Spain and watch over their father.

Later, many strange stories came to me about Jilly. Whether they were true or not I never found out. Later I heard that she had left David, left Spain and gone to live on the other side of the world.

There was another sad postscript. Our friend Tim Willoughby was drowned. He went out in a small boat with a friend, and although he knew all about the sea and the tides, they disappeared. We hated being without Tim, and I worried even more about David now that this good friend was no longer living near to him.

For years I'd been tantalized by offers to star in a show in New York. It had nearly happened in 1939, with *Nine Sharp*, and then the war intervened. It happened many times afterwards. I would be all ready to go and then something would happen to spoil things. To get permission to appear in New York, I would have to go over as principal in a play, doing a role that could not be played by an American. There had always been something inside me that wanted to prove that I could reign on Broadway, just as I had queened it in London. I had suffered when I was made bankrupt and in some subconscious way I had to put the blame on someone or something; so I chose to think to myself that I hadn't been fairly treated and that I would do much better in another country where they would appreciate me more. That, I know, was one of the reasons I wanted to get to America.

Still, the next offer I got was to do a film with Laurence Harvey called *Room At The Top*. I was in Brighton when the phone rang one afternoon – I'd moved to a lovely little cottage in Black Lion Lane. It was my agent. He wasn't at all sure about the showy little part I had been offered – the money wasn't even very good and it certainly wasn't the break I had been looking for. But then it occurred to me that Larry had probably suggested me for the part and I thought how stupid I would be to let an agent interfere. It would be great fun working with Larry again. Life was too short to pass up a chance like this. When I spoke to Larry about it over the telephone, he told me that there was a lovely scene we would be doing together, very tender and romantic. I laughed and then he laughed. I know we both remembered those mad, rumbustious days back at Chester Square.

I did two days work. My friend Joan Assheton-Smith came to the studios with me. Joan, who is a tender soul and had always been very fond of Larry, worried about Simone Signoret, one of the female leads. Simone, even in those days was putting on weight, and in the script Larry had to carry Simone around. Joan thought she would do him an injury. But Larry survived and *Room At The Top* turned out to be a great success. It was the story of a man who claws his way to the top, and much as I loved Larry I have always thought that he was very like the character he played in the film – tough, but with a side to his character that is irresistible to women.

For my part in *Room At The Top* I was nominated for two awards: one in London, and the other in Hollywood where I was nominated as a featured player for the Academy Award. Naturally I was very glad that I had done it against my agent's advice. I was also glad to have worked with Larry again. I had been hurt when our love affair ended and I had missed having his support when I needed someone in my times of trouble. We always remained friends, but this little episode rounded off what had been, I must say, a very happy time in my life.

Chapter Sixteen

When Francis de Moleyns returned from America, where his wife Joan had so sadly died, he was anxious to look me up. But he had not seen me since my bankruptcy and despite lengthy enquiries he was quite unable to find my address for some time. He finally caught up with me in Sloane Gardens and was like a delighted puppy at seeing me again. It was lovely to see him and we got on just as well as we had always done. He immediately invited Ciggie and me to stay in his castle in Scotland. He hadn't very much money to run it with, but what he had he used very well. There were some other people there and we were all having a lovely time when my agent rang up. Laurence Olivier wanted me to go and do a play with him in America.

In the sweetest way, Larry Olivier often disrupts my life, so I was on my guard when he did ring me. The play he was proposing was by Benn Levy and had only four parts. Trevor Howard was to be one, but I was concerned to hear that Larry was not. He was going to direct. When I put the phone down and told everyone, there were one or two uncertain looks. Larry is the most wonderful actor in the world, but his qualities as a director were not recognized to the same extent and I knew that he would be a stern taskmaster. Lord Ancaster, a great friend of Joan Assheton Smith's said that Olivier should be in the play, not directing it, and everyone agreed.

The script came – just a bit pretentious, I decided. Then a wire came to say that Trevor Howard was otherwise engaged, but Charlton Heston was going to take his part. Here I was, having a perfectly lovely time in a beautiful castle, yet planning to go over to America and act in a heavy play with Charlton Heston, who is a great movie actor but not in the same league as a stage performer. I rang up Larry Olivier and told him I wasn't too crazy about the play and had a lovely revue being written for me and so . . .

But Larry had a very persuasive way. I should have stayed in Scotland because the play turned out to be a disaster. I could soon see that *The Tumbler* was going down the drain and nothing anyone did could put it right. My agents over there, MCA, were of the same opinion. If I could get out of it, they had some television for me in New York with Rex Harrison. It would pay much more than if *The Tumbler* ran for three months – and I was sure it would not so I left by mutual consent during the final week in Boston and a very fine actress called Martha Scott took my place. Rosemary Harris was the lead and she was wonderful, but I told her, as I've told many actresses, not to give it all out before opening night. Rosemary was giving too much emotionally in Boston and later at the dress rehearsal in New York. I think that sometimes you give that little extra of yourself too soon, and it isn't there when you need it on opening night. Instead, there's a deadness in the play because the actors are drained and weary.

The play lasted two nights on Broadway. Afterwards, Larry was sweet enough to invite me to a little farewell party. Charlton Heston arrived and he'd lost so much weight that his suit looked about two sizes too large for him. Larry stood in front of us all and apologized in a doleful voice. It was a sad, but sweet failure. I didn't get to New York in Larry Olivier's play but my trip to America did turn out to be well worthwhile for me. I had laid the foundations for the next time – the television I did in New York proved to be very important for my future. When I'd been in *Fallen Angels* in London, a gentleman called Arnold Weissberger brought his mother to see me. They came over every year to see the plays and they were great fans of mine. Weissberger and Harris were big lawyers in New York, and they told me about the need to apply for a Green Card. This permit to work in America and pay your social security is vitally important. I did go to New York later as a principal in a play, but when the play closed I knew that I would not be allowed to work unless I had a Green Card. I applied at once and the television people in New York were very helpful. I was lucky my Green Card came through comparatively quickly – I have friends out there who have waited for ten years or more.

The play that took me back to America was called *A Taste Of Honey*. It had first been put on in London by Joan Littlewood in her East End Stratford theatre and it was a big hit. I went to see it with

Vivien Leigh and every time the mother came on, Viv would nudge me and tell me that was the part for me. Although lots of other people told me the same thing, I knew that Joan Littlewood liked to give unknowns a chance. It was an unusual play in that it touched on two sensitive subjects: homosexuality and inter-racial love, but the character of the mother, flighty and funny, torn between her lover and her daughter, was right up my street. *A Taste Of Honey* moved from Stratford East to the West End and later it went over to New York with the mother played by Angela Lansbury and the daughter by Joan Plowright. One day David Merrick, the producer of the New York show, rang up my agent and asked if I would replace Angela Lansbury who was leaving the cast to go back to her children in California.

My agent didn't like the idea of me 'replacing' anyone and said I should go to New York as a star. Besides, the play wasn't doing very good business. Maybe I was what they needed, I thought to myself. I wanted to go to New York and I wanted to play in *A Taste Of Honey*, but when I got there and saw how it all was, I felt like getting on the next flight back to London. However, I did arrive in some style. Larry Olivier had arranged very good rates for me at the Algonquin Hotel. He had, I knew, a special interest in *A Taste Of Honey*, for he was very close to Joan Plowright at the time and later married her. In those days he used to wear two watches, one with London time and the other with New York time. I was told that this wasn't because his heart lay in old New York, but because that was the type of man he was.

I went round to the Booth Theatre, slipped into my seat and prepared to enjoy *A Taste Of Honey*, New York style. I remembered Noël Coward when he watched what we had done to *Fallen Angels* and had to get up and pace back and forth at the back of the stalls. It wasn't quite as bad as that for me, but I kept saying to myself that they were doing it all wrong, I couldn't possibly act the part like that, I must get on a plane back to London the very next day. I watched Angela Lansbury playing the part of the mother with growing concern. She was good all right, but it was all so different to the London production. Angela kept addressing the audience, which I found very odd. As I walked round to her dressing room afterwards, I couldn't think what I would say.

Angela smiled at me. 'How did you like it?' Angela is a lovely person; she'd asked me a straight question and I decided to give her a straight answer. I told her exactly what I thought of it. To my delight, she laughed and said she didn't like it all that much either. Angela told me to play it just the way I wanted to.

Next day I found that there had been quite a bit of backstage manoeuvring. Tony Richardson, the director, was leaving and George Devine was taking over. At least the stage manager was a very nice American called Ben Strobach, who ran through my lines with me. We started to rehearse and I blurted out that I couldn't do it the way Angela had. That was fine by him. What I liked, he liked, and we got on perfectly.

On the last day of rehearsal, Joan Plowright came down to go through it with us. She stopped after a few lines. Wasn't I going to do it the way Angela had? I tried to explain to her that I'd watched the play several times since I'd arrived, and I thought that my way was right. But I could see that she wasn't convinced. It wasn't the best of beginnings; our two parts, the young pregnant daughter deserted by her black sailor lover and the flighty working class mother, had to go well together otherwise the play would fall apart.

The afternoon try-out performance made me very happy because an ecstatic note came from David Merrick saying he was delighted. That relaxed me considerably and gave me the confidence to put in a good performance when my opening night arrived.

On the third night Ruth Gordon was in the audience and came backstage afterwards. In she walked to my dressing room talking at the top of her voice – and Ruth's voice had plenty of carrying power. 'I saw the play on the first night, but I prefer the way it is now. You and Plowright are so unbelievably real together,' she bellowed. I knew that Joan in the next dressing room couldn't have helped overhearing. But she must have agreed with Ruth, because from then on Joan and I worked happily together and I began to enjoy acting with her.

Looking back, I can see that I probably arrived in New York nervous and over-excited about appearing on Broadway for the first time. I turned mole-hills into mountains, but in Angela Lansbury and Joan Plowright I was fortunate enough to have two very nice people to help me through. Everything went perfectly that first time in New York. I met Herbert Machiz, the theatre director, who was just off on tour and he agreed to rent his garden apartment to me. It was in the East seventies, next door to Dag Hammarskjold, the United Nations Secretary General, so we were well guarded! When it looked as if we were in for a good long run, I asked my friend, Joan Assheton-Smith, to come on over and bring Lottie, my French bulldog.

It was marvellous to have Lottie with me. I have always been a great dog-lover, even as a child. I was once caught climbing upstairs with a huge leg of lamb stuffed down my bloomers for my first dog – a whippet. Soon after Lottie arrived, the Chase Manhattan Bank gave a competition for their clients who owned dogs. A little silver bowl would be awarded to the dog which behaved best in public. Madam Lottie trotted round, wobbling her backside like Marilyn Monroe. This must have caught the judge's eye, for the silver bowl was hers. I kept Lottie with me during the year the play ran in New York, and afterwards took her on tour. But when *A Taste of Honey* finally came off, I realized we had a problem on our hands in the shape of this lovable little dog. If you want to bring an animal into England, you have to put it into quarantine, and I just couldn't bear the thought of Lottie stuck for months and months in some miserable kennels. Where could I leave her?

An old friend, Madame Mireille, who had a yacht moored in the north of France had an idea. She wrote to me saying that if I could get Lottie to France she would look after her. Another friend who shall be nameless took charge of arrangements. I was delayed in America so she flew to France with Lottie. Without telling me her plans she persuaded Madame to take a trip to England and slipped on board Madame's yacht with Lottie tucked out of sight. Feeling very much like smugglers they set off for England. Upon arriving in Poole harbour they were boarded by a stern customs official. Did they have any animals on board? Madame who was not a great actress blushed scarlet. My other friend had a sudden attack of remorse and sanity. She knew they couldn't possibly go through with the crazy plot they had concocted. 'I've got a French bulldog aboard,' she blurted out, 'but we're taking her straight back to France'. Lottie, the prospective illegal immigrant sailed back to France where she lived happily with Madame until I eventually took her to Italy and then back to the States. It was a crazy escapade and I was shocked when I found out. But Lottie didn't turn a hair. France after all was her ancestral home.

Lottie had originally been named Salote, after Queen Salote Tupou of Tonga, who had visited England about the time I acquired this enchanting animal. Queen Salote was the inspiration for one of Noël Cowards better-known witticisms. On her royal tour, she was always accompanied by a tiny little dignitary of some kind. She was a large and stately woman and they made an amusing spectacle together. Anyway, Noël and his companion were watching Queen Salote arrive at an official function. 'Who is that man standing next to Salote?' asked Noël's companion. 'That is her lunch,' replied Noël. We had to stop calling my dog Salote after a while. I was up in Edinburgh doing a play at the festival and naturally I had my dog with me. She was not very obedient and was constantly running off on some business of her own, so no doubt I could be heard calling 'Salote! Salote, come here!' all over the hotel. One day the chambermaid came into my room and asked me if I was acquainted with the Queen of Tonga. I assured her that I was not. Then why did I keep calling her name? It was then that I learnt that Queen Salote was staying at the same hotel as us and must have heard me yelling her name a dozen times a day! I thought how awful it would have been if the real Queen Salote had answered one of my frantic calls. From that moment on, my dog became just plain Lottie.

Another visitor from England while I was in New York was Bill Sitwell, and when he went back, we wrote each other long, affectionate letters; but long distance did weaken the bonds between us. It's hard to carry on a love affair for a long time when you have the Atlantic ocean between you.

New York was filled with amusing and interesting people. An acquaintance of mine called Irving Strauss once gave a farewell party – he was about to marry a wealthy lady from Texas and was going to give up his theatrical agency. He took me on one side and pointed out the young man who had sat next to me at dinner – he had seen how well we got on together. Irving said he had charm, good looks and was a great actor who was going to be a big success. But he had the wrong name – Carol Keeling! 'It's all wrong,' said Irving. 'What do you think of Johny Keeling?'

Johny was better than Carol, but still not a name with obvious star quality. Then Irving asked me whether I liked this young man. He was tall and good-looking in a dark, thin way, and in fact I did rather like him. What all this was leading up to was that Irving wanted me to help him make his way in the theatre. I was rather mystified – I couldn't make out what it was I was supposed to do.

'The boy's straight,' said Irving. 'The unfortunate thing is that young actors don't always get on in the theatre if they're straight.' In the end I agreed to take him round with me and teach him what I could about the theatre. It all sounded very strange, but in its own strange way, it worked. Johnny knew all about the New York scene and could give me advice. We English think we can walk into America and it's exactly like home, but it isn't, of course. This young man became my guide. I used to ask him what to do and he always gave me the right answer. I found I liked having a man around again. Getting an escort to take you to parties and things like that is easy – they seem to come out of the ceiling – but having someone with your interests at heart is different.

As time went by Joan, who had also become very friendly with Johnny Keeling, had to go back to England for a visit and somehow, almost without knowing, Johnny and I slid into an affair. It was the last thing I wanted, but it wasn't at all serious and eventually what started out as a love affair turned into a good, enduring relationship. When Joan came back from England, Johnny had joined our household. He'd also found a new name for himself – Johnny Rebel. I think that some Americans are rather like cats: if they find somewhere they like, then they stay. Johnny was a bit like that. He wasn't around all the time, but he'd always come back when you needed him.

When we went on tour after the Broadway run of *A Taste Of Honey* was over, Johnny came with us. We started off in places like Washington, Philadelphia and Kansas City. For some of the audiences, the sight of a black boy kissing a white girl was anathema and in some of the towns the black boy who was playing the sailor was given a hard time. If he was eating with the rest of the cast and the restaurant owner gave us trouble, we, the cast, would get up and leave. This was way back in 1960, and I'm sure that things have changed by now.

When we returned to New York I found an invitation to go out to Hollywood waiting for me. I had been nominated for an Academy Award as best supporting actress in the film *Room At The Top*. I asked Johnny Rebel what to do, and he told me that it was unlikely I would get the award. They invariably give the Oscar to someone they think should have won it the year before. So I wrote and told them I couldn't come. I wasn't going all the way from New York to Los Angeles for nothing. The people in Hollywood telephoned to say how disappointed they were over my decision not to come. It doesn't look good if the nominees don't turn up to Academy Award ceremonies and they wanted as many people as possible to come so they asked me whether I would come if they found me a small part in a film. That would at least make the trip to Los Angeles worthwhile, so I agreed. The film was a Universal Studios production starring Doris Day, and my part would only take an afternoon to film. I could hardly believe my ears when they told me I would be paid $6,000 for that few hours' work. It was my introduction to the high prices that Hollywood pay.

I didn't get the Academy Award – I didn't expect to. But I did this part in *Midnight Lace* with Doris Day and I saw how it was in the big studios in Hollywood. Very different to England: in Hollywood the big star is protected by a solid front of advisers, helpers and, of course, hangers-on.

Our tour with *A Taste Of Honey* was over, Hollywood was over and it was time to go back to England. The new theatre at Chichester was about to open and Laurence Olivier had asked me to appear with him in a Restoration play. Herbert Machiz had his lovely garden flat back, so I was packing in a little hotel when two exciting things happened. The first was that I was offered an apartment on the East Side. It had everything, it was rent-controlled at the unbelievably low rent of $250 a month and, as an added bonus, it was almost next door to where Greta Garbo lived.

'But I have to go home,' I told the two kind people from the cast of *A Taste Of Honey* who had found it for me. 'Isn't it a shame.' As soon as I put the phone down I had another call from Herbert Machiz. Tennessee Williams had just given Herbert his latest play and he wanted me to come over and read it for him. This time I didn't say I had to go home. I went round to see Herbert Machiz. The play was called *The Milk Train Doesn't Stop Here Any More*, and Herbert told me that Tennessee had written it with me in mind.

Into the life of a lucky actress one day comes a play that she knows is her own, that she must cover with her own signature. As I read the play, the fascination of this strange character I was to play, Flora Goforth, gripped me. I felt the tremendous force of the play which was a combination of bitter sadness and high comedy. It was the story of a rich widow who has got through many husbands and is now writing her autobiography. She is a woman with hardly a bit of nobility and filled with absurd pretensions, but who is fiercely resistant to her next awful adventure – that of dying. The story of Mrs Flora Goforth, said Tennessee Williams, is the story of the death of a female clown.

Tennessee came over to Herbert's apartment and I read the play for him. I expected to be terribly nervous reading this great play out loud for the first time, with Tennessee listening and comparing his idea of the character with mine, but I felt quite at home with the part of Flora Goforth from the very first line. Tennessee told me that it was when he came backstage at the Booth Theatre where I was playing *A Taste Of Honey* that he had decided to write *The Milk Train Doesn't Stop Here Any More* for me. All I knew was that this play was like an earthquake smashing into my life. And then I remembered Laurence Olivier and my promise to do the Restoration play. I telephoned him and told him what had happened. I left it up to him – professionally, I couldn't do anything else. He understood completely and let me go without a grumble. Someone else wanted to play Flora Goforth very badly – Tallulah Bankhead! She had played Blanche in *A Streetcar Named Desire* and Tennessee was getting a barrage of telephone calls from her. She never let him alone.

Tennessee wanted the initial performance of *The Milk Train . . .* to take place under circumstances that would allow him tranquillity. At first there was talk of us going to Australia, but there were plenty of difficulties. Then Gian Carlo Menotti telephoned to say that the town of Spoleto in Italy would be honoured to present the first performance at its festival. The offer was accepted. Mildred Dunnock, Paul Roebling, Herbert Machiz, Tennessee Williams and myself flew to Rome. Mildred and Paul were in the cast, Herbert was the director and Tennessee was to attend rehearsals. Spoleto was about sixty miles north-east of Rome. As our cars wound up the mountainside, we glimpsed the high walls of a medieval town dominated by a vast castle.

197

The charming Italian who had met us at the airport told us we would be staying at the castle. Home from home!

Rehearsals began in a wonderful atmosphere. The town seemed to breathe culture and be filled with writers and painters. Tennessee was there all the time: we all had lunch together, dinner together, and saw the sights together. Whatever Tennessee did was fun – he made us laugh with happiness. But at rehearsals, Tennessee stayed completely in the background; he offered no advice, he asked no questions. He was simply there, and that was splendid.

Joan arrived from New York and moved into the castle too – she was to act as my dresser. With her she brought four suitcases and in each one she had thoughtfully packed a bottle of champagne, just in case one suitcase got lost, she told me. She also sent off a telegram to Robin Maugham, who was staying in his villa in Ischia and signed it Lottie, which had Robin flummoxed for a long time. When he caught on, he sent a telegram back to Spoleto to say he was on his way. Robin Maugham was one of my great friends from Brighton, so he had to remember Lottie. She had walked in and out of his home often enough. I admired Robin tremendously, he was one of the best people I had ever known. He had been badly wounded during the war and had a heart condition, but he rarely complained.

Robin arrived an hour or two before the opening. We walked down the street from the castle. It is always a very nervous time for any actress walking into an empty theatre that will soon be the scene of her triumph – or her despair. By the time I was dressed, the auditorium was full. I could feel the tense atmosphere of expectancy. The curtain rose on the villa of the rich, ageing American, Flora, in the hills above Amalfi. To achieve Tennessee's intentions, I had to encourage the audience to laugh at this unwitting female clown, but also pity and understand this flamboyant, vain woman. I did my best to achieve that and I think I succeeded.

I can't tell it myself because I was on the stage, but Robin who was in the audience wrote a dramatic notice of the play. It read:

Hermione made Flora Goforth both exciting and compelling. Her performance was a triumph of virtuosity. She portrayed greed and lust and bitterness. Yet underlying it all was pathos and tenderness.

When the curtain fell on the last Act there was complete silence. Then when Hermione appeared for her first curtain-call as if impelled by some invisible power the whole audience rose and shouted for her. I have never seen or heard such an ovation.

Later I was told that Tennessee Williams now considered her one of the four greatest stage actresses he had ever seen: Laurette Taylor, Geraldine Page, Anna Magnani and now Hermione Baddeley.

The Milk Train Doesn't Stop Here Anymore was at Spoleto for three weeks; amongst those who came to see the play were Elizabeth Taylor and Richard Burton and we had a party for them after the show. We never dreamed that they would try and do a film of the play. They were completely wrong: she was too young to play Flora and he was too old to play the young man. This is a situation that often crops up when one actress sees another in a part that she covets. She watches the other actress play a highly dramatic role and says to herself: 'I must do it.' If she has the financial means, she can do it, but what suits one actress can be a calamity for another. In the hands of the film people *The Milk Train* . . . was the most colossal flop. It was called *Boom* and became totally incomprehensible. Noël Coward hopped in and out of the film with them, but he was no help. I am only sorry that such a beautiful play met such an unkind fate, and that Tennessee's film script didn't have a chance.

But that was all much later. After our performances of *The Milk Train* . . . in Spoleto, we left the festival with high hopes and great happiness. When we got back to New York, the play would open on Broadway. If all went well and it had a long run like *A Streetcar Named Desire,* my dream would be fulfilled and I would make my name on Broadway.

Before Joan and I went back to the new apartment waiting for us on the East Side of New York we were invited to go and stay with Robin Maugham in Ischia. For the first few days, Joan and I lay in the sun wearing our bikinis. Then, suntanned and rested, we sat up and took notice. Robin Maugham was a wonderful host. Like Tennessee Williams, he found laughter in everything and his dry sense of humour made everything we did more interesting and lively.

199

Sir William Walton and his South American wife were Robin's neighbours. They came over to see us and Sir William was telling us about a remarkable artist who lived in the village. He was a local man and quite brilliant, William told us. Then he decided that I simply must be painted by him. Robin and Joan were all for it and arrangements were made for me to sit for my portrait. Joan dressed me up in a frilled costume bikini she had with a little jacket to cover the bare parts. Then I stuck a little straw hat banded with bright ribbons on the back of my head. 'Just like a Matisse,' declared Robin.

In the studio, I was a little taken aback to discover that the artist didn't speak a word of English. As my Italian consisted of about three words – 'ecco, bene and ciao – we communicated in gestures and nods. I sat on the artist's throne and found my silent thoughts going back to Spoleto and Flora Goforth in The Milk Train . . . When the portrait was finished, Robin and Joan came round to have a look. I could see by their odd expressions that something was wrong. I went round to have a look for myself at the portrait, still on the artist's easel. I had kept away because I think it is unfair to look at an artist's work before it is finished.

The woman in the portrait was not me. A stern face with hard eyes and pursed lips stared back at me. Even the little straw hat had taken on another dimension – it looked like a halo. Robin and Joan agreed that the woman in the portrait was a stranger. In rather cross Italian, the artist said he could only paint what he saw. I was not flattered.

That evening we were invited to a cocktail party at the William Waltons. As I was getting into the car that was to drive us there, I suddenly realized who the woman in the portrait was – Flora Goforth. I had sat for those hours on the model's throne remembering my role, remembering the play and unconsciously I must have drawn my face into the petulant unhappy lines of the doomed widow. I hadn't yet unwound properly from that tremendously powerful play.

'We'll buy the picture anyway,' said Robin.

'No, I couldn't bear to look at it,' I replied. 'It's the portrait of a dead woman.'

William Walton thought the portrait was wonderful, no matter if it didn't look at all like me. He bought it and some time later, when

Joan went back to Ischia, there it was hanging in the hall of the Walton's house. She told me that it was a strange, haunting picture and she couldn't take her eyes off it, but she was very glad to get away from it.

Chapter Seventeen

As soon as we arrived in New York, there were the usual rumours of catastrophe swirling around. As always, no one seemed to trust anybody's word, but the theatre in New York is often like that. I did know for a fact that Tallulah Bankhead was driving the producer, the director and the writer crazy, announcing that she would surely die if she couldn't play Flora. It was true that the Morosco Theatre, where we were to open, wasn't ready for us, but we'd get there eventually. And Roger Stevens, the producer, told me not to bother my head about Tallulah. 'We're all standing firmly behind you, Hermione,' he assured me. What a very nice man Mr Stevens is!

I could cope with all the ordinary happenings, it was the extra-ordinary ones that upset me. I had come to New York to realize a dream, to create a new role on Broadway, to make *The Milk Train* . . . my play, one I should always be remembered for – nothing could really go wrong, could it?

Yes, it most certainly could. As soon as I got to New York, the government closed down the Music Corporation of America because the agency was considered to have too powerful a monopoly. One day our dear kind agents at MCA were leading actors and actresses all over the civilized world by the hand, fighting to make managements pay us well over the living wage; the next day they were gone. Their offices were closed down, our telephones were silent. With most of the New York theatre crowd rushing around like scalded cats looking for a new agent, the choice was limited, but I found one eventually and, like all new agents, he promised me the earth. Not only was I to do the play *The Milk Train* . . ., I was to do the film as well, he promised.

The company went off to Boston and New Haven for the try-outs: all went very well. We came back to New York, moved into the Morosco Theatre and opening night was upon us. The first night was everything we hoped it would be; you could have heard a pin drop the audience were so engrossed in the play. We all went out with Tennessee afterwards and waited for the early editions of the newspapers. They weren't as large as usual – there was some talk of trouble with the unions – but when they came, Tennessee read out glorious notices and the whole company was thrilled. One of them said, to my joy, that I was even better than Laurette Taylor had been in *The Glass Menagerie*. I remember Tennessee saying that *The Milk Train* . . . was by no means one of his best plays, but that I had woven magic into it.

I think I was the happiest actress in New York. All my friends came to see the show. Even Hermione Gingold came backstage to congratulate me and a real tear trickled down her cheek. This euphoria lasted for exactly four days. Dark forebodings about a newspaper strike had been hanging over our heads, but we prayed that the print unions would work something out with the newspaper bosses. On the fourth day, the newspapers had shrunk to scrappy bits of paper. On the fifth day there was not a newspaper in the whole of New York.

The public were bewildered, but we were stunned. Without newspapers Broadway would suffer a mortal blow. No theatre advertisements, no reviews, no gossip columns. The heart of the entertainment business had stopped beating. The New York newspaper strike lasted for four and a half months; our poor play crawled along for about four, but it was crippled and finally killed by the lack of publicity. If the theatre-going public doesn't know what's on, you don't get big audiences. *Time* magazine ran a wonderful review of the play, but that was a nationwide magazine and didn't help the Broadway scene. Mildred Dunnock was wonderful. She begged Roger Stevens not to take it off before the newspapers came back. But when the strike did end, it was too late to save us.

When we came off, Hollywood reached out and grabbed me. My new agent told me to forget the play and go into films. George Cukor, the director, asked me out to Hollywood and Rex Harrison, with whom I had done television in New York, suggested me for a role. Stanley Holloway and Cecil Beaton and many other English stars had come out to do *My Fair Lady* and Hollywood was suddenly filled with English accents. I was offered the part of housekeeper.

I didn't like the idea of another housekeeper part in films, so I talked to Walt Disney about appearing in *Mary Poppins*. The very next day, I was offered a part by another company in *The Unsinkable Molly Brown*. Since the two did not clash, I signed both contracts.

Months later, I had a telephone call from Tennessee Williams. They were going to revive *The Milk Train Doesn't Stop Here Any More* and wanted me for Flora again. My agent had told them that I wasn't available, but Tennessee wanted to make sure. If only I had known about this before signing those contracts, but it couldn't be helped.

The Milk Train . . . opened again in New York with Tallulah Bankhead and it ran for just three nights. Tennessee wrote later: 'I wrote it for Hermione Baddeley and she was wonderful. Then I did it with Tallulah Bankhead. She was dying and she couldn't project past the third row.'

Poor play. I'd had such enormous luck to go into it and land a star role in New York. It had all gone so well and then it was as if some bad fairy had put a curse on me.

Walt Disney, when I arrived in Hollywood, was a young-looking man filled with vitality and ideas. He looked at me, soon after we met, and said that he had found Mrs 'Arris. He had always wanted to make a film of Paul Gallico's *Mrs 'Arris Goes To Paris*. Walt had been telling me how much he loved England, how often he went there and how he was enchanted with life in London – particularly the cockneys and the ebullient charladies. These were the type of parts I could play with my eyes shut and, as far as the movies were concerned, they were my speciality. Walt Disney wanted me for Mrs 'Arris and I, of course, was delighted to say, yes. It couldn't happen straight away. Walt had to get it all set up and, above all, he had to buy the rights from Paul Gallico, which might take some time. While I was waiting he would put me in *Mary Poppins*.

The set-up seemed really marvellous. I had nothing to worry about, Walt told me, I was not going to be let down and it was just a matter of time before *Mrs 'Arris* . . . was begun. Working at the Walt Disney Studios was different – there was a very special atmosphere there. Julie Andrews and Dick van Dyke were a joy to work with. I loved Julie and I thought that Dick van Dyke was touched with genius. *Mary Poppins* was a very happy film to make and it certainly deserved its huge success.

When I was working on the second picture I had contracted to do, *The Unsinkable Molly Brown,* which was about an Irish girl who comes to America, I had to learn a good Irish accent. A very pleasant woman was engaged to help me, and it was she who suggested that instead of living in expensive hotels, I should buy myself a house. It did seem to make sense. I knew that *Mrs 'Arris . . .* was going to be an important film and, if all went well, I should be financially secure; and it would be lovely to have a home of my own again.

I liked what I saw of Hollywood when I came out to do these films in 1964. I must admit that I thought it was a strange part of the world where con-men proliferated, but I knew that with time I could learn to deal with that. I liked the way everything was altogether in one place. In New York and London, the entertainment business is just a small part of the whole. You can live in the city, work in the theatre, and then go home and forget about it. But not Hollywood: everything in Los Angeles is concentrated around the great god entertainment. The film factories are there, the TV studios, the scriptwriters, the journalists and the gossip columnists. Someone always knows anyone you might want to meet and at parties you bump into all the important people in the film industry – the producers, the directors and the actors. The talk in Hollywood isn't about what Reagan or Thatcher are up to, its about your next role and your future career. You take a taxi and the driver will say that he saw you in a late movie the night before. His brother, cousin or sister-in-law is sure to work in some studio. There are always fans waiting outside all the big restaurants, discos and entertainment places, and it's very good for the ego when they rush up to you and actually know your name.

Going back to 1964, the woman who coached me in my Irish accent introduced me to a gentleman who she was sure would find me exactly the right kind of house. His name was Mr Khoury and he was dark and dapper with a smooth line of talk and had a nice big car to drive me around in. He came, I believe from the Lebanon. He told me that the place to live was up in the canyons, where the air was fresh and dry. Smog was just beginning to creep into the Los

Angeles Boulevards and people were beginning to say that it was the only place where an arrow fired into the air would get stuck.

Canyons, I learned, are ravines, valleys, gorges or chasms in the mountains. Houses are built clinging to the edges of these canyons and they have breathtaking views all over Hollywood. The better the view, the higher the price. I felt rather a novice in the matter of real estate, so I was delighted when my friend Joan came out to join me in Hollywood – she arrived, as she often does, just when I needed advice and support. I didn't want to buy a house unless Joan liked it, for she would be coming out to stay with me frequently and I valued her opinion. One of the houses Mr Khoury took us to see was in Coldwater Canyon and had a superlative view. It was a lovely rambling house set in four acres of garden on the edge of a canyon. It had six bedrooms, six bathrooms and a swimming pool, and was built by the English actor, Aubrey Smith. Joan and I fell in love with it instantly. 'How much?' we asked. Mr Khoury told us and we signed.

Joan and I couldn't keep away from that house. We used to drive up there, climb over the wall and sit in the garden and think up ways to try and raise the money. Joan had some money in England and I was hoping that *Mrs 'Arris . . .* would soon get off the ground. There'd been another hold-up about getting the rights from Paul Gallico, but Walt assured me that all was going well.

'Let's buy it,' said Joan, and she immediately started working out how we could finance the deal. I tried to think up reasons why we shouldn't buy it: there were no neighbours, and the house itself was out on a promontory; and what about the coyotes, prairie wolves that have made the canyons of Hollywood their own. They creep about at night drinking water from the swimming pools and laying in wait for unwary pet animals. 'Let's buy it,' I said.

We got mixed up in all kinds of weird schemes getting the money together to pay for the house. Before we signed the contract, I asked Walt Disney once more if he was sure about *Mrs 'Arris . . .* Not only was Walt sure, but he had also commissioned the music and was making plans for a sequel called *Mrs 'Arris Goes To New York.* But while he was getting *Mrs 'Arris . . .* worked out, I was to do another film, *The Happiest Millionaire,* with Tommy Steele.

I must admit that I did wonder just a little. How many more films was I going to do while I waited? In *The Happiest Millionaire* I played Mrs Worth, the long-suffering cook to the household of an eccentric millionaire. It had a very starry cast with Greer Garson, Geraldine Page and of course Tommy Steele. I was always very interested to watch Tommy Steele work: he put everything he had into it, and yet it always seemed that he was looking for that little bit extra. It wasn't star quality, he already had that, but he was not easily satisfied.

Joan and I moved into the house in Coldwater Canyon with Lottie, the French bulldog, and no furniture at all. We'd spent and mortgaged everything we had just to buy the house. Funnily enough, money isn't all that important when you want to furnish a house. The most important thing is time. I had made a friend called Larry Bordeaux, and Larry knew all about buying antiques and second-hand furniture. He used to take me along to a wonderful sales room where I found the loveliest furniture at knock-down prices. I had plenty of time now, just to sit around in my empty house and wait for my big film to start and my big salary to come rolling in.

While I waited, I went to the sales room and bought a Napoleonic bed for my room, found some chairs and a table and did some interior decorating. There was a huge room in the house with fabulous views and it had a great open fireplace. This room I painted pale orange and it looked very good. The weeks went by and I went on furnishing the house. I heard that Frank Marcus was writing a play with me in mind – it was to be called *The Killing Of Sister George* and he wrote and asked me to come back to London and appear in it. I had to turn it down. I was going to do this Walt Disney film.

At last it looked as if the film was to go into production. I went down to the Walt Disney studios the morning I heard the good news. It was always a happy place to go to: I met all my old friends – the technicians, wardrobe people, actors, actresses, producers and directors. I'm not quite sure when the news hit the studio. The year before, the news of President Kennedy's assassination had hit the world and everyone reeled back in horror. What happened at the Disney studios that day was comparable.

'Walt is dead,' someone whispered. Walt Disney had died suddenly, and with him died a big part of the film industry. The shock in the Walt Disney studios that day was terrible. He was the man who ran everything, the man with the vision, the ideas. He was the man who was to make me the star of *Mrs 'Arris* . . . I'd been waiting around all these months, doing little character roles in pictures to keep me going. What will happen now? I remember thinking. Without Walt Disney, it was unlikely that the studios would go on producing and I had this Hollywood mansion up in the mountains to maintain. My first thought was to sell it. My reason for buying it, for staying in Hollywood, was gone. Walt Disney was a great loss, not only was he a lovely man, but his death ended many careers.

Johnny Rebel came out from New York. As soon as he saw the house he advised me not to sell it, feeling sure that it would become a very valuable property in time. If I sold it now, with all the trouble in Vietnam, I could only lose money. I had to go back to England, though, so I decided to rent it out. At least the house would still be mine when I came back. Johnny Rebel said he had a feeling about the house and he was right. It was sold again last year for two million dollars, but of course I'd sold it long long ago.

I had received an offer from London to do *The Killing Of Sister George,* the play I'd turned down because I was to do the Walt Disney film. Although I was very happy to accept the offer, there was a little shadow over it for me. I wouldn't be creating the role, for Beryl Reid had already done that. While I was in Hollywood, the play had scored a huge triumph at the Duke of York's. Beryl Reid did a marvellous job and she deserved all the plaudits. She had worked with the playwright and the director re-writing prior to the opening in London, helping to turn it into a brilliant play. Beryl was going to New York with the play, while in London it was being transferred to the St Martin's. Nowadays people do create a role, then hand it over to someone else, but this is quite new. Everyone told me how funny Beryl had been in the part, but of course the play also had a tragic side. There was drama and pathos in the story of a middle-aged woman who is slowly being written out of her star role in a television soap opera. Sister George, the fictional district nurse, is going to be killed off by the writers and the woman starts a losing battle to save her career.

Before I left for London, I set about renting the house in Cold-water Canyon. The smooth Mr Khoury wasn't half as interested in renting the house as he had been in selling it, but eventually he came up with some clients, a black soul band. I wasn't at all sure that I wanted a whole band in my house, but Mr Khoury assured me that it was really only their manager who would live there. He gave me a take-it-or-leave-it lecture, and asked me where I expected to find that kind of money except in this new entertainment phenomenon of young men with swivelling hips and guitars?

I went over to London and soon fell in love with the part of Sister George; I enjoyed every performance. The play was going to run for a long time. While I was there, David came over from Spain. He was very ill, having had some kind of nervous breakdown. Just as I had thought, the life in Spain hadn't been good for him – too many pills and too much to drink. He went into a nursing home in Hampstead and slowly got better. When he was convalescent we used to have dinner together now and then and go to the theatre. I remember us sobbing together over Olivier's magnificent rendition of Othello.

Over dinner in a restaurant one evening, he told me that he was thinking of giving up his life in Spain. He wouldn't come back to England, because he said he could never stand the climate. Instead, he had to go out and see that island in the West Indies called Mustique. Oliver Messel and Colin Tennant had bought some land there and David rather liked the idea of being on an island with them. We talked about it and it seemed a lovely idea. Pauline had said that she would go with him and, if he liked Mustique, he would build a house there. 'You must come out,' David told me. 'Not just for a holiday. Come out there and live.'

I came off stage after the last curtain call at the St Martin's one night to find a wonderful surprise in my dressing room. Sitting perfectly posed in my chair was another French bulldog to replace my beloved Lottie, who had recently died. I called him George and he was a delightful character. I used to take him to the Wig and Pen Club, where we often went between rehearsals in those days, and deposit him in the cloakroom there. He behaved so well that he became a great favourite with all the staff. One day, they asked me for George's full name and address – they had decided to make him an honorary life member of the club. They sent him a membership card, which George signed with his paw print – he must have been the first dog ever to be a member of a London club. Whenever I had to go out for the afternoon, all I need do was put George into a taxi and he would spend some time at his club, where he was always very well fed and looked after.

When *Sister George* finished, I had other offers of work in England, but first I wanted to go back to Hollywood and see what had happened to my house in Coldwater Canyon. I'd heard from Mr Khoury that the house was empty. The band had gone and Mr Khoury had sub-let the house to some new tenants who had gone back to New York leaving a great deal of rent unpaid. My poor house! Ten people had lived there with six dogs and the chaos and destruction was unbelievable. Furniture was smashed and broken and a lot of it had strange water marks over it. According to the gardener, these people had had a fight one night and thrown it in the swimming pool. They had also erected hideous concrete posts all over the garden as part of some game. And the dogs! The gardener was very upset about the destruction and mess that six large dogs had made. The by-laws up in the canyons are strict. Usually only two dogs per household are allowed and for the sake of hygiene there is a dog park for which you pay $20 a year. You run your dog down there in the car and take a bucket and spade to clear up after him. The highways of the Canyons are pristine.

Mr Khoury was very cool about the whole affair. When I said I was going to sue the tenant, not only for the unpaid rent but also for the destruction of my furniture, all he could say was: 'How do we find him?' He'd left the state. I moved back in and started to clear up the mess. One afternoon, I was in the kitchen making a cup of tea when I saw a bright red sports car turn into my driveway. There, sitting in the driving seat, was the rich man who managed the black band. I think he thought that the house was still empty and he was quite surprised when I appeared.

We chatted quite affably and I asked him where he was staying. He gave me the name of his hotel and as soon as the car was out of the drive I got on to my lawyer. A writ was served on him at once and the case came to court. My poor mis-treated furniture was brought into the courtroom. The judge examined a lovely old eighteenth century screen that had been kicked in. He was quite sympathetic and awarded me more than the statutory minimum.

I didn't learn – I was still an easy touch for the con-men of Hollywood. The Coldwater Canyon house was now in order again and I had to leave; I either had to rent it or find someone trustworthy to look after it for me. I met a man at a party called Ed. He told me that he was writing a film script for a Laurence Harvey film and that

Larry was very keen on it. He said he was in the middle of re-writing it but that his apartment was so noisy he could hardly think. Where did I live? I told him I lived in Coldwater Canyon but that I was leaving for England very soon and must find a good place to board my two cats. 'Do you know one?' I enquired.

What a silly question. 'But of course I do,' he said with great conviction. 'Me! I love cats.' I couldn't see my cats loving his noisy apartment, but Ed had other ideas. He wanted to move into my home, finish Laurence Harvey's script, and give my cats all the care and love they needed.

I rang Laurence Harvey, who was about to marry the wealthy widow of Harry Cohn the film tycoon. I found his future bride, Joan, very pleasant; she was an expensive looking Hollywood blonde with lots of money with which to go to expensive hair-dressers and buy expensive clothes. I remember she asked me what she should buy Larry for his birthday: 'I gave him a Range Rover for Christmas, but I'm not sure if he liked it? Should I buy him a Rolls?'

I chatted with Larry for a minute or two and then I brought up the subject of Ed. Was this man really writing a script for him? Could I trust him? According to Larry, this Ed had been hanging around for ages. He had read a bit of the script but really didn't know much about Ed.

Against my better judgement, I left Ed and the cats up in Cold-water Canyon. Before eventually returning to Hollywood, I rang Ed to tell him that my friend Joan and I would be arriving on a certain date and would he vacate the premises by then. Ed was horrified. He claimed that his sick father was living in the house and that he was under strict instructions not to move him an inch. There was nothing else for it. Joan and I moved into the Chateau Marmont, a hotel, and waited for Ed's dying father either to recover or die. We had no sooner unpacked our bags than our friends and acquaint-ance came dashing into the hotel to report on Ed.

Evidently he had thrown a large party as soon as my taxi had disappeared down the Canyon. It was his house-warming, said Ed, for he had bought the house from me. He was the new owner. Bills were unpaid, neighbours had been quarrelled with, and he'd sacked my very decent gardener. But what about his sick father. I wanted to know. It seems that Ed's sick father was a figment of Ed's sick imagination.

It took another lawyer to get Ed out of the house. Hollywood, they say, is one big steal, and I think there are more con-men in Los Angeles than anywhere else on earth. The tales they tell of the houses they own and the money they earn are highly ingenious; perhaps it's because they see so much wealth around that they have to invent some of their own.

While I was in Hollywood that time, letters came to me from David and Pauline saying that David had decided to build his house not at Mustique but at St Lucia, a beautiful island nearby. 'He's making all kinds of plans,' Pauline wrote. 'He's thinking of having a plane that would fly from island to island. He wants to start some kind of business.' I was so pleased that David had got over his breakdown, recovered from the terrible depression, and left what he himself called 'a rotten part of the world' to start afresh in the beautiful West Indies. David wrote me a charming letter saying, 'When are you coming out to join us? The house is nearly ready. We want you to choose the furniture.'

At once I cancelled some film work I was due to start and prepared to leave. I really thought that everything would come together and we could live together as a family again. Then the telephone rang at Coldwater Canyon: Pauline was calling from St Lucia. Something awful had happened, I could tell immediately. Pauline told me that David had been unwell and a doctor had provisionally diagnosed cancer of the lung. I was heartbroken. Everything was off, cancelled. David was flying straight to London for tests and treatment.

A few days later, Pauline rang again. Good news! The doctors in London had found that there was not a shadow on David's lung and he was perfectly healthy. I hoped that he would pick up again where he had left off – fly back to St Lucia and finish the beautiful house on the bay, install the furniture that he had ordered. But David was a strange bird. He couldn't bear to go back to St Lucia where he'd been given a probable death sentence. He just left everything! No matter that Pauline was upset, that I was disappointed, that God knows how many people on the island were let down; David abandoned St Lucia. He went back to the villa in Mijas and an uncertain fate. I felt very unhappy and worried about him.

When I'd been in England finishing the run of *The Killing Of Sister George*, I'd had an offer to do a national American tour of the play, going from big city to big city. It sounded lovely and I was ready to accept when a Mr Roy Moseley and a Mr Epstein changed my mind for me. Roy Moseley had been a friend and occasional agent of mine for a long time and was now doing something in films; he introduced Mr Epstein to me. Mr Epstein wanted me for the film of *The Adding Machine* and Roy said I'd be much better doing that than going on the national tour. Film production has a way of going on and on for months before the contract is signed and the job is yours; *The Adding Machine* was no exception. In the end, in desperation, I went back to Los Angeles to find out what was happening to my house in Coldwater Canyon.

While I was there I tried to contact Roy Moseley or Mr Epstein, but they both seemed to be lost without trace. I felt very sad that I'd given up a tour with a part I loved for an apparently non-existent film.

Then a very strange and unusual thing happened. The William Morris office rang me up and told me that Claire Trevor, who had taken the role of Sister George on tour, was ailing. She wasn't strong enough for this strenuous part and was getting terrible notices. Would I consider taking over? As I could still find no trace of Mr Moseley or Mr Epstein, I accepted gladly. No matter that I'd missed a lot of the tour, I'd be delighted to got to Chicago. As I said before, it is always very tricky taking over from another actress who has been fired. When you take over, you usually try and avoid meeting the person in an attempt to save hurt feelings.

I hadn't met Claire Trevor, but I'd always admired her films, and I felt very sorry about the bad notices she'd been receiving. I had a feeling that something must have gone wrong somewhere. Film actresses often need a lot of direction; they are used to it in films and they're wonderful when they get it.

My friend Joan Assheton-Smith was staying with me in Coldwater Canyon so she decided to come along to Chicago with me. We checked in at the Blackstone Hotel and naturally enough gravitated to the bar. We were feeling a bit strange in a new town with new people, but Joan, who is quite an assertive personality, was soon chatting with two businessmen at the bar. She explained to them that I had come to Chicago to take over from Claire Trevor.

'Claire Trevor!' cried the man. 'Oh what a doll! My favourite screen actress. Oh, I'd just love to meet her.'

I knew that Claire would be feeling depressed and that her self-confidence would need bolstering so I telephoned the theatre and asked if Miss Trevor could possibly come to my room at the Blackstone after the show that night. I had friends with me who would love to meet her. A message came back saying that she would be happy to come.

Our two new friends turned out to be quite rich business men. They insisted on setting up hors d'oeuvres and a table of drinks in my room – they quite took our breath away. Then this pretty little thing, looking exactly as she used to in all those films, walks in and immediately took their breath away. 'I saw you in *Stagecoach*,' said one. 'Oh boy! What a film!' Claire absolutely bloomed. It was exactly what she needed. We'd all got so much to say to each other that the time flew by and we talked to the early hours. At the end of the evening, she said she wished I had been on the tour with them from the beginning. 'But darling,' I said, 'you know I couldn't have done – I'm taking your place!' We both laughed happily. Claire had clean forgotten the circumstances of our meeting.

She stayed and watched me play the part of Sister George and then she came backstage and wanted to know why she hadn't been told to do all the little things I did. Just as I had thought, Claire, with her film background, was used to getting a lot of direction. She went off to her lovely home in Palm Beach quite happily, knowing that she wasn't to blame, and leaving us invitations to stay with her. So what could have been a tricky situation ended very well.

While I was appearing in *The Killing Of Sister George* in Chicago, I received some very sad news. David had died suddenly in Spain. His health had deteriorated and he had gone downhill rapidly. He was being brought home to be buried in the churchyard at Wilsford, next to his mother and father. I flew straight over to attend David's funeral – I felt the loss very deeply and felt utterly bereft, as if I had lost a husband and was now a widow. Virginia, the Invisible Lady, revealed herself at the funeral: her hair was swept right back and she wept and wept. Christopher Glenconner asked me to come and stay with him in Corfu whenever I wanted – I was very touched.

Some time later, when the tour was over, I went up to La Jolla in California for an art exhibition. Someone said: 'I've a friend here who wants to meet you. Here she is, Lady Charles Cavendish.' A small lady I remembered as Adele Astaire turned round. 'And Adele, this is Miss Hermione Baddeley.' Adele made a deep curtsey, 'No,' she said, 'this is my friend, the Honourable Mrs David Tennant. It's so lovely to see you again.'

And that was the last time anyone ever called me that.

One of the drawbacks of Coldwater Canyon was the remoteness – there were no near neighbours. One evening, Joan and I were in the kitchen putting together some supper, when we heard a noise from the back of the house near the library. Joan went out into the hall to see what it was, while I hovered near the kitchen door listening. Suddenly three extraordinary looking men stormed into the hall from the back. They were dirty and dishevelled with long hair and weird-looking clothes, and were all obviously high on drugs. Joan was very brave, and asked them what they wanted in a perfectly normal voice.

'We've come to our house.' shouted one of the men. The other two took up the chant. 'This is our house! This is our house!'

'Why do you say it's your house?' asked Joan reasonably.

They hadn't seen me, so I slipped back into the kitchen, closed the door softly and rang the police from the kitchen phone. I've never known anyone arrive so quickly. The police cars were up that hill in three and a half minutes flat. They rounded the men up and took them away, but they left one young policeman with us. He searched the grounds and found a fourth man sitting in the garage reading a bible. Written across the open pages of the bible were the words: 'Thou shalt kill!'

About three weeks later, my lawyer came up to the house to take me to a cocktail party. He stood by the window looking down over the panoramic view, down past the canyons to Los Angeles. 'Isn't it frightful about all these murders?' he said. I didn't know what he meant, for we didn't have newspapers delivered to our house in Coldwater Canyon. He pointed down to another canyon and indicated the place where poor, Sharon Tate had been horribly murdered the day before. He had learned from the police all the ghastly details of the murder and of the messages written in the victim's blood.

An icy finger went down my spine as I remembered the man with the open bible and the words scrawled across the page, 'Thou shalt kill!' Charles Manson and his family were captured and tried for murder, but I often wonder if our visitors that night were part of this sadistic group called 'the family' and what a lucky escape we might have had.

That was about the time I started to think about selling the house in Coldwater Canyon.

Chapter Eighteen

American audiences finally got to know me when a Saturday night series called *The Good Life* appeared on their screens. I was supposed to be a very rich woman with a very rich brother and we were supposed to be surrounded by luxury, so we played in sets weighed down with props that really were expensive: fine silver, china, antiques and magnificent rugs. The Columbia studios were proud of themselves. 'Other studios may have their stars, 'ran their publicity, 'but we've got the genuine antiques.' As it happened, they also had a big future star in *The Good Life*, Larry Hagman, who played the butler and afterwards became J. R., the round-faced villain in *Dallas*. Larry was an easy person to work with. He had a great deal of charm and talent, but a mind of his own. 'I don't really like this series,' he said every other day. I agreed that it wasn't earth-shaking but it did push me to the front somewhat and I got to like the people I worked with.

I didn't try very hard to become a celebrity. When my agent told me that Norman Lear, who was just about the biggest name in Hollywood TV wanted to see me about a role, I said it would be a waste of time going along. I was off to England to do a fourteen-week serial. But the agent would insist; I'd just had a swim in the pool, so I shoved my wet hair into a cotton cap, picked up my handbag and off we went. In the car, the agent groaned and shook his head: no make-up, no false eyelashes! He was right, I looked terrible, but I got the part because I was just what they wanted – a woman who didn't look like a Hollywood doll.

At that time I was always popping back and forth across the Atlantic if I was offered a good play. Let's be honest, I've never ever stopped. One of the plays I was offered was *Mother Adam* by Charles Dyer. He'd written *Rattle Of A Simple Man*, then *Staircase* and finally *Mother Adam* to form a trilogy, and he called them plays of loneliness. His theme was that action cannot heal loneliness, it is cured only by sharing an action. *Mother Adam* was a wonderful play; it didn't get its fair due at that time and I feel it is just waiting to be done again. I loved Charles Dyer's story of a man and his mother and their courage and optimism. Peter Wyngarde was my schizophrenic son, Adam, and I was his arthritic mother.

We toured with the play, but the nearest we got to the West End was the Hampstead Theatre Club at Swiss Cottage. While I was sitting in my dressing room the telephone rang. It was a property man from Hollywood; he had a client who wanted to buy my Coldwater Canyon house for $180,000. Since that was about what I had paid for it I protested that it couldn't be enough. There followed a long diatribe about the Vietnam War, the Dow Jones index, the Wall Street blues. The man who was offering to buy it was Isaac Hayes, the singer and writer. I knew him and liked him, and after all the trouble it had been through, I felt that my house deserved someone good. So I relented privately, and told the agent that I would think about it when I got the contract. I went over to California to complete the sale, but soon afterwards discovered that not only had my house been sold, but the selling price included all the furniture. 'It was all down there in the contract you signed,' said the property man blandly. Of course it was all down in the small print, which I had asked this same property man to read to me before I signed. He had carefully omitted the important bits and this was the result.

However, Isaac Hayes believed my story, and he asked me to come round and choose whatever furniture I wanted. I didn't choose much because it all had to go into store. I had no idea when I'd return to America. In England I was going to make a TV serial, *South Riding,* and more television was planned after that. It was during this my final week in Hollywood that I went to see Norman Lear with my wet hair tucked into a little cotton cap I had once bought in Malta. I looked anything but chic, but it was that little cotton cap that caught Norman Lear's eye. We drove out to the CBS television studios – a big white edifice out by Farmer's Market. When I walked into Norman Lear's office, I realized that it wasn't just an ordinary little interview. There were a whole crowd of writers there, big names, important television people.

'It's for a kind of maid part,' said Norman Lear, 'a housekeeper.' I noticed that everyone was watching me, looking me up and down, listening to me. 'We're going to create a new character.' I protested that I was leaving for England the following week and would be away for three or four months. There was a pause. Norman Lear looked round the room as if to see what the rest of the crowd thought. Then he said that in three months time I would be invited to join the series, which was called *Maude*. But I was used to Hollywood promises. I'd first stayed in Hollywood because of a promise given me by Walt Disney. There's something in the Hollywood air that makes promises evaporate, so I didn't really expect anything to come of it.

When *South Riding* was over, Norman Lear sent for me and I returned to California. I wanted to feel the hot sun again – *South Riding* had been a story about Yorkshire in the depression, not the most cheerful environment. Almost as soon as I arrived, Norman Lear telephoned and asked me to come over, wearing my Maltese cap. The same group of writers were there. They were going to create a new character around me, a housekeeper called Mrs Naugatuck. One of the writers handed me a script and asked me to try reading it. I started off in a rather genteel, carefully-spoken voice, but was soon interrupted by a chorus of objections. They wanted this woman to be a brash cockney, eccentric and nutty. I read the part that way, and they all liked it. Norman Lear was pleased and I was asked to join *Maude*. Mrs Naugatuck had been created.

In the mid-seventies, *Maude* was big in television. It was a series that had the Norman Lear 'developed' touch – a spin-off of a spin-off. It had started in England with the rough and raucous *Till Death Us Do Part*, changed into *All In The Family* in America (rough Bronx instead of rough cockney), and now they were taking one of the characters and giving her a series of her own. Maude, played by Bea Arthur, was an overbearing, bossy woman, looking for trouble – a female Captain Bligh without the Bounty. I was the other female character sent to clash with her, make the sparks of comedy fly. Mrs Naugatuck was the cockney ingrate who was employed to keep house, but who usually ended up wrecking the house.

The opening scene of the first show had Bea Arthur waiting for the high-class English housekeeper to trip in, and she gets Mrs

Naugatuck in her cotton cap and beads. 'Here I am expecting Greer Garson to walk in, and what do I get – you!' Bea Arthur was a tall, statuesque woman with a pretty face and a voice that rippled beautifully. When we first met, she told me I had such beautiful eyes, and I told her she had a beautiful voice. We got on very well.

I had no idea that the character of Mrs Naugatuck – it was a weird name – would be such a hit. I had to stay in Hollywood, but I had nowhere to live for I'd sold my house in Coldwater Canyon just at the wrong time. There was no doubt that I was not going to move from California for a long time to come, so the only thing to do was buy another house. This I did, but while the house up in Coldwater had been too big, this one was too small. It was still in the Hollywood Hills, but it had only one spare bedroom and a small guest studio in the garden. It was a lovely place, but just too small.

One of the reasons I liked working in television in preference to films is that the hours you work are so civilized. You get to the television studios about nine in the morning and by the late afternoon you are home again. As Wilfred Hyde White once said to me: 'I'm getting a bit long in the tooth to get up with the birds. I'll take television any day.'

Every week while you are doing a series, the schedule is exactly the same. On Saturday the new script arrives at your house and you learn it over the weekend. On Monday there's a read-through, but you don't concentrate too much in case the writers alter it. Next day, the dialogue has been sharpened up and tightened. On Wednesday the altered dialogue is frozen and the final rehearsal takes place on Thursday. On Friday we do two shows live to an invited audience. I liked this, because I work naturally to an audience. Next day, Saturday, the whole procedure starts again, and you do this week by week without a break until the series is finished.

Between shows, Norman Lear would come in and make very good suggestions. Americans in television are really perfectionists, although there is always the risk that they might overdo the perfection just a little bit and ruin the whole thing. When the series is finished there is what they call a 'hiatus' – a break of about three months when you can do other work if you want; then the series starts up again.

Television is performed at great speed. After the theatre and films, the lack of time can be frightening, and the way the brilliant writers and directors seemed to create at lightning speed made me worry that I wasn't fast enough. But with every episode, as I got into the character, I found it easier. The dialogue in American television is very fast. Of course, in time you find who are your favourite writers and I had two; I called them the two Bobs. They expanded my role and thought up bizarre happenings every week. With their scripts I became an outrageous liar and my claims to a lurid past got more and more extreme. In one episode, I declared that I had had a wartime love affair with Winston Churchill in a bomb shelter; in another that I had run a bawdy house in Australia; in another that I wasn't really a housekeeper down on my luck but an English Duchess and the Duke, my husband had drowned when falling overboard from our yacht.

My room in Maude's house, which I called 'a corner of olde Englande', was invaded one night by a suspicious Maude who discovered a naked Englishman there called Alfie. Maude screams at me: 'You're blackening the reputation of our home.' I retort: 'Hell's Angels couldn't blacken the reputation of this home.' It all made up for great comedy. The newspapers wrote a lot about the outrageous character, Mrs Naugatuck, and I was always being asked on chat-shows to talk about myself. Interviewers asked me when I was going to have a show of my own, when Norman Lear was going to spin me off. All I could say was that I hoped so, but that only Mr Lear knew that.

As I became a bigger and bigger hit, I did begin to expect a series of my own. I was beginning to feel embarrassed that the newspapers wrote about Mrs Naugatuck and not the rest of the cast. The first inkling I had that my popularity wasn't going down too well came at one of the script meetings. The cast, the writers, the director and the producer sit around and discuss what's going to happen next. I noticed this time that some new writers were sitting in, young and clever with bright expressions and eyes that darted back and forth.

I listened to them and made a mental note that Mrs Naugatuck was not going to be quite so funny in the next episode. I couldn't help remembering *The Killing Of Sister George* and the part I'd played of the actress who is slowly written out of her soap opera. But it won't happen in real life, I thought to myself. Why should they kill off the most popular character?

Norman Lear gave a lovely lunch for us all at the beginning of the next series. I'd been in *Maude* for over three years and it looked as if it would go on forever. My favourite writers, the two Bobs, were sitting near me. Just before we all got up to leave, one of them leaned over and whispered that he and his colleague, the other Bob, were leaving *Maude*. This was the most unpleasant news for me. The two Bobs had been entirely responsible for the character of the dotty housekeeper who couldn't even make a cup of coffee. But nothing stands still. I looked over to the bevy of bright young writers sitting round Norman Lear and left that lunch party feeling very depressed. Maybe truth did emulate fiction, maybe I would be written out.

I was in *Maude* for four years, but in the last year my part was made progressively smaller. Fans wrote in and demanded to know why Mrs Naugatuck wasn't around so much. Some of these letters were produced at the next script meeting, but to no avail. My agent called in to see Norman Lear. He said that the audience were happy to know that Mrs Naugatuck was there in the background. She would keep on putting her nose round the door.

I grew tired of putting my nose around the door, carrying in a tray and disappearing and we all agreed that I would be written out. Norman Lear brought in a younger actress from the film *Network* to take my place. The original Mrs Naugatuck went to Ireland and never came back. When I had left, Bea Arthur used to ring me up and complain that things weren't what they used to be. The ratings dropped and Maude finished at the end of the season.

I didn't stop working in television – there are always good character parts – but I've always remembered what Laurence Olivier once said to me: 'It's all right to do films and television but never forget that the theatre is where you learned your craft. It is the reason you are able to do films and television, so don't ever give it up.' Of course I agree with him completely and that was why, when we had these 'hiatus' periods in *Maude,* I often went back to the theatre. Once I was asked to do *Fallen Angels* at a delightful theatre near Chicago. I was asked to play the role of Jane, the one I'd done in London, and they wanted to know who I thought should play Julia. I chose Joan Blondell, because she is such a lovely, funny actress and so pretty in her movies.

When I met her in Santa Monica, I found her as pretty as ever but she did admit that she had arthritis and said she hoped it wouldn't flare up and ruin the play for everyone. We agreed that I should go down and rehearse with her about three times a week. I knew my lines backwards, of course, having done the role for over a year. After a few visits, I was disappointed because for some reason or other Joan just didn't know her lines. At one point she said she thought it might be her arthritis playing up, so she rested for a day or two.

This seemed to work and when we rehearsed next time she knew most of her lines, but then next time someone came in to listen and they were all gone again. I knew what she felt like because my own memory can fail now and then these days. Even so, I was beginning to be a little apprehensive. By the time opening night at the Pheasant Run in Chicago came round, I had become very apprehensive. The very worst happened: Joan dried up at the most important part of the story and there was only one thing I could do – take over, play the two parts and speak the dialogue for both of us. I felt like a sort of ventriloquist, but by some miracle the audience seemed to accept what I was doing and we even got some laughs. That performance is carved into my memory. It was one of the worst things I have ever been through.

The party that followed opening night was rather fraught and unhappy, but next morning everyone was calm again. We all made rather a joke of it and a lot of people, including the stage manager, offered to hear her read the part and get it right. But Joan opted to have a friend of ours fly in from LA. However I don't think that poor Joan got through a performance word perfect, or without drying up somewhere. I didn't want to appear to be making a fuss. We all kept saying to each other: 'I think she'll get to know the part in a few days.'

Unfortunately that never happened. Joan had a bad attack of arthritis one night and dried up as she had done on opening night. There was only a week of our run left, but we knew she'd never get through it. We had to ring up an English friend of mine called Emma Dempster; she flew in from LA, learned the part in three days and then played it for another three days without drying up once. She did it very well. Joan Blondell was a charming person and we all loved her. She was so upset and in so much pain that at the end I know she wished she had never agreed to appear in *Fallen Angels*.

Angela came out for a holiday in 1975 – she needed a rest. She was not strong and suffered from diabetes and bronchitis. Angela, who had had a great career as a dramatic actress, who had played everything from Chekhov to Shakespeare, had suddenly found international fame as Mrs Bridges, the cook in the TV serial *Upstairs, Downstairs.*

I'd seen her in most of her plays, but in *The Wild Duck* she gave the most amazing performance. I sat there unable to take my eyes off her, filled with tremendous emotion. I can honestly say that Angela made me feel more strongly that night than any other actress has ever done. She was made of the great stuff, but Angela wasn't selfish enough. To be really great, to get to that peak, you have to be selfish, and Angela gave too much of herself – both to Glen, her husband, and to her children – for that. She was offered wonderful parts, but she would turn them down to be at Stratford with Glen.

She stayed with me in my little green and white house near the top of Doheny, sat in the sun by the swimming pool and after a month I thought she didn't look quite so frail. One day, she said to me that if it wasn't for her wonderful family, her Glen and the children, she wouldn't care all that much about leaving. At first, I couldn't see what she meant and asked her to explain.

She made a little gesture with her hand: 'Leaving everything. I'm so very tired. Everything is such an effort these days.'

'Oh don't say that,' I protested. 'There's so much left for us. We've still got so much to do.'

Angela smiled. She was the one who had always said that I had the star quality and she repeated it now, saying perhaps star quality meant that extra little bit of life that others didn't have. When Angela went home I had a lovely letter from Glen, who was now a director of the English National Opera Company. He thanked me sweetly for looking after Angela.

Angela died quite suddenly in 1976. It was a great and awful shock for all the family. She had gone back to the theatre and was appearing in Sondheim's *A Little Night Music* in the West End, and having a great success. She caught a bad cold and had to leave the show because it turned to bronchitis, and then to pneumonia. To everyone's relief she pulled through and she went off to a convalescent home to recuperate. Quite unexpectedly and to our great sorrow, she died. Poor Glen was heartbroken – I don't think he will ever get over the loss of Angela.

There had also been tragedy in the life of Muriel, my eldest sister. Her marriage hadn't been good for some years and she and her husband parted; she kept their two beautiful children, though. Her daughter, Anne, joined the Ballet Rambert and then, to everyone's horror, she died of cancer at the age of twenty-one. As if that wasn't tragic enough, Muriel also lost her son John. He was married to an Italian girl and they had small children when he too died. I don't know how she managed it, but she seemed to develop some wonderful inner strength that got her through these terrible tragedies.

Ciggie was the last of us to marry, perhaps because she was the one who stayed home to keep our mother company. When she did marry, she had two daughters and the family went to America. Something went wrong and, after about twenty years of marriage, Ciggie eventually divorced her husband and came home. Her two daughters live in the States and whenever she can Ciggie combines a visit to see them with a visit to see me. Ciggie was very different to the rest of us girls. We used to tease her and say that she had the wild look of the wicked old Judge Clinton Baddeley, one of our ancestors. Her life has certainly been eventful in its own way. For a while, Ciggie ran a stall in the Portobello Road market. When Mummy died, Ciggie found many little knick-knacks, bits of china, pieces of silver and so on that she didn't want. She took them down to the Caledonian Market to sell, but then had the bright idea of selling them herself. She set up a stall and enjoyed it so much that she did it for many years after. Her exquisite collection of old scent bottles is quite well-known in collector's circles.

As for my children, young David has grown up to look very like his handsome father, but with quite a different personality. He's very witty and awfully good company, but his life is very different to the life that David led. He loves outdoor life more than anything and I think that began when he was a little boy and used to stay at Wilsford, and was then encouraged by Francis de Moleyns, my Irish lover. Snodde, the butler at Wilsford was a great outdoor man and a very good shot. He taught David everything there is to know about shooting and fishing. When, after Eton, he should have gone to Cambridge like his father, David, my husband, said that he just wasted his time there, and young David would be better off joining the family business.

First, David joined the Irish Guards and the army seemed to suit him far better than it had his father; then he went into the family business – Charles Tennant & Sons. Very soon it was quite apparent that we'd done the wrong thing; David just wasn't happy there. He is married with children, but now he and his wife have separated. He still remains a very good father to his children and nowadays he enjoys the outdoor life in Norfolk, where he shoots and fishes to his heart's content.

Pauline remarried; her husband was Sir Anthony Rumbold and they adopted a son. Since she loves the country, they live in a very pretty house near Wilsford, where my brother-in-law Stephen still lives. Bill, my half brother, has retired with his wife to Suffolk. I still say that when Bill went into the church, the theatre lost a fine actor, but, I suppose his voice has stood him in good stead in the pulpit. Christopher Glenconner died in Corfu last year and my nephew Colin became Lord Glenconner. Colin is a darling and always comes to my first nights – he is the kind of person who makes me feel inclined to come home and settle down.

Having a house in Los Angeles means that I meet a lot of old friends coming out to Hollywood to work. One of them was Peter Finch, who whenever he came to Hollywood would ring me up just to say that he was all right, as if I was his mother. And yet if anyone needed worrying over it was Peter Finch. He was the nicest of men, very funny and very sweet, but he had one fatal flaw – he used to get very drunk.

I met him first ages ago in England when he was very keen on Vivien Leigh and we had the same agent at MCA. He was a beautiful actor, his really was a gift from the Gods and it was a gift he should have cherished instead of squandering.

He came calling to my little bungalow at the Chateau Marmont one day, I was sitting around waiting for the call to make a certain film. He had been told by the film company to look me up, but not to say that we were about to start work. The message was that they had no intention of putting Peter and me together in the same film because they didn't think we would be good for each other. I didn't mind too much; I knew it wouldn't be a very good film and it wasn't. I saw Peter every day while he was making this film and I think one of the reasons was The Liquor Locker, a lovely booze shop next door to the Chateau Marmont. We were a happy little group, a good mixture. Most of us were in films, and although it was demanding work, we always found time to relax and enjoy ourselves. Amongst us were Larry and Norma Storch, Sidney Poitier and Tony Curtis; my friend Joan came over from England and mothered us all. We would meet in the evening at our bungalow, 'Bungalow B', having bought in the necessary bottles from The Liquor Locker, then go out in search of a new French restaurant. We used to get very jolly and were always clinking glasses rather heartily and finding a few broken glasses on the bill.

In spite of our happy parties, Peter watched his drinking while he was making the film. As soon as it was over, he got in his car, drove off and had plenty to drink. Soon after, he was stopped by the police. They pulled him out of his car, slammed him up against the side and handcuffed his hands behind his back.

'What absolute cads, these cops,' said Peter to me later. 'They might at least have handcuffed my hands in front of me. How do they expect a chap to answer a call of nature?'

Peter's career went up and down for the next few years, but when he came to Hollywood last, his career was doing fine. He was working on a major film called *Network* and he was going to be a much sought-after actor again. By this time he had married Eleutha, a darling little Jamaican girl who looked, in fact, rather like a little boy. Peter had become very relaxed and Eleutha obviously made him very happy. His attitude had changed – he was very serious about this film for he knew it was going to be good. They were planning a holiday when it was over, for Peter had a heart condition and needed to relax.

When it was finished, Joan and I gave a party and Peter and Eleutha came along. Peter walked in holding a tiny girl by the hand. He was very proud of his daughter and Eleutha and Peter asked if I would be her godmother. The night after our party, Eleutha told me, she and Peter had been sitting in the living room of their house when Peter said he felt very cold and strange. Suddenly she felt the same way and had the frightening feeling that someone was trying to get into the house. She ran round closing all the doors and windows in spite of the mild Californian air.

Next day Peter had an appointment at one of the Hollywood hotels. It was a pleasant day, so he decided to walk and Eleutha said she'd join him in the hotel later. As soon as Peter walked into the hotel lobby, he collapsed and died. It was the most shattering blow for little Eleutha, but she took it very well. Peter was awarded a posthumous Oscar for his part in *Network*.

Anything to do with illness is shunned in Hollywood. No one wants to know for whom the bells are tolling and there is a reason why illness is kept so quiet. It happened to me and I wasn't even ill. If the scandal sheets – and there are a couple of really hot ones in Hollywood – get a whisper or a rumour of a star's failing health, they can cause untold trouble. I remember that one of the so-called investigative journalists came to interview me about a television series I was in. He arrived early and I wasn't home yet, so Joan let him in. She told him innocently that I had gone to see my doctor.

When I came in, I was full of the amusing things that had happened to me that morning. I had received some new kind of treatment that was supposed to be very good for the hair. The journalist made copious notes. When his article appeared, I was very surprised to learn that I was at death's door, having chemotherapy for a dread disease, but I was hoping to save my hair. It was all completely untrue. What do you do? Sue the newspaper? Spend a lot of money on lawyers? No, you try and laugh it off and make sure that you are very careful what you say in front of journalists, and don't make jokes that they won't understand.

But I didn't find it at all funny when for six months after that article appeared I didn't have a single offer for television or films. It took that long for the powerful tycoons of Hollywood to really believe that Hermione Baddeley was hale and hearty and longing to work. Getting work and staying out of the unemployment queues is just as hard in Hollywood as it is in Hartlepool, even for the very big stars. About five or six years ago, I was sitting in the hairdressers when Julie Andrews popped up next to me. Julie hadn't been working very much – she'd been a victim of the 'drop-out' system. In Hollywood they can drop you just like that; and then sometimes they pick you up again, just like that. Julie's husband is a producer so her chances of being 'picked-up' are better than most.

Everyone applauded Bette Davis when she put an advertisement in the newspapers: 'Bette Davis is out of work and would welcome any offers'.

I moved to a new house in the Santa Monica mountains in 1980. It's way above Laurel Canyon, with a wide patio and a pool built at the edge of a mountain. I never mind changing house because I get so much pleasure out of doing them up. My little green and white house in Doheny was just too small, but this one is big, with spare bedrooms and bathrooms. As with so many Californian houses, the swimming pool is the focal point: you can step out of either the living room or my bedroom onto the patio and dive right in. There are big white tubs spilling over with geraniums and hibiscus and yellow daisies. In the garden at the edge of the mountain are palm trees, eucalyptus and jacaranda trees with hanging branches for shade.

Below is a great unspoilt panorama of wooded hills. In the distance, little white roads thread their way across the hills and tiny cars scurry down them, hell bent for Los Angeles and Santa Monica. Now and then, the wail of a police car siren cuts through the still air, and overhead the odd helicopter chops its way to a pad in a garden in Bel Air or Beverly Hills.

There are three dogs in residence at the moment, but only one is really mine. Peaches is a lithe Saluki-like dog who can stand up, put her paws about your shoulders and waltz with you. Lucky is part German-shepherd and part Coyote, and really belongs to Johnny Rebel – she has inherited a touch of madness from her coyote forebears and likes to lie on the steps of the pool and soak up the water in her fur, then rush round the house dispensing pools of water all over the best carpets. If the coyotes creep up the mountains late at night and drink from the swimming pool, Lucky nearly goes off her head trying to get out to them. Then there is Oliver, who is a huge red setter and a wonderful watch dog. Oliver is a lodger; his owner hadn't anywhere to live and Oliver was sleeping in the back of his car, so Oliver moved in with Peaches and Lucky. After a time, Oliver's owner, Pat, moved in too. I like to have a man living on the premises and it takes someone young with a lot of energy to get three big dogs in the car and drive them down to the dog-park every day.

For a time, Wally Crisham, my old friend from the revues in the thirties and ENSA days lived in my house. He'd had trouble down in his flat in Hollywood – an armed mugger broke into his apartment twice – so Wally came up to stay in the mountains for a while.

Sometimes I think of those far off days when I took over from Bea Lillie at the Café de Paris and wonder what I'm doing in this town of film stars. I still wonder if it's a happy way of life for them. I know that my daughter Pauline decided to turn down the film offers she had received when she met Rita Hayworth and Ali Khan. She thought they looked terribly sad. Rita Hayworth had come up to my house with some friends. She was a pale ghost of the beauty she had once been, and she sat in a corner all alone until I went over and spoke to her. Poor Rita was soon so ill that she couldn't go out anymore.

Marrying a rich and famous man like Ali Khan was, I think, one of the breaking points for Rita. I've met many women who were married to very rich men and very few of them seemed happy. There were some very tough ladies in Hollywood who made their millions themselves, but even that didn't seem to bring them much contentment. I used to know Joan Crawford, who was extremely successful, but at the end it was religion that gave her some happiness.

One of my best friends here is the comedienne Martha Raye. In private life, she isn't at all the same as her film persona: she is a charming and funny woman, one of the kindest people in show business, and I was very fortunate to be introduced to her when I first came out to Hollywood.

I meet many Hollywood stars when I go to parties, although the scene has changed now and I don't know quite as many of the new actors and actresses as I used to. Most of the big studios have gone over to making television films and those who remain are into 'bedroom-movies', as the taxi-drivers call them – soft porn, really. I get quite a few of these weird scripts sent to me and I always send them back. I was talking to one of the leading film actors the other day: he had been asked to appear in one of these films with me. We were to be the parents of some of the sexually liberated young who did nothing but romp in the hay. We both agreed that the scripts were boring – and short – and that we didn't want to be saying 'Oh shit!' every other line.

I went to a party with Lee Graham, the Hollywood columnist, some time ago where some of the stars who made their name in the thirties, forties and fifties were invited. Tom Cooper who owns a film theatre where he shows movies of yesteryear was our host. We were invited to meet Rex Reed, the drama critic who was in from New York. For a man who writes such cutting prose, Rex Reed was surprisingly young and good-looking. Reuben Mamoulian and the beautiful woman he has been married to for thirty-five years was there. He is one of the real 'greats', having directed all the great beauties and great actresses – Greta Garbo, Vivien Leigh, Marlene Dietrich. Esther Williams turned up looking larger than she used to, but amazingly beautiful still with two gigantic sons over six foot eight. There was Marsha Hunt, Joan Leslie and Ella Raines, all looking about thirty years old.

As often happens at these parties everyone is asked to sing. Marsha Hunt sang a very wistful song and Betty Garrett and Guy Nash did 'Baby it's cold outside' and were fantastic. Then they asked me to sing. I had a red handkerchief in my hand which I knotted around my neck and I sang 'Je suis' by Alan Melville. It is the kind of song that French chanteuses sing in Parisian nightclubs. The music has an air of nostalgia and sentimentality, but the lyric that sounded so Parisian was really a lot of gibberish: 'Je suis . . . tu es . . . nous sommes . . . la plume de ma tante . . . le jardin de mon oncle . . .' The humour lay in the gestures I used as I sang this gibberish – the French sniffs, the quick finger across the nose, the scratching of the behind . . . Here I was in Hollywood, California, singing Alan's song from the revue *A La Carte* which had been written for me over thirty years before.

It was, as it was intended to be, a party filled with nostalgia.

They have all been wonderfully good years. All of them in England and America. I have spent most of my life working in the theatre – which is always my greatest love, but the films and the television were the providers of a lot of the little luxuries of life.

Joan comes out to stay with me a great deal and when I'm in England we share a flat or a house. In Hollywood she is called Saint Joan because she's such a fantastic person and so ready and willing to help anyone in trouble. If someone is ill, Joan will find the name of the right doctor. She'll get out her black book and look up a herbalist, a faith healer or a guardian angel priest. Joan is a great believer in the wonderful powers of the Catholic priest, Padre Pio, who lived in Italy. Our friendship is as strong as ever; if anything, it has grown more steadfast with the passing of time.

In 1982, I went to England to do William Douglas Home's *Mother Came Too,* and before I'd finished the run, my New York agent telephoned to say that he'd signed me for a play on Broadway called *Whodunnit* by Anthony Shaffer. I was rather cross about this. I had read the play through and thought that on balance I would rather see it than act in it. But my agent had signed me up for it without so much as a 'by your leave' and there was no way out. The play ran until May 1983.

I have found out that often nothing turns out quite as you think it will, but you must search for the advantages and ignore the disadvantages. I always think that people are much happier if they don't take life too seriously. At least no one seems to take me too seriously. I was shopping in Ralph's Supermarket, a vast store near the Cedars of Lebanon Hospital, where everything is super big, the mangoes and the pineapples and the peaches as big as pumpkins.

Near one entrance is a little tea and coffee bar where you can sit down and have a rest before going down another long aisle with your trolley. I was with a friend who was going back to England next day and she was rather annoying me because she was taking so much time choosing every conceivable thing she thought she wouldn't find in England. 'Let's have a cup of tea,' I suggested.

It was just a little place with a few plastic-topped tables and tip-up chairs, but as soon as we sat down with our plastic cups of tea and bran muffins we found ourselves chatting away to other shoppers. We talked about the heat and the high cost of food in supermarkets – it was quite a jolly little gathering, but when we'd finished our tea we got up to go.

'Hi!' called one of the jolly ladies as I found my trolley. 'Don't I know you? Weren't you Mrs Naugatuck in *Maude*?'

My friend gave the game away. 'Yes, she's Hermione Baddeley.'

'My! My!' said the lady shaking her head in mock surprise. 'I never thought I'd ever see you pushing a trolley in Ralph's. I thought you'd be on your yacht in the Caribbean.'

'I usually am,' I said.

Backword

There is a question I am often asked – do you prefer living in England or in the United States? Let me put it like this: I like working back and forth. I love both countries. My grandchildren are in England but my dogs are in America.

And I love America because I have so many friends out there – people like Baron Freddy von Soosten, Baron Herbert Hirschmuller and Gary Weelock. Then there are my girl friends, Lynne, Jill, Kabrina and Eleanor.

And I do have past connections with America as well. It is a source of pride to me that my great-great-grandfather, Sir Henry Clinton, a distinguished soldier, fought in the American War of Independence. In fact he was the general who took New York.

Another ancestor I should mention is Robert Baddeley, a pastry cook. He was also a talented actor and appeared with David Garrick at Drury Lane. When he died he left a request in his will that every year on Twelfth Night an iced fruit cake should be given to the company playing at Drury Lane. This cake should be called the Baddeley cake and the management should provide a bowl of punch. For nearly two hundred years someone has been cutting the Baddeley cake on Twelfth Night. One year Angela had this honour and one year it was me. The cast of *My Fair Lady* even donated a silver punch bowl for the ceremony.

Angela Baddeley, my sister, was both famous and honoured. I remember a day at my home in Los Angeles when we were so excited because a letter arrived from the Queen. Angela was to be made a Commander of the Order of the British Empire. She read the letter then handed it to me. 'This honour should be for you, darling,' she said. 'You deserve it just as much as I do.'

As to the title of this book; at first, I thought *The Unsinkable Hermione* sounded more like the war service and hard times of a battleship than the story of my life. But now I think it may be an apt title. There have been so many ups and downs in my life, so many disadvantages squeezed into advantages.

Let's just say that the unsinkable Hermione is still afloat and so far I've managed to keep my head above water.

Index

Ace of Hearts 54, 56–7
Adding Machine, The 213
A La Carte (Melville) 147, 148, 149, 231
Albanesi, Meggie 30, 32
Albert, Duke of York 40
Allen, Lady Phyllis 118, 177
Ambassadors Theatre 151
Andrews, Julie 228
Ancaster, Lord 189
Apollo Theatre 145, 146
Armstrong-Jones, Meg 119
Armstrong-Jones, Tony (later 1st Earl of
    Snowdon) 179, 180
Arnold, Tom 125–6
Arthur, Bea 178, 219–20, 222
Arts League of Service 26, 29
Ashley, Tony 71–2
Ashton, Frederick 98, 108
Asquith, Margot 11–12, 37
Assheton-Smith, Lady Joan 118, 188, 193,
    195, 198, 199–200, 201, 206–7, 211,
    213, 215, 227, 228, 231
Astaire, Adele (later Cavendish) 215
Astor, Bill 34–5
Attenborough, Richard 128–9, 148
At the Lyric (Melville) 178

Baddeley, Angela 39; childhood 10, 14,
    19, 21, 99–100; career 22–4, 25–7, 60,
    70, 71, 96, 98, 99, 100, 141–2, 148,
    153, 223–4; private life 25–6, 28, 31,
    60–1, 63, 160–1, 170, 224
Baddeley, Cynthia ('Ciggie') 14, 19, 21,
    28, 31, 39, 101, 189, 225
Baddeley, Muriel 14, 19, 21, 28, 31, 39,
    101, 225
Baddeley family see also Clinton-Baddeley
'Baggs, Mr' (spaniel) 114–16, 120–1,
    132–3

Ballyhoo 98–9
Balnagowan Castle 172–3, 183
Bankhead, Tallulah 150, 161, 197, 202,
    204
Banks, Leslie 32, 33, 141, 145
Barr, Mr 153
Barrie, Sir James 73
Barry, Joan 61
Bath, Marquess of 173
Beaton, Cecil 68, 203
Beaumont, Binkie 142, 169, 182
Beaverbrook, Max 47–8
Beecham, Sir Thomas 23
Beedon, Mrs 64
Beit, Sir Alfred 85–6, 123
Benny, Jack 149
Best, Edna 151
Blackburn, Raymond 140
Blaney, Norah 37, 38
Blondell, Joan 153, 222–3
Bogarde, Dirk 148
Boom 199
Bordeaux, Larry 207
Bourdin, Louise see Clinton-Baddeley
Bow, Clara 58
Bowes-Lyon, Elizabeth 36–7, 40,
    111
Bowes-Lyon, Johnny 111–13, 114
Bowes-Lyon, Timothy 112
Brighton Rock (Greene) 128–9,
    148
Britneva, Maria ('Little Brit') 122, 168,
    178
Bryan, Dora 178
Burgess, Guy 128
Burnaby, Dave 40
Burton, Richard 199
Byam Shaw, Glen 63, 160–1, 162, 170,
    171, 224

Caesar, Sid 109
Café de Paris cabaret 167–8, 229
Cambridge Theatre 100
Campbell, Mrs Patrick 62, 64
Carlyon, Gillian 175
Carmichael, Ian 178
Carroll, Madeleine 59, 60
Cavendish Hotel 83–4, 114, 126–7
Channon, Chips 179
Charlot, André 42–3
Childs, Freddy 88–90, 91, 104, 105, 109, 110
Childs, Gilbert 40, 41–2
Christie, Major-General Campbell 138
Churchill, Winston 140–1
Clare, Mary 30, 32
Clinton-Baddeley, Louise: family life 10, 14–16, 18–22, 35–6, 39, 50–1, 61, 70–1, 100–2; and HB's career 10, 21, 30–1, 33, 42, 45, 49, 56, 77, 102; background 16–17, 36
Clinton-Baddeley, Victor 86
Clinton-Baddeley, William Herman 17–20, 24
Cochran, C. B. 42–3, 44–5, 49, 52, 54, 97
Collins, Joan 170
Comedy Theatre 98
Conan Doyle, Sir Arthur 46
Conway, Tom 99
Cooch Behar, Maharajah of 168, 169
Cooper, Edward 123
Cooper, Tom 230
Co-optimists 40–2
Coward, Noel 28, 44–5, 75, 132, 138, 150, 151, 152–3, 191, 194, 199
Crawford, Joan 230
Crewe, Colin 180
Crewe, Quentin 180
Crisham, Wally 98, 103, 124, 125, 126, 130, 133, 134, 135–6, 148, 229
Cukor, George 203
Cunard, Emerald 54
Cunard, Nancy 76
Curtis, Tony 227

Daubeny, Peter 151, 152, 153
Davis, Bette 228
Dawn of Happiness, The 23
Dean, Basil 29–30, 31–2, 33–4, 37, 42, 130, 160

Dean, Paul, Brenda 65–6, 69, 76–8, 79
Dear Mr Prohack 148
de Bath, Christopher 75, 76, 77
de Beer, Archie 37, 40
de Leon, Jack 122, 123, 124
Delysia, Alice 45, 49
de Moleyns, Francis 142–3, 144–5, 146–8, 149, 153, 158–9, 171–3, 183, 189
Dempster, Emma 223
Desmond Hurst, Brian 158
Devine, George 192
Disney, Walt 204, 206, 207–8, 219
Douglas, Sir Sholto 120
'Dozey' see Willis, Major J. H.
Drummond, John 159, 160, 177
Drummond, Violet 159, 177
Duchess of Duke Street, The 84
Duke of York's Theatre 100
Dunnock, Mildred 197, 203
Dwyer, Leslie 155
Dyer, Charles 217–18

Ed (script writer) 210–12
Edward, Prince of Wales 10, 38, 54, 103
Elder, Eleanor 25, 26, 29
Elmsmere, Lady 86
Elsom, Anita 40
ENSA tours 129–30, 131–41
Epstein, Mr 213
Escape Me Never (Kennedy) 97

Fairbanks, Douglas 72
Fallen Angels (Coward) 150–4, 190, 191, 222–3
Farjeon, Herbert 107, 108, 109–10, 110–11
Farraday, Miss 20
Farrar, Gwen 37, 38
Farringdon, Lord 118
Fielding, Daphne 84
Fields, Gracie 34
Finch, Eleutha 227–8
Finch, Peter 226–8
Five O'Clock Girl, The 77, 79
Forest, The (Galsworthy) 32, 33
For Love or Money 168
Furness, Thelma 54

Gable, Clark 72
Gallico, Paul 204, 206

Gandarias, Tony 94–5
Garbo, Greta 58, 231
Gargoyle Club 53–4, 62, 65–6, 76, 82–3, 103, 105, 106–7, 127–8, 140, 142
Garrett, Betty 231
Garson, Greer 207
Gate Revue, The 123
Gay, Molly 133, 134, 137
George (bulldog) 209
Gielgud, John 63–4, 70
Gingold, Hermione 123–6, 130, 149, 151–3, 203
Gish, Dorothy 117
Glenconner, Lord Christopher ('Kit') 35, 36–7, 40, 47, 61, 62, 67, 79, 80–1, 111, 177, 214, 226
Glenconner, Lady Pamela 62
Glyn, Prudence 130
Going To Town 178
Golden Biscuit Award 109
Good Life, The 217
Gordon, Gavin 130, 136
Gordon, Ruth 192
Gosse, Edmund 17, 25
Gosse, Reginald 25–6, 34
Graham, Lee 230
Grand National Night (Christie) 138, 141–2, 145–6
Grant, Mark Ogilvy 111
Gray, Dulcie 128
Greeks Had A Word For It, The 98, 99–100, 107
Greene, Graham 128
Grenfell, Joyce 111, 135
Grey of Fallodon, Lord 12, 47
Grey, Lady 12–13, 45–7, 48, 51, 56, 57–8, 61, 62, 64–5, 66, 67–9
Guinness, Merrod 57–8
Gurney, Claud 145
Gwen (Welsh maid) 81–2, 93, 94–5, 105, 115–16, 119

Hagman, Larry 217
Hale, Sonny 38, 40
Hall, Edward Marshall 17
Halliday, Angela 175
Hamilton, Lance 150, 152
Happiest Millionaire, The 206–7
Hardy, Thomas 26–7
Harris, Rosemary 190
Harrison, Rex 203

Harvey, Laurence 154, 155–65, 167, 169, 170–1, 172, 173, 182, 188, 210–11
Hassan 160–1
Hawkes, Sylvia 71–2
Hawkins, Jack 60
Hayes, Isaac 218
Hayworth, Rita 230
Henderson, Dickie 147
Henson, Leslie 113, 129–30, 131–2, 133, 137, 139, 171, 172
Heston, Charlton 190
Hitler, Adolf 82
Holding Out The Apple 63–4
Holloway, Brownie 74
Holloway, Stanley 40, 41, 150, 203
Howard, Brian 76
Howard, Trevor 189
Howland, Ian 73–4
Hunt, Marsha 231
Hutchinson, David 130, 133, 134, 135
Hyams, Elizabeth 52
Hyde White, Wilfrid 220

'Invisible Lady' 9–10, 103, 214
It Always Rains On Sunday 148

Jacob, Naomi 133
'Jilly' 185–7
Jocelyn, Captain 114–16
John, Augustus 93, 104
Johns, Glynis 148
Johnson, Amy 82

Keane, Doris 97
Kee, Robert 157
Keeling, Carol see Johnny Rebel
Kendall, Henry 123, 124–5, 147, 149, 168
Kennedy, Margaret 97
Khoury, Mr 205–6, 208–9, 210
Killing of Sister George, The 207, 208, 209, 212, 213–14, 221
Kite, The 148
Knight, Decima 130
Knight of the Burning Pestle 28

Lanchester, Elsa 22
Langley, Noel 170
Lansbury, Angela 191–2
Laughton, Charles 22
Lawrence, D. H. 39

Lawrence, T. E. 94
Laye, Evelyn 38
Lear, Norman 217, 218–19, 220, 221, 222
Leigh, Vivien 132, 184–5, 191, 226, 231
Leighton, Margaret 170–1, 182–3
Leslie, Joan 231
Lester, Alfred 39
Lewis, Rosa 53, 83–4, 113–14, 121, 126–7
Likes of 'Er, The (McEvoy) 10, 30, 32, 34, 60, 97
Lillie, Bea 123, 132, 167, 168, 229
Lincoln, Diana 151
Linnet and Dunfee 128
'Little Brit' *see* Britneva
Little Night Music, A 224
Little Revue, The 112, 122
Little Theatre 109
Littlewood, Joan 190–1
Lodge, Sir Oliver 46
Lord Babs 57, 61
Lottie (bulldog) 193–4, 207, 209
Lucky (dog) 229
Lughalore 171, 172
Lyric Theatre 27, 28, 178

MacDonald, Ramsay 39
Machiz, Herbert 192, 196, 197
Mackay, Hugh 26
Mackeson, Tony 61
Make Believe (Milne) 27
Mamoulian, Reuben 230–1
Mann, Christopher 59–60
Manson 'family' 216
Marcus, Frank 207
Margaret Morris School 21–2, 23, 25, 27, 29
Marriage of Figaro, The 23–4
Marshall, Norman 123
Mary Poppins 204, 205
Matthews, Jessie 38
Maude 219–22, 232
Maugham, Robin 198, 199–200
Maugham, Syrie 11, 34, 38
Maxwell-Stuart family 16, 17, 18
Mayer, Freddy 105
Mayer, Louis B. 13, 58
Melville, Alan 122, 125, 128, 130, 147, 231
Menotti, Gian Carlo 197

Merrick, David 191, 192
Merson, Billy 61
Messel, Oliver 209
Metcalfe, 'Fruity' 103
Meyrick's nightclub 71
MGM 58–60
Mickey, Brian 123, 124
Midnight Lace 196
Milbank, Sir John ('Buffles') 138–9
Milinaire, Madame 74
Milk Train Doesn't Stop Here Any More, The (Williams) 196–9, 202–3, 204
Millet, Jack 144–5
Mills, Johnny 77
Mrs 'Arris Goes To Paris (Gallico) 204, 205, 206, 208
Mitchell Colts, Sir Campbell 180–2
Mitford, Nancy 82
Mitford, Unity 82
Mollison, Jim 82
Monkman, Phyllis 40
Morosco Theater, New York 202, 203
Morris, Margaret 21, 22
Morton, Clive 100
Moseley, Roy 213
Mosley, Cynthia 95
Mosley, Sir Oswald 95
Mother Adam 217–18
Mother Came Too (Douglas Home) 231
Mount, Robin 92
Music Corporation of America (MCA) 202
My Fair Lady 203

Nash, Guy 231
Network 227, 228
Newton, Natalie 157
Newton, Robert 97–8
Nichols, Beverley 162–3
Nine Sharp (Farjeon) 107, 108–11, 112, 123, 187
1926 Revue, The 52
No Room At The Inn 148

Old Vic Theatre 60, 70, 71
Oliver (dog) 229
Olivier, Laurence 60, 70, 184, 185, 189–90, 191, 196, 197, 209, 222
O'Neill, Miss 65, 82–3
On With The Dance (Coward) 44–5, 49, 52

Oranmore and Browne, Lady Oonagh 171, 172

Page, Geraldine 207
Parker, Cecil 148
Parsons, Alan 103
Parsons, Virginia (*later* Tennant) 103–4, 105, 106–7, 173, 214
Passport to Pimlico 149, 150
Pat 229
Patton, General 137
Payne, Graham 138
Peaches (dog) 229
Pearson Gee, Hugh 28
Phoenix Theatre 125
Pike, Stanley 20, 21
Pillar of Ice 173
Pink Room, The 183
Pio, Padre 231
Pitt-Rivers, Julian 146, 156
Pitt-Rivers, Pauline *see* Tennant
Playfair, Giles 28–9
Playfair, Nigel 28
Plowright, Joan 184, 191, 192
Poitier, Sidney 227
Porter, Bob 158, 165
Porter, Ronnie 52–3, 65–6, 69, 76, 82–3
Price, Dennis 166
Pritchard, Matt 51, 52, 127
Pritchett, John 167, 168
Punchbowl, The 37–9
Pye, William 22, 28, 36, 101
Pye-Baddeley, William 28, 31, 86, 101, 226

Quartet (Maugham) 148

Raines, Ella 231
Rattigan, Terence 183
Rawlings, Margaret 100
Raye, Martha 230
Rea, Alec 31
Rebel, Johnny (Carol Keeling) 194–6, 208, 229
Redhead, Barbara 85
Redhead, Peggy 85
Reed, Maxwell 170
Reed, Rex 230
Reid, Beryl 208
Reinhardt, Max 171
Reith, Lord 51

Ribblesdale, Lord 83, 84
Richardson, Tony 192
Rise Above It 122–5
Ritchard, Cyril 108–9
Robey, George 139
Robson, Flora 45
Roebling, Paul 197
Romulus Films 161
Room At The Top 188, 195
Rose Tattoo (Williams) 122, 168–9
Ross, Lady Jean (*later* de Moleyns) 171–2, 183, 189
Rothermere, Lord 85
Royal Court Theatre 29, 30
Rumbold, Sir Anthony 226
Rumbold, Hugo 23
Rumbold, Pauline *see* Tennant
Russel, Charles 150, 152
Russell, Bertrand 62
Russell & Russell, solicitors 10, 77, 106
Russler, Nanny 46
Rutherford, Margaret 149

St Hellier, Ivy 110
St Just, Lord 122
St Just, Lady Maris *see* Britneva
St Martin's Theatre 30, 31, 208, 209
Salote, Queen of Tonga 193–4
Sanders, George 98–9
Sargent, John Singer 45–6, 178
Savoy Theatre 147
Scott, Martha 190
Seafield, Nina, Countess of 85, 88
Separate Tables (Rattigan) 183
Shaw, George Bernard 62, 64
Shaw, Susan 155
Shilling Theatre 98, 100
Signoret, Simone 188
Simpson, Wallis 103
Sitwell, Bill 181–2, 184, 185, 194
Sky High 125–6
Slings and Arrows 148
Smith, Aubrey 206
South Riding 218, 219
Spencer, Barbara 170, 193
Spinelli, Mlle 52
Stamp, Lord 12
Stanley, Lord Edward 72, 85
Steele, Tommy 206–7
Stevens, Roger 202, 203
Still Dancing 52

Storch, Larry 227
Storch, Norma 227
Strauss, Irving 194–5
Strobach, Ben 192
Swaffer, Hannen 109
Swan Lake, parody 108
Sweet and Low (Melville) 128, 129, 130

Taste of Honey, A, 190–2, 193, 196, 197
Tate, Sharon 215
Taylor, Elizabeth 199
Taylor, Laurette 203
Teffont Manor 9, 92–5, 103, 105
Tempest, Marie 18
Tennant, Charles 37
Tennant, Christopher see Glenconner
Tennant, Colin 209, 226
Tennant, David (husband) 37, 51–2,
    52–4, 127–8, 139, 140, 142–3, 185–7,
    209, 212, 214; marriage 9–10, 58,
    61–6, 67–73, 74–8, 79, 86–7, 89–91,
    103–6; courtship 11, 12–13, 34–7, 38,
    39–40, 41, 45–8, 50–1, 54–5, 56–7;
    and HB's career 59; divorce 104–7,
    109, 110, 114, 117, 173
Tennant, David (son) 87, 106, 113, 141,
    146, 156, 179, 225–6
Tennant, Edward ('Bimbo') 46, 64
Tennant, Georgia 106
Tennant, Michael 71
Tennant, Pauline 57, 64, 77, 79, 80, 113,
    119, 141, 146, 157, 185, 209, 212,
    226, 230
Tennant, Stephen 13, 47, 61, 68–9, 86,
    226
Tennant, Virginia see Parsons
Thomas, Charles 25, 28–30, 34
Thomas, Stephen 25–6, 28, 60–1
Tickeridge Mill 88
Travelling Theatre of the Arts League of
    Service 25–6, 29
Tree, Viola 104
Trevor, Claire 213–14

Tumbler, The (Levy) 190

Unsinkable Molly Brown, The 204, 205
Upstairs, Downstairs 224

Valerie (secretary) 178–9, 180, 181
Vaudeville Theatre 57
Van Dyke, Dick 205
Vazetti, Signor 17
Ventry, Lord 144, 158
Vosper, Frank 96–7

Walton, Sir William 200–1
Watergate Theatre 123
Webber-Douglas School 141, 146
Weissberger, Arnold 190
Whodunnit (Shaeffer) 231–2
Who's Afraid of Virginia Woolf 183
Wig and Pen Club 209
Wild Duck, The (Ibsen) 224
Wilding, Michael 182–3
Williams, Esther 231
Williams, Hugh 29, 34, 60
Williams, Tennessee 27, 122, 168–9,
    196–7, 198, 199, 203, 204
Wilsford House 45, 46, 47, 57, 64–5,
    67–9, 91–2, 214
Willis, Major J. H. ('Dozey', husband)
    114, 117–18, 120–2, 124, 126, 132–3,
    139, 141
Willoughby, Tim 186, 187
Wilson, Harriet 121
Wilson, Martin 70
Wilson, Sir Matthew 70
Winnie (maid) 93
Wood, Miss 20
Woolf, Jimmy 161–2
Woolf, John 161
Wooly, Mrs 84–5
Wyndham family 12, 45
Wyndham, Dick 88, 94
Wyndham, Violet 138, 139
Wyngarde, Peter 218